The 33rd
an anthology

Editor — Gail D. Rosen

Drexel Publishing Group Director — Scott Stein

Book Designer — Andrew Turner

Editorial Co-ops — Madison La Mountain
Caitlyn McGonigal

Senior Editorial Assistant — Sanjana Ramanathan

Student Interns — Stephanie Cugine
Michaela Graf
Sushmit Kuchana
Charlie Massey
Sanjana Ramanathan
Daniel Sadler
Aailyah Sesay
Leonie Staartjes

Sponsors

Drexel University
The College of Arts and Sciences at Drexel University
The Department of English and Philosophy at Drexel University

Dr. Norma Bouchard, Dean, College of Arts and Sciences, Drexel University
Dr. J. Roger Kurtz, Department Head, English and Philosophy, Drexel University

The 33rd Volume 13
Drexel University
Department of English and Philosophy
3141 Chestnut Street
Philadelphia, PA 19104
drexelpublishing.com

Cover photo by Dylan Lam

Copyright © 2020 by the Drexel Publishing Group. All rights reserved.

The 33rd is published once a year.

Submissions are open in the spring, winter, and fall terms of each academic year. Manuscripts must be submitted as an e-mail attachment (MS Word). Visit drexelpublishing.com for submission guidelines.

ISBN 978-1-7324500-2-8

Deepest thanks to: Dr. Norma Bouchard; Dr. J. Roger Kurtz; all the judges from the Drexel Publishing Group Creative Writing Contest (Stacey Ake, Valerie Booth, andré carrington, Judith Curlee, Lisa DiMaio, Valerie Fox, Henry Israeli, Lea Jacobson, Deirdre McMahon, Karen Nulton, Margene Petersen, Donald Riggs, Donna Rondolone, Doreen Saar, Sheila Sandapen, Fred Siegel, Errol Sull, Robert Wetherill); the Drexel Publishing Group Essay Contest (Stacey Ake, Jessica Cohen, Jordan Hyatt, Jay Jolles, Elizabeth Kimball, Craig McClure, Karen Nulton, Donna Rondolone, Doreen Saar, James Stieb, Errol Sull, Kathleen Volk Miller, Fengqing (Zoe) Zhang); the First-Year Writing Contest (Jan Armon, Valerie Booth, Rachel Kolman, Roger Kurtz, Jackie Landau, Leah Mele, Chris Nielson, Karen Nulton, Margene Petersen, Gail D. Rosen, Doreen Saar, Sheila Sandapen, Fred Siegel, Scott Stein, Errol Sull, Robert Wetherill); the Department of English and Philosophy, especially Mary Beth Beyer and Eileen Brennen; contest participants; and the Drexel Publishing Group staff.

The fonts used within this publication are Laski Slab and Source Sans Pro.

Credits

Ake, Stacey. "'If You Are All Christians, then I Am Not': How Kierkegaard Helped Me Survive a Christian College" was presented at the International Kierkegaard Conference in June 2018.

Chnaraki, Maria. "'Teach me to Dance!': Speaking without Words in Zorba's Culture" was published in *2BOARD* (The official Athens airport magazine): Blue Issue No 46, August 2019 - October 2019, 112-118.

Cohen, Paula Marantz. "The Divine Artistic Hand in My Late Mother's Beauty" was published in *The Wall Street Journal*, April 22, 2019.

Fitts, Tim. "You Have Ruined This Car" and "Spring Break" originally appeared in *Boulevard* in 2019 and "Sugar" was published in *The Jellyfish Review* in March, 2020.

Fox, Valerie. "Blue Horses" appeared in 2020 in *New Flash Fiction Review*. "The not so distant future" appeared in the *A3 Review* in 2020. "Girard Avenue" was published in *Philadelphia Stories* in 2019.

Hirsch, Cassandra. "Twenty-Five Years in a Writers Group" was published on *Write Now Philly*, 23 Jan. 2020.

Hunold, Christian. "Green Infrastructure and Urban Wildlife: Toward a Politics of Sight" appeared in *Humanimalia*, 11(1), (2019) pp 150-169.

Kotzin, Miriam. "In This Poem Only," "The Lace Maker," and "Notice" were published in *Boulevard*, Fall 2019.

Katerinaskis, Theodoros. "Dyeing Eggs and Baking Ties: Connected Customs and Manners Reinforce Cultures in 'E-cake and E-Eggbattle' Social Networks" was presented at the 4th European Conference on Social Networks (EUSN 2019, Presentation booklet).

Levin, Lynn. "The Lady with a Hundred Pockets" first appeared in the March 13, 2020 edition of *The Saturday Evening Post* online.

McCourt, Richard. "Surprising Discovery of Civil War Plant" was published on *The Academy of Natural Sciences of Drexel University* (www.anspblog.org/surprising-discovery-of-civil-war-plant), Aug. 20, 2018.

Miller, Jonson. "The 1869 Avondale Mine Disaster: A Transatlantic Welsh Tragedy" was originally published in two parts in *Ninnau* (The North American Welsh Newspaper) 43, no. 4 (September 2018) and no. 6 (November 2018).

Ottinger, Gwen. "Scientist Legislators Are No Cure for Bad Science Policy" was published by *Undark* (undark.org) January 3, 2019.

Piety, M.G. "On 'Going Low'" originally appeared in an issue of the online political journal *Counterpunch*, November 1, 2019.

Riggs, Don. "Covid-19 Sonnets" was published in *North of Oxford - The Pandemic Issue # 3*.

Sandapen, Sheila. "An Ungolden Silence. Danger, Detours, and Damnation in Narnia?" was delivered at the IRSCL (International Research Society for Children's Literature) 2019 Congress Stockholm, Sweden, August 2019.

Stein, Scott. *The Great American Deception* was published by Tiny Fox Press, 2020.

Thury, Eva. "Fairytales with Grownup Rage" appeared in *Write Now Philly*, 2020.

Volk Miller, Kathleen. "Mothering and Young Adult Covid Anxiety" was published as "Helping My Already Anxious Daughter Through These Times" in *Grown & Flown*, May 22, 2020.

Warnock, Scott. "Whupping the Teenage Boy Literacy Crisis with the Vacation Journal" was originally published on *When Falls the Coliseum*, July 31, 2019.

Welcome

The College of Arts and Sciences is the most diverse of Drexel University's schools and colleges, and nowhere is that more embodied than in the pages of *The 33rd*.

Like any great anthology, *The 33rd* speaks with many voices and offers many perspectives. Overlaid with CoAS' signature combination of interdisciplinary collaboration, field experience, and community engagement, the submissions in this volume are a testament to the creativity, collegiality and talent of the College's students and faculty.

This edition of *The 33rd* is the first produced since I became dean. I am already eagerly awaiting future editions. Happy reading!

Norma Bouchard, Ph.D.
Dean, College of Arts and Sciences

Preface

Each year the Drexel Publishing Group collects and publishes outstanding writing by students and faculty from across our university to create this unique anthology that we call *The 33rd*. In your hands is our thirteenth volume.

All the essays and stories in this collection are adjudicated through a competitive process. After publication, we use this volume as a textbook in many of our writing classes. It's different every year, with new and creative surprises each time. What remains constant is the way that *The 33rd* embodies our mission of promoting imaginative and effective writing, starting right here on the street that gives the publication its name, and reaching out into a world that is limited only by our creative imagination.

We are especially proud that one of the entries in last year's edition of *The 33rd* was noticed and selected for re-publication in a major composition textbook from W.W. Norton. Sanjana Ramanathan's essay "An End to Sexism in Gaming Communities" will appear in the fifth edition of *They Say/I Say: The Moves that Matter in Academic Writing, with Readings*. Congratulations to Sanjana, and congratulations to all the writers whose work was selected for this year's volume!

Cultivating curiosity and creativity in a supportive environment is the hallmark of the Department of English and Philosophy. Whether it's through our MFA in fiction writing, through our community-based learning courses that connect with organizations and institutions in greater Philadelphia, through our many internships, or through other initiatives from the Drexel Publishing Group like *The 33rd*, our students find multiple outlets for their writing to reach the world.

Enjoy!

J. Roger Kurtz, Ph.D.
Professor and Department Head
Department of English and Philosophy

Table of Contents

First-Year Writing

Nominees — 2
Introduction — 5

Winner
LingAn Zheng — Women and Girls — 7

First Runner-up
Laura Klouda — Why does America Keep Running out of Drugs? — 10

Second Runner-up
Jorina Teneqexshiu — Calloused Hands — 14

Honorable Mention
David Ahn — Suspension of Disbelief in Professional Wrestling — 16
Qwuacii Cousins — Behind the Closed Door — 19
Yasemin Dayi — ABDUL: The Inventor of Apple — 25
Mark Fazzolari — Muscle Memory — 28
Colin Latch — Home Sweet Home — 31
Marshall Nisselbaum — The Perils of Gifted Education — 33
Kalahne Serpanchy — Involuntary Disguises — 38
Ibim Sobiharry — Hustler's Paradise — 41
Renae Tingling — Sleepless Nights of a University Student — 44
Najifa Zaman — Dancing in The Rain — 48

Drexel Publishing Group Essays

Introduction — 55

Humanities

First Place
Sanjana Ramanathan — The Story of Philomela in Eliot's *The Waste Land* — 57

Second Place
Priya Dudhat — Flight as Escape or Confrontation; Mercy the Unspoken Wish of the Novel's Population — 61

Honorable Mention
María José Garcia — Haunted Houses and the Subjugation of Women — 65

Social Sciences

First Place
Jillian D'Souza — Cross Cultural Comparison of Gender Roles: Prevalence of Gender Roles in Indian Versus Indian American Culture — 70

Second Place
Megan Peng — The Culture of Education — 74

Honorable Mention
Steven Zhao — The Different Effects of Parental Expectations — 79

Zelda Provenzano Endowed STEM Writing Award

First Place
Lee Feinman — Geoengineering: The Climate Change Solution — 83

Honorable Mention
Meghan Mohnot — Genetic Modification: The Future of Curing Disease? — 87

Drexel Publishing Group Creative Writing

Introduction — 95

Creative Nonfiction

First Place
Sara Beinish — Cut Ties — 97

Second Place (tie)
Yasemin Dayi — The Good, The Bad, The Evil — 101
Sana'i Parker — The Signs of Disruption — 104

Fiction

First Place
Ferishta (Freshta) Rahmani — Mass — 109

Second Place
Samantha Nicole Johnson — Show and Tell — 112

Honorable Mention
Luis Cruz — La Llorona: The Weeping Woman — 119

Humor

First Place
Timothy Hanlon — The Prince of Trashlandia — 128

Second Place
Aaron Jeong — An Invitation to Laugh — 132

Op-Ed

First Place
Ciara Richards — Taking Action on Climate Change — 136

Poetry

First Place
Sanjana Ramanathan — Immortality 101 — 139

Second Place
Bella Randazzo — Nuclear/Winter — 140

Honorable Mention
Sanjana Ramanathan · Fickle Roots · 142

Writers Room
Introduction · 147
Norman Cain · Haiku · 149
Bella Randazzo · That Which Holds Atlas · 150
Teigha VanHester · Say Her Name, Live Her Story, Speak Her Truth · 151
Alex Wasalinko · January in the News · 152
Devin Welsh · Sick Daze · 153

Faculty Writing
Introduction · 157
Stacey E. Ake · "If You Are All Christians, then I Am Not": How Kierkegaard Helped Me Survive a Christian College · 159

Maria Chnaraki · "Teach me to Dance!": Speaking without Words in Zorba's Culture · 166

Paula Marantz Cohen · The Divine Artistic Hand in My Late Mother's Beauty · 171

Tim Fitts
- Spring Break · 173
- Sugar · 174
- You Have Ruined This Car · 175

Valerie Fox
- Blue Horses · 176
- Girard Avenue · 177
- The not so distant future · 178

Cassandra Hirsch · Twenty-Five Years in a Writers Group · 179

Christian Hunold · Green Infrastructure and Urban Wildlife: Toward a Politics of Sight · 181

Theodoros Katerinakis · Dyeing Eggs and Baking Ties: Connected Customs and Manners Reinforce Cultures in "E-cake and E-Eggbattle" Social Networks · 198

Miriam Kotzin
- In This Poem Only · 205
- Notice · 206
- The Lace Maker · 207

Lynn Levin · The Lady with a Hundred Pockets · 208

Richard McCourt · Surprising Discovery of Civil War Plant · 215

Jonson Miller · The 1869 Avondale Mine Disaster: A Transatlantic Welsh Tragedy · 218

Gwen Ottinger	Scientist Legislators Are No Cure for Bad Science Policy	223
M.G. Piety	On "Going Low"	226
Don Riggs	Covid-19 Sonnets	230
Sheila Sandapen	An Ungolden Silence. Danger, Detours, and Damnation in Narnia?	233
Scott Stein	Excerpt from *The Great American Deception* (Chapter 2)	243
Eva Thury	Fairytales with a Grownup Rage	248
Kathleen Volk Miller	Mothering and Young Adult Covid Anxiety	250
Scott Warnock	Whupping the Teenage Boy Literacy Crisis with the Vacation Journal	252

Contributors 257

Writings Arranged by Context

Argument

David Ahn	Suspension of Disbelief in Professional Wrestling	16
Jillian D'Souza	Cross Cultural Comparison of Gender Roles: Prevalence of Gender Roles in Indian Versus Indian American Culture	70
Lee Feinman	Geoengineering: The Climate Change Solution	83
Christian Hunold	Green Infrastructure and Urban Wildlife: Toward a Politics of Sight	181
Laura Klouda	Why Does America Keep Running out of Drugs?	10
Meghan Mohnot	Genetic Modification: The Future of Curing Disease?	87
Marshall Nisselbaum	The Perils of Gifted Education	33
Gwen Ottinger	Scientist Legislators Are No Cure for Bad Science Policy	223
Sana'i Parker	The Signs of Disruption	104
M.G. Piety	On "Going Low"	226
Ciara Richards	Taking Action on Climate Change	136

Education

Mark Fazzolari	Muscle Memory	28
Marshall Nisselbaum	The Perils of Gifted Education	33
Megan Peng	The Culture of Education	74
M.G. Piety	On "Going Low"	226
Scott Warnock	Whupping the Teenage Boy Literacy Crisis with the Vacation Journal	252
Steven Zhao	The Different Effects of Parental Expectations	79

Environment

Lee Feinman	Geoengineering: The Climate Change Solution	83
Christian Hunold	Green Infrastructure and Urban Wildlife: Toward a Politics of Sight	181
Ciara Richards	Taking Action on Climate Change	136

Ethics / Philosophy

Stacey E. Ake	"If You Are All Christians, then I Am Not": How Kierkegaard Helped Me Survive a Christian College	159
M.G. Piety	On "Going Low"	226

Explanatory Writing

David Ahn	Suspension of Disbelief in Professional Wrestling	16
Aaron Jeong	An Invitation to Laugh	132
Richard McCourt	Surprising Discovery of Civil War Plant	215
Jonson Miller	The 1869 Avondale Mine Disaster: A Transatlantic Welsh Tragedy	218

Exploratory Writing

Stacey E. Ake	"If You Are All Christians, then I Am Not": How Kierkegaard Helped Me Survive a Christian College	159
Maria Chnaraki	"Teach me to Dance!": Speaking without Words in Zorba's Culture	166
Jillian D'Souza	Cross Cultural Comparison of Gender Roles: Prevalence of Gender Roles in Indian Versus Indian American Culture	70
Theodoros Katernaskis	Dyeing Eggs and Baking Ties: Connected Customs and Manners Reinforce Cultures in "E-cake and E-Eggbattle" Social Networks	198
Laura Klouda	Why Does America Keep Running out of Drugs?	10
Megan Peng	The Culture of Education	74
Renae Tingling	Sleepless Nights of a University Student	44
Steven Zhao	The Different Effects of Parental Expectations	79

Fiction

Luis Cruz	La Llorona: The Weeping Woman	119
Timothy Fitts	Spring Break	173
	Sugar	174
	You Have Ruined this Car	175
Samantha Nicole Johnson	Show & Tell	112
Lynn Levin	The Lady with a Hundred Pockets	208
Ferishta (Freshta) Rahmani	Mass	109
Scott Stein	Excerpt from The *Great American Deception* (Chapter 2)	243

Gender, Race, and Culture

Maria Chnaraki	"Teach me to Dance!": Speaking without Words in Zorba's Culture	166
Luis Cruz	La Llorona: The Weeping Woman	119
Jillian D'Souza	Cross Cultural Comparison of Gender Roles: Prevalence of Gender Roles in Indian Versus Indian American Culture	70
Yasemin Dayi	ABDUL: The Inventor of Apple	25
Priya Dudhat	Flight as Escape or Confrontation; Mercy The Unspoken Wish of the Novel's Population	61
María José Garcia	Haunted Houses and The Subjugation of Women	65
Jonson Miller	The 1869 Avondale Mine Disaster: A Transatlantic Welsh Tragedy	210
Megan Peng	The Culture of Education	74
Ferishta (Freshta) Rahmani	Mass	109
Kalahne Serpanchy	Involuntary Disguises	38
Ibim Sobiharry	Hustler's Paradise	41
Teigha VanHester	Say Her Name, Live Her Story, Speak Her Truth	151
Najifa Zaman	Dancing in the Rain	48
Steven Zhao	The Different Effects of Parental Expectations	79
LingAn Zheng	Women and Girls	7

Literary Criticism

Priya Dudhat	Flight as Escape or Confrontation; Mercy The Unspoken Wish of the Novel's Population	61
María José Garcia	Haunted Houses and The Subjugation of Women	65
Sanjana Ramanathan	The Story of Philomela in Eliot's *The Waste Land*	57
Sheila Sandapen	An Ungolden Silence. Danger, Detours, and Damnation in Narnia?	233
Eva Thury	Fairytales with a Grownup Rage	248

Memoir / Personal Narrative

Sara Beinish	Cut Ties	97
Paula Marantz Cohen	The Divine Artistic Hand in My Late Mother's Beauty	171
Qwuacii Cousins	Behind the Closed Door	19
Yasemin Dayi	The Good The Bad The Evil	101
Yasemin Dayi	ABDUL: The Inventor of Apple	25
Mark Fazzolari	Muscle Memory	28
Timothy Hanlon	The Prince of Trashlandia	128
Cassandra Hirsch	Twenty-Five Years in a Writers Group	179
Aaron Jeong	An Invitation to Laugh	132
Colin Latch	Home Sweet Home	31
Kathleen Volk Miller	Mothering and Young Adult Covid Anxiety	250
Sana'i Parker	The Signs of Disruption	104
Jorina Teneqexhiu	Calloused Hands	14
Renae Tingling	Sleepless Nights of a University Student	44
Teigha VanHester	Say Her Name, Live Her Story, Speak Her Truth	151
Scott Warnock	Whupping the Teenage Boy Literacy Crisis with the Vacation Journal	252
LingAn Zheng	Women and Girls	7

Poetry

Norman Cain	Haiku	149
Valerie Fox	Blue Horses	176
	Girard Avenue	177
	The not so distant future	178
Miriam Kotzin	In This Poem Only	205
	Notice	206
	The Lace Maker	207
Sanjana Ramanathan	Immortality 101	139
	Fickle Roots	142
Bella Randazzo	Nuclear/Winter	140
	That Which Holds Atlas	150
Donald Riggs	Covid-19 Sonnets	230
Alex Wasalinko	January in the News	152
Devin Welsh	Sick Daze	153

Politics

Christian Hunold	Green Infrastructure and Urban Wildlife: Toward a Politics of Sight	181
Gwen Ottinger	Scientist Legislators Are No Cure for Bad Science Policy	223

Popular Culture

David Ahn	Suspension of Disbelief in Professional Wrestling	16
Maria Chnaraki	"Teach me to Dance!": Speaking without Words in Zorba's Culture	166
Theodoros Katernaskis	Dyeing Eggs and Baking Ties: Connected Customs and Manners Reinforce Cultures in "E-cake and E-Eggbattle" Social Networks	198
Sheila Sandapen	An Ungolden Silence. Danger, Detours, and Damnation in Narnia?	233
Eva Thury	Fairytales with a Grownup Rage	248

Profile

Yasemin Dayi	ABDUL: The Inventor of Apple	25
Kalahne Serpanchy	Involuntary Disguises	38
Ibim Sobiharry	Hustler's Paradise	41

Najifa Zaman	Dancing in the Rain	48
LingAn Zheng	Women and Girls	7

Science

Lee Feinman	Geoengineering: The Climate Change Solution	83
Christian Hunold	Green Infrastructure and Urban Wildlife: Toward a Politics of Sight	181
Richard McCourt	Surprising Discovery of Civil War Plant	215
Meghan Mohnot	Genetic Modification: The Future of Curing Disease?	87
Gwen Ottinger	Scientist Legislators Are No Cure for Bad Science Policy	223

First-Year Writing

First-Year Writing Nominees

The following students were nominated for the
First-Year Writing Contest.
Congratulations to all!

Sanjana Ahmed	Kaleigh Gillooly
Valentina Angelkova	Emily Gioacchini
Nicole Audi	Brian Glogower
Adeloa Awotunde	Eitan Goldberg
Sungminn Bae	Abigail Greskovic
Sarah Barker	Amber Gunderson-Smith
John Barnitt	Mekkah Harris
Caroline Bayliss	Tasmia Hasan
Sara Beinish	Courtney Heffelfinger
Aaron Herbert Bernard	Danielle Hight
James Berner	Jacob Hoffpauir
Ariana Berrios	Chiamaka Ibe
Alyssa Bohorquez	Matthew Jones
Julian (iulian) Buzila	Harrison Jones
Desmond Cheung	Liam Kane
Wiliam Christine	Hemani Kapoor
Rea Chroneos	Ali Zain Khan
Kevin Cisneros-Velasquez	Jaehoon Kim
Sean David	Grace Knauss
Minh Chau (Jade) Dinh	Serena Kothari
Hannah Dong	Michal Koutamonov
Jevaughn Victor Zedan Edwards	Danielle Larkin
Temuujin Erdenebayar	Annie Le
Neranjana Fernando	Jess Li
Luke Forwood	Christina Ludwig
Bhavna Ganesan	Valery Luo

Liam Mailley	Samantha Santos
Leo McIlvain	Emily Schatzman
Chloe McLaughlin	Daniel Schraeter
Harrison Nguyen	Samantha Seiden
Jack Nguyen	Naomi Shifman
Katie Nguyen	Armen Shirozian
Kyle Nguyen	Julia Silva
Lauren Nibbio	Gwyneth Steele
Nicole Nowakowski	Isabella Stoll
Ian Onuska	Toby Sullivan
Jade Owens	Horia Tagouma
Rachana Panchal	Vishal Tailor
Seo Yeong Park	Zaria Thomas
Sana'I Parker	Robert Togna
Megan Peng	Willy Tran
Dan Phan	Melissa Tuley
Inara Pirani	Nicholas Vennitti
Emily Pummer	Francis Virtucio
Isabella Randazzo	Cheryl Vo
Marisela Rechner	John Voll
Carson Rendahl	Caroline Wang
Eli Richards	Amanda Warkow
Liam Rondon	Yonatan Wiese-Namir
Niki Roseborough	Feben Wolde-Semayat
Mason Rothstein	
Kejsi Ruka	

Introduction

As the Director of the First-Year Writing Program, I work with over 60 dedicated instructors who coach, cajole, and mentor close to 3,000 incoming students who produce tens of thousands of pages of writing. One of the best parts of my job is working with Sheila Sandapen, our Assistant Director, on the First-Year Writing Contest.

This section of *The 33rd* includes essays written by the winners, runners-up, and honorable mentions from the contest that ran in the 2019-2020 academic year. Here is how the essays get from the classroom into this book:

- Students work very hard in their classes to produce lively, engaging writing about themselves and the world around them. Their instructors work hard, too, giving advice and encouragement throughout the writing process.

- Towards the end of the fall term and again in the middle of the spring term, we ask instructors to invite no more than two students from each of their sections to submit their best work to the First-Year Writing Contest. Last year, we got 127 excellent entries.

- With the help of 15-20 faculty members, we go through a two-step judging process. After much deliberation, the judges come up with a winner, a first runner-up, a second runner-up, and ten honorable mentions.

- During the spring term, the winners, runners-up, and honorable mentions are announced at the English Awards Ceremony, along with the winners of various other contests. Furthermore, our winners receive prizes supported by a very generous endowment from the Erika Guenther and Gertrud Daemmrich Memorial Prizes.

- Finally, the editors of *The 33rd* step in to get permissions, to edit, and to create the book you are holding.

So, here is *The 33rd*. Your instructors in the First-Year Writing Program will ask you to read essays that won prizes last year so you can discuss them, debate them, and learn from them.

Are you interested in writing? Will you be in this book next year? On behalf of the First-Year Writing Program, we look forward to reading your work.

Fred Siegel, Ph.D.
Director of the First-Year Writing Program

Winner—First-Year Writing

Write a profile.

— Professor Cassandra Hirsch

LingAn Zheng
Women and Girls

It was a cool autumn in the year 1977 in China. Leaves wrinkled and fell from the tree tops, away from the sky that was still bright and blue. The wind came and carried leaves in spirals. One leaf fell out of the spiral and fell on a little girl's hair.

Her hair had an auburn highlight that did not match her dull-colored dress. At the age of eight, she was popular among her neighbors. She loved to help neighbors and get praise and food from them. Her family also spoiled her with food, even though the food was scarce. Her friends nicknamed her "Wudun," which means five meals in Chinese, because of how often she ate.

One day, she held her head high as she reached out her arm, showing her new watch to her friend. Wudun stood proudly and seemed to not notice how wide her smile was, "My mom bought it for me." She was so proud because no one else her age had a watch, especially a girl.

After they had a short conversation about the watch, Wudun noticed a bag in her friend's hand.

"Is...is that a dumpling?" Her eyes opened wide and she unconsciously pursed her lips for a second.

"That's for my brother." Her friend mumbled as she looked to her feet.

"What about you?"

The other girl bit her lip and did not say a word. Wudun came home with the question lingering in her head: "Why was it only for her brother?" She asked her quiet mother, and the answer was that boys were more valuable to some families. "Really? But you told me it's all the same." She frowned in confusion. Her mother smiled and did not answer.

Poverty grew in this land. Most children's dreams, including her dreams, were delicious sweets, meat, or even just plain rice. Among those children, girls were more unfortunate than others. Many families gave only meat to boys and then gave worse food or sometimes no food to girls.

"I'm lucky," Wudun thought. She only had two older brothers, a relatively small number of siblings compared to her friends. Her family was much more gender-equal compared to other families at the time. She was also her parents' favorite because she was the youngest.

Wudun grew up and married a man she had only met a few times before marriage. At the age of twenty, she already had two daughters. On the birth bed in her house, she heard her husband sigh. He frowned and took his eyes off the baby. He walked out of the room and lit up a cigarette.

"Next one will be a boy." The midwife comforted. Wudun looked at her with slight disbelief and nodded.

Her mother, the quiet and yet strong woman, the grandma of the newborn, held her hand and said, "It's all the same."

Her husband soon left for a job opportunity in the Netherlands. After eleven years, he returned and said to her, "I want a son." In the year 2000, the one-child policy was still strictly enforced. Exceptions were made for families with only one daughter to have a second try, but certainly not for a third try. During her pregnancy, Wudun hid in different places in different cities where no one knew their background to prevent getting caught. They knew that once caught, the government will force an abortion upon her. The government killed many fetuses, including those that were mature enough to survive outside of the womb. In the winter of 2000, in a small and cold apartment they rented, she gently stroked her belly and pondered the possibility of this baby being a son. This will mark all her hard work with a beautiful period. Although she had already checked the gender illegally with a doctor and found the gender to be female, she still wished it to be a mistake.

"I should be lucky." Wudun smiled at some posters of cute twin baby boys. People believed that things women see during pregnancy influence unborn babies.

A few months after, the baby was born and, to everyone's disappointment, it was a girl. After hours of giving birth, Wudun saw the disappointment on their faces and heard them walk outside to talk about solutions. They talked about giving the baby to another family, actually taking care of the baby, or... drowning the baby. It was a common practice at the time. Millions of fetuses and newborns were murdered every year simply because they were girls. She wanted to curse at them, but she soon lost consciousness because of the blood she lost. Fortunately, the baby was saved and was decided to be raised in this family. However, this child did not mark an end to her pregnancy and hiding due to her husband's dream. After another year of hiding, her fourth daughter was born. At this time, the newborn was given to another family. Wudun planned another child, but, unfortunately, she was caught. Her child was aborted, and she was forced to do a surgery that prevented her from pregnancy.

I am her third child, the one that stayed in the family and cost them thousands of dollars in fines to the government. Whenever Mother talks about her fourth child, she regrets how she did not keep the fourth child with her. She said that if she knew she would not have any more children, she would try her best to keep the child. However, she had to complete the mission of having a son who would carry on the family name and lineage. Families with only daughters were looked down upon as weak and as not having a future because of how little expectations they have on girls. People considered daughters useless and only meant to become someone else's wife. My mother was raised in this cultural environment, and she told me that if she could, she would continue trying until she was too old to give birth.

Unlike the end of many novels, she did not fight like a superhero and live out of the frame of a gender unequal age. She is just like every common woman of her time. She perhaps had tried fighting, but failed to go against everyone. She tried hard to provide me with a more equal environment than her time. She worked full time and provided for the family when my father did not work for years. She took care and paid for her parents when they were old and sick. Now people know that women could do much more than just being a wife. She did not fight and win glamorously like a superhero, but she still won. Isn't that something that many common people do? We see and experience injustice. We fight for change. We fail. We continue to live with injustice, but we do not surrender to the darkness. Like seeds under thick soil, we gradually find our way to the brightness.

First Runner-up—First-Year Writing

Evaluating and Solving Problems: For this assignment, you will research a problematic issue, propose one or more solutions to the problem, and present an argument supporting your solution. One effective way to approach this assignment is to identify a problem in a profession or discipline of interest to you. Another is to deal with a problem local to Drexel, Philadelphia or your hometown, and relevant to your experience there. The topic should be original and significant.

— Professor Robert Finegan

Laura Klouda
Why does America Keep Running out of Drugs?

On September 5, 2014, my dad was diagnosed with cancer. After receiving the news, all I could think about was that there would be no cure and he would die. This turned out to be half-true. His chronic neuroendocrine cancer is currently incurable, but it has been treatable. He is alive and relatively well. His oncologists have new options to tackle each new complication as it comes. Yet even today, five years later, my family feels persistent anxiety that maybe someday there will be nothing else medicine can do.

Our 21st-century beacon of hope is medical researchers, whose revolutionary discoveries provide new treatments and cures. Yet these profound advancements of medicine are being set back by a deceivingly simple issue: a lack of drugs. Critical drug shortages are a widespread issue across the United States, posing significant risks for patient health and placing severe strain on hospitals. John M. Maris M.D., chief of the Division of Oncology at The Children's Hospital of Philadelphia (CHOP), explains how awful it is to have to tell patients that a cure exists, but "one of the key essential ingredients" is unavailable. When this occurs, patients must either suffer through an unknown waiting period or settle for substitutes that may be less effective and more toxic (United States 72). Despite incremental legislative steps in the right direction, drug shortages remain an expensive, stressful, and dangerous issue for United States healthcare systems. In order to fix this, the root causes must be identified, analyzed, and prevented. When prevention is impossible, protections must be in place to buffer the impact. Essentially, demand cannot rely on supply; there must be adequate safety nets and backup plans to ensure that patients can always be treated quickly, without compromising the quality or safety of their medicine.

Unfortunately, demand usually outweighs supply. Due to the expensive and complex systems necessary for production, most drugs are only sold by one or two manufacturers. This creates numerous problems, including sky-high prices, products disappearing from the market, and bottlenecks in the supply chain. The American Society of Health-Systems Pharmacists reports that 30% of shortages are caused by manufacturing issues and another 10% from product discontinuation. A disruption as simple as a routine US Food & Drug Administration (FDA) inspection can halt production, leaving the country with only half of their product supply. The limited number of manufacturers also influences the market prices of drugs, which are often too expensive for smaller hospitals and clinics. Conversely, manufacturers cease the production of drugs that aren't profitable anymore. Thanks to inadequate communication during these struggles, everyone down the supply chain is blindsided. By the time hospitals are made aware of these shortages, they must scramble to find solutions, "a procedure which is highly complex, resource intensive, and frankly highly subject to human error" (United States 74). This frenzy wastes resources and increases the chances of fatal mistakes.

Desperate to help their patients, some doctors turn to questionable sources, fueling a "grey market" that sells imported brand-name drugs for cheaper prices. Due to copyright laws, the U.S. Supreme Court has ruled these transactions legal (Kirtsaeng v John Wiley), despite knowing that this process creates an opening where low-quality or counterfeit drugs can slip under the FDA's radar (Berkrot). These doctors may be well-meaning, but this shady practice puts patients at a much higher risk due to the lack of regulated oversight. Emmy award-winning journalist Armen Keteyian reported in 2012 that the FDA discovered a huge counterfeit supply of Avastin, a life-saving cancer drug. Most samples were merely salty starch water, containing no active ingredients. FDA investigation revealed that the "Avastin" originated from an unknown location in Turkey, was transported to Egypt, then the UK, and was finally imported to the US for purchase (Keteyian). Although the counterfeiting was discovered before causing any long-term damage to patient health, it appears as negligent that healthcare professionals would place such immense trust in mysterious third parties when the stakes are so high. Then again, fear and desperation often drive people to take extreme risks. Until drug shortages are eliminated, America's medical community may continue to make such reckless decisions.

The foundation of stopping drug shortages is transparency from manufacturers. Maryann E. Mazer Amirshahi, PharmD, MD, noted that manufacturers do not report the cause of over half of their drug shortages. This secrecy stunts progress by preventing analysis. The Drug Shortage Task Force, announced in 2018 by former FDA commissioner Scott Gottlieb, investigates innovative ways to tackle shortages, but must be well informed to do so. Transparency is also crucial for hospitals. Without proper warning or information about impending shortages, hospitals cannot ration supplies, plan patient treatments, or prepare viable alternatives. By providing honest public reports about potential problems, manufacturers could allow hospitals to take strategic action well ahead of time to prevent or mitigate adverse effects on their patients.

After open communication between manufacturers, the FDA, and hospitals is established, the drug market must be improved. The World Health Organization (WHO) insists that "a fair medicines price must be viable for the supplier and affordable for the buyer." Negotiating this balance is tricky, but an increase in manufacturers and financial support will help. The FDA Task Force plans to organize a critical drugs list, provide incentives for manufacturers, and encourage contributions from private investors. Investing in current and new manufacturers will increase market competition, while taking the burden off individual companies who currently have "very little margin for error" (Gottlieb). This will also let manufacturers take the time needed to upgrade facilities, while ensuring ample supply for patients. Over time, market improvement will keep critical drugs on the market, affordable for all without dependency on one or two manufacturers.

The fight against drug shortages requires collaboration between manufacturers, the government, and hospitals. The priority must be guaranteeing that patients always receive the best care possible. Only transparency, followed by communication, investments, and support of drug manufacturers will prepare hospitals and improve the market supply of critical drugs. These actions will combat shortages and contribute to their long-term prevention, allowing the advancements of medicine to benefit those who need it most.

Works Cited

Berkrot, Bill. "Fake Avastin Shows Little Protection of Drug Supply." *Reuters Health News*, 12 March, 2012, www.reuters.com/article/us-avastin-drug-fake/fake-avastin-shows-little-protection-of-drug-supply-idUSBRE82B0YY20120312. Accessed 10 October 2019.

"Drug Shortages Statistics." *American Society of Health-System Pharmacists*, September 2019, www.ashp.org/Drug-Shortages/Shortage-Resources/Drug-Shortages-Statistics. Accessed 10 October 2019.

Gottlieb, Scott. "Statement by FDA Commissioner Scott Gottlieb, M.D., on formation of a new drug shortages task force and FDA's efforts to advance long-term solutions to prevent shortages." *U.S. Food & Drug Administration*, 12 July 2018, www.fda.gov/news-events/press-announcements/statement-fda-commissioner-scott-gottlieb-md-formation-new-drug-shortages-task-force-and-fdas. Accessed 8 October, 2019.

Keteyian, Armen. "How Fake Avastin from Overseas Ends Up in U.S." *CBS News*, 21 March, 2012, www.cbsnews.com/news/how-fake-avastin-from-overseas-ends-up-in-us/. Accessed 10 October 2019.

"Kirtsaeng v. John Wiley & Sons, Inc." *Oyez*, www.oyes.org/cases/2012/11-697. Accessed 18 October 2019.

Mazer-Amirshahi, Maryann E. "U.S. drug shortages for medications used in adult critical care (2001–2016)." *Journal of Critical Care*, vol. 41, October 2017, pg. 283-288. *ScienceDirect*. www-sciencedirect-com.ezproxy2.library.drexel.edu/science/article/pii/S0883944117302344. Accessed 17 Oct. 2019.

"Medicine Shortages." WHO Drug Information, vol. 30, no. 2, 2016, www.who.int/medicines/publications/druginformation/WHO_DI_30-2_Medicines.pdf?ua=1. Accessed 10 October 2019.

United States. Cong. Senate. Committee on Health, Education, Labor, and Pensions. *Hearing on Examining the Prescription Drug Shortages, Focusing on Examining a Public Health Concern and Potential Solutions, and if the Food and Drug Administration's Ability to Respond should be Strengthened Dec. 15, 2011*. 112th Cong. 1st sess. Washington: GPO, 2014 (statement of John M. Maris, M.D., Chief, Division of Oncology, Children's Hospital of Philadelphia, PA), www.govinfo.gov/content/pkg/CHRG-112shrg88253/pdf/CHRG-112shrg88253.pdf. Accessed 10 October 2019.

Second Runner-up—First-Year Writing

Memoir: For this assignment, you will write a personal narrative style essay that details a significant or memorable experience from your life – or simply an incident that you'd like to explore further in writing.

— Professor Rachel Kolman

Jorina Teneqexshiu
Calloused Hands

I have walked through it before: the filthy alley with the abandoned shoe; the crushed beer cans decorated with wild weeds that sprout from cracked concrete and surround the abandoned taxi cabs. I've seen the line of auto repair shops along the alley many times. Yes, I've been to my father's rented garage—the one where he does his welding for his Iron Works business every day—several times before.

My father calls me into this shop to help him most weeks after school. I go to help translate a customer's questions and concerns. I go to call the industrial hardware company to order more steel. I even go to help pay the rent to the landlord. But I always do this with a certain degree of resentment. I do it because my father needs help, and I will disappoint him if I do not. And as a sophomore, what I *want* to do is to stay after school with my friends. I *want* to fulfill my duties as team captain of the Lady Griffins volleyball team. I *want* to be as carefree as my peers and not have to worry about *his* responsibilities in addition to my own.

Passing the chaotic alley and entering the threshold of my father's garage is like entering a battlefield. But on this cold November day, I really notice where I am. The nearly constant loud noise of cutting metal pierces my ears. Steel bars and metal scraps litter the floor. The ceiling lights flicker interminably and an icy wind blows through the open garage door.

When my father hears me enter, he approaches with a faint smile, kisses my forehead, and asks about my day as he searches his pockets for the supply list. My ears tune in to his weariness. He finds the list, and I notice the fatigue on his low, dark eyelids and the wrinkles at the corners of his eyes. He hands me the list and that is when I see his hands.

Every week for as long as I can remember, my immigrant father comes home with a new cut, burn, or bruise on those hands. I have known their roughness for years but have never considered their fragility. They are worn and exhausted from more than ten years of relentless labor of operating metal cutting machinery and carrying steel twice the weight they were designed to handle. When I grab the order request from his hand, I feel his rough, calloused skin as if I am feeling my father's hands for the first time. I am immobilized.

These calloused hands that have never faltered in their craft are beginning to weaken with age, I realize. But I realize something more profound too, something that has shaped my relationship with my father ever since: I realize how privileged I am. Unlike my father, I never had to undergo the chafing of my bare skin against sharp steel or the blistering heat of the welding gun. I never had to endure the harsh winters with a small portable heater or the scorching heat of the summer months with no real fan.

I take the list into my own unscathed hands and watch my father's back curl into his labor. Shame washes over me. I hold back tears as I dial the number of the industrial hardware company.

I never realized how much sacrifice was in my father's hands. Like many immigrants, he abandoned his home for a completely unfamiliar country so that his daughters could have the opportunities in life that he never did. And he never even spoke about it.

I no longer take for granted the opportunity to make him proud. His calloused hands are my reminder to utilize my education to the greatest extent, to take advantage of every opportunity I can as I work to achieve a life where his hands may rest.

Honorable Mention—First-Year Writing

For this assignment, use the chapters "Arguing a Position" and "Arguing" in *The Norton Field Guide,* to argue a position having to do with some aspect of deception.

— Dr. Fred Siegel

David Ahn
Suspension of Disbelief in Professional Wrestling

  Bong! The bell tolls, the lights go out. Bong! The bell tolls, the purple mist rises. Bong! The bell tolls, the funeral march commences. An eerie figure wearing a trench coat and a wide brim hat emerges from the mist. Hailing from Death Valley, weighing in at 299 pounds, The Undertaker enters the ring. In the world of professional wrestling, The Undertaker is truly like no other; his presence alone can send shivers down the spine of any hardened combatant. In reality, however, the concept of the man called The Undertaker is utterly ridiculous. An undead funeral director with the ability to control creepy druids and lightning who for some reason in the early 2000s decided to go through a biker phase breaks all conventional logic. Did I mention that he has a demon brother, named Kane, who the Undertaker tried to kill by burning their house down as children, who is now the mayor of Knox County, Tennessee? Knowing all of this, why would anyone want to be a fan of professional wrestling? It's so far-fetched that any sports-like appeal has disappeared. Much like a reality television show, professional wrestling requires its audience to cooperate in order to create the best version of its product. To willingly suspend your disbelief in order to enjoy professional wrestling is a form of self-deception where the audience needs to deceive themselves for a period of time to become immersed in the pro wrestling world.

  What actually is the willing suspension of disbelief? Coined by Samuel Taylor Coleridge, the term refers to when "the audience accepts fiction as reality so as to experience a catharsis" (Safire). Assuming that the work of fiction motivated the audience enough to engage in the process, that the illusion was represented and that the illusion is a gradual process; willing suspension of disbelief occurs within the audience to enhance their enjoyment (Ferri). Normand Holland, a literary critic, stated that "poetic faith" described how suspension of disbelief worked, with the audience believing in two inconsistent things. The audience feels as though they are a part of what is happening in fiction but since they know that it is fiction, the brain doesn't activate any motor impulses that might happen in a real situation (Mueller). This would account for why in professional wrestling, when Triple H "drugged" Stephanie McMahon and then married her while she was "unconscious," no one reported him to the authorities. While the viewer deceives himself that what he is watching is, momentarily, reality in order to get the most out of the entertainment, the brain knows the truth and stops the body from acting how it would normally. The term, suspension of disbelief, is most often used in discussions about theatrical productions whether they be dramas or films. As wrestling is more akin to theater than actual sport, the application of this term in a dialogue about deception in professional wrestling seems appropriate.

Ever since the secret of the century was revealed at Madison Square Garden in the mid-1990s, almost everyone knows the truth about wrestling. With the secret out, professional wrestling seemed doomed, any appeal of realistic combat was thrown out the window. So how did a wrestling boom in the late 90s, known as the Attitude Era, even happen? Wasn't wrestling supposed to have died? Four words: Stone Cold Steve Austin. The toughest S.O.B. on the planet who rose hell whenever the glass shattered and he stepped through the curtains. The appeal of Steve Austin was that he didn't take any crap from any of the higher ups, and in a time when people were fed up with their jobs they saw Stone Cold, who would literally beat up his boss on live TV, as their outlet. Even so, the same audience who relished the fact that Stone Cold would pummel the boss, Vince McMahon, every week also knew that Stone Cold was an employee under McMahon's payroll and it wouldn't make sense for him to get away with what would, in reality, be weekly assault and battery charges. The audience knows that Stone Cold is not actually out to destroy his boss but instead that this is an entertaining story between the good guy and the bad guy. Much like a melodrama, wrestling uses the drama created by these characters and its connection to the audience in order to succeed (Levi). Wrestling fans, for the sake of the experience, willingly believes in these pro wrestling characters and tropes, being completely aware of the truth but choosing to believe in a false reality for the moment (Craven, Moseley). Japanese philosopher Motoyoshi Irifuji argues that due to the nature of professional wrestling and how fakery is essential to the product, the audience's knowledge and cooperation with the performers is what allows the spectacle to exist (Tsutsui, Ito).

The major criticism against the concept of willing suspension of belief proposed by Kendall Walton, an aesthetic philosopher, is that the term does not accurately depict the relationship between the audience and the work of fiction. Using an example of a man being scared of a slime monster in a film, Walton rejects the idea of "part" of a person believes something that the other "part" doesn't. One argument he refutes is that half of the person believes in the monster while the other half doesn't because that implies that the person is unsure on whether or not the monster is real which would be false. Rather, Walton proposes that what is actually happening is a sort of make-believe situation similar to where a child runs away from their father when playing a game where he plays a monster (Walton). However, Walton's make-believe example would be difficult to transition for professional wrestling. To make-believe everything happening inside the squared circle would be to deny it any legitimacy which would be problematic since the performers do get injured from time to time. The association with the performers and the audience is also too close for the audience to just make-believe in wrestling. Without the audience's full support by suspending their disbelief, wrestling would just turn into acrobatics and powerlifting inside a ring.

Without the willing suspension of disbelief, professional wrestling would not have been able to remain as popular as it is now with over 10 million fans around the world. Some argue that suspension of disbelief doesn't correctly represent the connection between the entertainment and the audience which may apply to other types of entertainment but not for pro wrestling as the core concept of kayfabe depends on it. Many people disregard professional wrestling as a form of entertainment, since it was revealed to them that the product wasn't real. What people don't seem to realize is that the wrestling industry hasn't tried to hide their fakeness in decades. If one were to allow themselves to be immersed in the world of wrestling by suspending their disbelief, maybe then they will be able to see why when Mark Calloway puts on his coat and the bell tolls, only "The Deadman" towers in the ring.

Works Cited

Craven, Gerald, and Richard Moseley. "Actors on the Canvas Stage: The Dramatic Conventions of Professional Wrestling." *The Journal of Popular Culture*, Sept. 1972, search.proquest.com/openview/ed204025b7243574b3eab9e6e2278a06/1?cbl=1819044&pq-origsite=gscholar.

Ferri, Anthony J. *Willing Suspension of Disbelief: Poetic Faith in Film*. Lexington Books, 2007. 9-12.

Levi, Heather. "Sport and Melodrama: The Case of Mexican Professional Wrestling." *Social Text,* no. 50, 1997, pp. 57–68., www.jstor.org/stable/466814.

Mueller, Michael. "What Brain Activity Can Explain Suspension of Disbelief?" *Scientific American*, Scientific American, 1 Jan. 2014, www.scientificamerican.com/article/what-brain-activity-can-explain-sus/.

Safire, William. "Suspension of Disbelief." *The New York Times*, The New York Times, 7 Oct. 2007, www.nytimes.com/2007/10/07/magazine/07wwln-safire-t.html.

Tsutsui, William, and Michiko Ito, eds. "Wrestling With Godzilla" *In Godzilla's Footsteps: Japanese Pop Culture Icons on the Global Stage*. Springer, 2006. 74-75.

Walton, Kendall L. "Fearing Fictions." *The Journal of Philosophy*, 1 Jan. 1978, www.jstor.org/stable/2025831?seq=9#metadata_info_tab_contents.

Honorable Mention—First-Year Writing

Write a memoir.

— Dr. Sheila Sandapen

Qwuacii Cousins
Behind the Closed Door

I remember it was dark

But the where eluded me.

I remember the tears

But the why escaped me.

I remember the tiredness

That overwhelmed me.

I remember the music

Lulling me to sleep.

Of course, there was none.

And yet a lullaby was repeating itself in my ear

And then,

The humming.

Or was it... singing,

At this ungodly hour?

I rolled onto my side, pressing my hands into something soft.

I pried one sleepy eye open.

Cushions ....

Why was I sleeping on the couch?

The singing started up again, not that I had noticed the interlude.

I tried to remember when I had fallen asleep on the couch.

A still small voice whispered in my ear.

"But you didn't." I couldn't catch what it was saying, it was there and gone again.

My brain had started thinking without me.

The singing yes, the singing.

Who was singing at this hour?

"No," a whisper.

I had caught it this time.

No? I repeated.

A light breeze scampered across the room pulling strands of hair over my face;

I wiped at them absently and pried the other eye open.

The room was painted in the hue of the waning sun, the white walls waxed gold shimmered under the glittering chandelier.

Curious....

I hadn't noticed that before?

"But it isn't."

It isn't? What do you mean it isn't?

"Shouldn't this be the first sign of madness?" The thought flittered across my mind.

I could feel the starchy linen of the couch as I traced the filigree design,

I could smell the earthy aroma of soil after rain

And I could hear the singing from behind the closed door.

I stared at it.

The voice sounded rough,

Coarse, cracking in some places,

An older person?

The tune was gay, happy, inviting.

Yes, this voice,

I know this voice.

She sounded happy.

I couldn't remember the last time I heard her sing.

Why was she singing in the kitchen?

Oh

I inhaled deeply, the delightful smell of good ole Jamaican food as it wafted into the room and perfumed the air.

Ooooo

That smelled good.

What was it? Jerk chicken, oxtail. My taste buds were standing on edge.

How had I missed the smells before?

"They weren't there."

Clearly my subconscious was sleep-deprived.

I could smell the scotch bonnet peppers, onions, scallion, thyme.

I tried to get up, to follow the smell and satiate my hunger.

I was all but drooling.

"Stay," commanding, yet gentle.

Yes. Perhaps I should.

Besides, Granny didn't like people in the kitchen when she was cooking.

Granny?

But it was,

I had heard her voice.

But yesterday….

Was It yesterday?

I tried to remember what day it was.

My head hurt.

I remembered trying to talk to her, but she wouldn't respond, she turned her back to me and shut her eyes; no longer acknowledging my presence. Feisty old Jamaican woman, I smiled at the memory; she did that sometimes. Stopped talking when the conversation didn't suit her.

Maybe she will want to play a round of cards later, Coon Can was it.

Yes, she liked that one, she learned it in Cape Cod.

I've never been to Cape Cod,

Maybe we can plan a trip.

I wish she would let us teach her how to play Ludo.

But she says she is an old woman now; her hand can't roll the dice.

Yes, Granny is feeling better.

She is singing and cooking in the kitchen.

I was so worried that she would waste away, lying there every day, too weak to move.

This little old woman, thinking about what was going to happen to everybody when she died, like that was going to be sometime soon.

Three scores and ten, the time allotted, now she is 95.

I think she will live to see 100.

The hairs twirled about my face again; I wiped them carelessly.

I should go keep her company.

Ask her about her time in St. Thomas, Jamaica, those bygone years, before I was born.

Yes, I should write down those stories before I forget them.

The Kumina and the Setups,

The drums beating by themselves under white sheets.

Hmmm….

Maybe I will leave that part out.

I don't believe it myself.

"The Diary of An Ole Black Ooman,"

the title could use some work, sounds familiar.

But the recipes,

Yes,

The smells tickled my nose again.

I should write down the recipes.

I still don't know what is Pacasah or how to spell it.

"Shhhh…."

"Don't shhhh me! I wasn't even talking out loud."

I was quarreling with my subconscious, maybe I should go back to sleep, gather my faculties.

"Listen."

Another voice.

Auntie must be keeping her company. I smiled. The conversation sounded cheerful. I could hear Granny's melodious laughter from behind the closed doors.

Yes, she will be alright.

She sounded so much happier now; I pictured the smile that she must have on her face, her soft silver-grey hair peeking out from under her head tie.

"Are you ready?"

"Yes, I am ready."

"Are you happy?"

"Yes, I am happy."

Yes, she is happy.

But ready? To go where?

Maybe it was Sunday and she was going to church.

The voice asking the questions sounded unfamiliar, oldened, wizened.

I tried to place it as I closed my eyes.

Maybe it was best if I let them talk.

I would see Granny later and I would ask her then.

More hairs flew across my face.

I swiped at them annoyed.

Wet....

"Why was my face wet?"

The still small voice didn't answer.

I opened my eyes.

There was no soft light, bathing the room gold.

No singing, or voices to be heard.

It was dark,

As it was before.

But this time,

I remembered the where and the why.

I was lying in my dorm room.

Tears streaming down my face.

And I realized,

That my heart had tried to spare, that which my mind could not.

How dreams imitate reality.

A beautiful nightmare,

To soothe my grief.

Recompense....

Well-intended, yet sardonic.

At least I had gotten to hear her laugh one last time.

At least I knew she was singing,

At least I knew she was happy.

From behind the closed door...

    .... having died the night before.

Honorable Mention—First-Year Writing

One of the goals of this course is for us to begin doing primary research. Using the guidelines in the "Profiles" chapter in *The Norton Field Guide*, write a profile of an interesting person, place, or event. You will be required to interview someone, go somewhere, and/or participate in a live event. Approximate length: 1200-1500 words.

— Dr. Meagan Poland

Yasemin Dayi
ABDUL: The Inventor of Apple

One day, I was walking to class through the crowds of people rushing about their daily lives in the busy streets of Philadelphia. I stumbled across an interesting sticker on a SEPTA bus sign that simply read, "Abdul Latif Jandali." Honestly, the first thing that crossed my mind was, "Is that a sticker with a pair of boobs on it?" From a far glance, that is what it looked like. I came to find out, at a closer look, that it was an odd balloon animation of a man with glasses. Being Syrian myself, I could recognize the last name. I felt I had to dig deeper into this because I was intrigued by the possibility that I might find something, or someone, related to me.

I went on my phone and searched, "Abdul Drexel." Nothing. I tried again and searched, "balloon Abdul." Bingo. This led me to an account named, "@balloon.jobs" on Instagram that is run by an eccentric Algerian woman named Riham Dib. I immediately reached out to her through direct message and we got to know one another. In the message Riham sent that struck me the most, she described the discrimination she and her family faced as immigrants from Algeria in 2003. She described her first few months in America as "scary and unsafe" and recalled acts of islamophobia against her mother, stating, "There was a lot of drunk harassment towards her because of her headscarf. Men outside of bars would try to rip my mother's hijab off as we walked past." Coming to the U.S. in 2003 was not an ideal time for Muslim immigrants because it was just two years after 9/11. After reading this, I saw these encounters as fuel to the fire for a strong Muslim woman on a mission to promote equality. The more I spoke with her, the more fascinated I became. wanted to get to know her personality. Riham's outlook on life is one of the most notable aspects about her. She also has the confidence to speak out whenever she sees any type of discrimination, or something unfair happening. Conveniently enough, she attends Drexel as a graphic design major in Westphal; however, her current focus is a documentary about a man named Abdul. After learning more about her current work, I knew that I wanted to profile Riham and her documentary. The real question is, who is Abdul?

First-Year Writing | 25

Soon after, I asked her if she was willing to meet up at Westphal to talk more about her passion for this documentary in person. I wanted to hear the story raw from Riham herself. I was in for a treat when I met a five-foot-tall girl who had afro-style hair, looked as if she had been electrocuted, bleached eyebrows, and henna-dipped brown fingertips. *This* was a character if I'd ever seen one, and her story on Abdul was just as peculiar as her. As a Muslim woman, I feel as though there is a matter of discrimination in society today. This discrimination is evidenced by the fact that people of color are less valued, compared to white Americans. Their contribution to society is often overlooked compared to their white counterparts. This matter is very important and needs to be recognized. That is why I feel very strongly about Riham, another Muslim woman, and her vision for this documentary: to bring to light our culture and prove that we are innovators, creators, and just as revolutionary as the white man.

Abdul Latif Jandali is the full birth name of Steve Jobs. Yes, *the* Steve Jobs that made the phone or computer you are likely using right now to read this profile. You may be wondering, how is it possible that a white man has such a classic Arabic name? The answer is because Steve Jobs is indeed Syrian. Steven Paul Jobs was born to Abdulfattah Jandali and Joanne Schieble but was later put up for adoption and adopted by Paul and Clara Jobs. According to Steve's uncle, "Abdulfattah had a baby boy out of wedlock with an American woman, Joanne, and they gave him up for adoption. Abdulfattah could not return to Syria because of this 'scandal'" (Jandaly).

We know the extent of Steve's Syrian decent from specific accounts by his uncle stating, "Abdulfattah John Jandali belongs to a prominent Sunni family from Homs. The family is a direct descendent of the Prophet Mohammad" (Jandaly). Riham focuses on the idea of his name because it is essential to determining how a name defines a person and can alter one's career path. His name is a clear determinant of his race. With that being said, the question Riham wants to answer is based on whether people would have taken Steve Jobs seriously if he was not labeled as a white man but rather, a Syrian man.

A person's name can influence the way the public will view them if their race can be inferred based upon their name. The general consensus is that people have already made their judgement on someone just by seeing their name. In a study conducted by two economists from Stockholm University, they found that, "immigrants had changed their Slavic, Asian, or African names, such as Kovacevic and Mohammed, to more Swedish-sounding, or neutral ones, like Lindberg and Johnson" (Konnikova). Immigrants change their birth names to white-washed versions in order to gain an advantage in financial areas. The two economists further explained this in the study by stating, "This kind of name change substantially improved earnings: the immigrants with new names made an average of twenty-six per cent more than those who chose to keep their names" (Konnikova). This is a clear representation of the public's discriminatory mindset.

Based on current stories surfacing in the media, it is possible that the public would not have taken Abdul Latif Jandali seriously when he went public with the Macintosh. He could have been slapped with the label "terrorist," and his dream of the Macintosh may have never been realized. Or, Americans may have become scared of Abdul, proclaiming him to be too smart for an immigrant Arab man, ultimately becoming a danger to society. Some questions Riham wanted to answer were: "Would anyone even buy his products? Would we have Apple today? Would people have listened and taken him seriously?" She hopes to find answers to these questions by conducting random, in-person questionnaires with everyday people on the streets of Philadelphia. *ABDUL* is far from finished though. Riham could not give an estimate on how far along she is but claims the documentary is a long-term project she will continually work on for life. Riham explains that her goal is to finish the initial documentary next year as part of her senior thesis project. She anticipates public viewings in galleries only in countries and cities where Syrian refugees are welcome, such as Istanbul, Turkey.

As I interviewed Riham, she explained to me how this idea came about, stating, "I'm not sure why I was looking up Apple, but I was really into Steve Jobs at the time and I stumbled upon his wiki page. On the side bar, where you have the picture, the name, date of birth, etc. I saw his real birth name listed as Abdul Latif Jandali." Riham then explained how she was shocked to find this as his name and initially laughed, "I thought it was a joke." She remembers her parents, "murmuring about him being Syrian, but I never paid attention to it." This threw her down a rabbit hole, researching "day and night" to find his roots and any documentation she could about Jobs and his biological parents' early lives. Riham also began researching studies on the psychological science of the impact of names. When I investigated these studies myself, I was very impressed to find research specifically tailored to the effect of Arabic immigrant names, and overall, proves xenophobia using science.

During this interview, Riham showed me all the propaganda stickers she was working on, including the one that originally led me to her. She also showed me a clip of her documentary, in which she hired a professional balloon artist to make a life-sized version of Jobs holding an Apple in his hand. She then carried the creation around all of Philadelphia, asking locals if they knew his name. The only answer she got was Steve Jobs, but she is working to change that with her documentary, *ABDUL*.

Works Cited

Dib, Riham. Personal Interview. 19 Nov 2019.

Jandaly, Bassma Al. "Steve Jobs: A Tribute to the Cousin I Never Met." *Technology – Gulf News,* Gulf News, 29 Oct. 2018, gulfnews.com/technology/steve-jobs-a-tribute-to-the-cousin-i-never-met-1.887022.

Konnikova, Maria. "Why Your Name Matters." *The New Yorker,* The New Yorker, 19 June 2017, www.newyorker.com/tech/annals-of-technology/why-your-name-matters.

Honorable Mention—First-Year Writing

Write a memoir.

— Professor Jill Moses

Mark Fazzolari
Muscle Memory

"Oh, this is *beyond* easy. You can learn this in ten minutes," Lucas reassured me as he handed me the sheet music. What Lucas didn't know was that my fingers hadn't touched a piano in two years. It's a crazy thought, that something you'd been studying for nearly a decade can revert to a new concept within weeks if you neglect it. But I had already promised Lucas I would help him; and as my little sister would always say, "a promise is a promise."

I was seven when I started taking lessons. It's not as if I had a choice; what mom said was the law in our house. My first lesson consisted of all the fundamentals: finding middle C, learning the lines and the spaces and the notes that filled them, and, most importantly, avoiding all the black keys. But as I was packing my things, my instructor stopped me and nonchalantly remarked, "I think you have perfect pitch."

It turned out he was right. We dedicated a few moments at the end of each lesson to a game. As I turned away from the piano, he would play a note, and I was tasked with guessing which note he played. Notes would then evolve into chords, and chords would turn into songs. Miraculously, I never guessed wrong. Everyone told me I had a gift. I considered it to be more of a party trick, but it didn't take long for me to figure out that I was musically inclined.

As time flew by, I started to develop other interests; interests that began to devour my time. Every grade I advanced in school proved to be more demanding and time-consuming than the previous. And, for some strange reason I still can't enumerate, I began to detest playing the piano in front of people. If any member of my family was in the house (and with four sisters, a mom, and a dad, someone was *always* there), I would freeze up and stop playing. Practicing became an ordeal—torturous at times—and I just couldn't find the time or the will to get better. So, after ten years of lessons, I quit.

I went almost two years without touching a piano, constantly wondering if I had made the right decision. *Was this really what I wanted?* The more I deprived myself of the piano, the more I forgot how to make it sing. I never forgot the basics, but the more advanced songs and techniques I had known inside and out were unlearned much faster than it took to learn and master them. Soon enough, it was a forgotten art…

…until one day.

"Hey, I need your help with something." Lucas approached me after ninth-period band. "You play piano, right?"

"Uh, if you use the term 'play' loosely," I replied sheepishly.

"I want you to accompany me for Open Mic Night." He handed me some foreign-looking paper. It was sheet music. *Love Is a Losing Game* by Amy Winehouse. "Practice tomorrow after school, okay?"

"Okay."

"You'd better not disappoint me."

Great. Just great. I'd been out of the accompaniment business for a while now. How was I supposed to learn a song within a week and play it perfectly in front of hundreds of people? But I took Lucas up on his offer. I mean, if I was being honest, a tiny part of me wanted to relearn the art.

So that's exactly what I did. To my surprise, it felt as if I had never taken a hiatus. Everything came back to me at once—the same amount of time it took for me to forget it all. I spent those next six nights practicing, and practicing, and practicing, until I could play it flawlessly every single time. I will admit, it was rough at first. "*You're telling me you took piano for ten years?! Come on, I could do this in my sleep!*" But by the end of night six, I had become so accustomed to the hand movements that I think I *was* doing them in my sleep.

"I'll be honest," Lucas started bluntly. "I thought the first day that we were screwed. But now I feel that the weight has been lifted. I feel better now." We were ready.

Open Mic Night was on a Friday night, and we were the first act after the intermission. I shouldn't have been so nervous. All we were doing was performing in front of a bunch of classmates. Simple, right? They shouldn't care if it goes awry! But I still hadn't overcome my discomfort with playing in front of people. Hell, it took a lot out of me to play in front of Lucas, who was one of my closest friends that year.

"Give it up for Lucas and Fazz!" The emcee's blaring words caught me off guard. Oh, God. There was no going back now. I glanced at Lucas, who gave me a nod.

And then, something amazing happened. The moment my right hand sounded that all too familiar C-major-7 chord, all my fears vanished. Even though there were hundreds of people watching, it felt like I was playing the song with nobody home. We were rolling. I looked up momentarily; everyone slowly waved their phones as if they were lighters at a concert. I didn't mind. In fact, I was thoroughly enjoying it! But all good things come to an end, and before I knew it, the song was over. We got a standing ovation. I took a bow, and then looked over to Lucas and mouthed the words, "thank you."

If it weren't for Lucas, who knows if I ever would've touched a piano again? I don't have trouble playing in front of people now. I play what I want, and I don't care who hears. If you ever catch me in the lobby of Bentley Hall playing the songs of my childhood and just so happen to like what you hear, you can thank Lucas, too.

Honorable Mention—First-Year Writing

For this assignment, you may choose to write in either of two genres: literacy narrative or memoir.

— Dr. Donna Rondolone

Colin Latch
Home Sweet Home

The familiar bumping of cracks in the pavement bounced the 14-year-old me in the backseat. I knew these bumps like the back of my hand. For as long as I could remember, they had meant home was near after a long drive. To this day, I could drive down Hickory Road with my eyes closed and know where each bump would be.

My childhood home sat atop a hill. As the car drove up the steep driveway, I had mixed feelings towards the cream colored building. My family and I had poured countless hours of work into the house in the last few months before selling it. Painting walls, ripping up carpet, and building a back deck were just a few of the many chores we performed. I had given up my summer, spending hours each day helping with whatever new thing my parents needed me to do. By the time I put down the paintbrush for good, I was done with my childhood home – ready to say goodbye and never look back. Nevertheless, as I got out of my mother's car on a crisp autumn day to say my final goodbye to 48 Hickory Road, I could not hold back the sadness of leaving behind such a large part of my life.

Before going inside, I took the time to wander through the surrounding property. The rough bark of my favorite climbing tree felt familiar under my fingers as I climbed through the branches. With each step the tree creaked – I was much bigger than the last time I had attempted the ascent. The rapidly cooling weather of New Hampshire pricked at my skin as I sat above the only home I had ever known. Across the street, my childhood best friend Caitlin was helping her mother carry boxes from their house. Her parents had moved in just three weeks before my parents. Caitlin and I had grown up together. Being born exactly three weeks before me, Caitlin was like my inseparable twin. Now, we were both leaving. Walking through the woods, I saw younger versions of ourselves running through the trees, chasing after the "bad guy." I saw long-forgotten fallen forts, trampled paths, and an old sled sticking out of woven branches. All remnants of our shared past.

"Beep! Beep!" the door announced my presence as I walked inside; a once annoying sound had become a thing to mourn the loss of. The smell of cleaning products and fresh paint assaulted my nose. The TV Room, as my mother had dubbed the small front room, was barren. The only remnants of my family's residence were the tick marks on either side of the freshly-painted door casing to measure my little sister's and my height throughout the years. "The new owners will have to paint over your height marks if they would like them gone," my mother had said. "I will not be the one to erase all of our years here." As such, while almost every other room had been graced with a fresh coat of paint, this room was left untouched. Seeing the height marks on the wall felt wrong, like they no longer belonged against all of the new surrounding them. Sadly, it no longer felt like my home. The sounds of everyday life were no longer echoing through the halls. And walking through the once vibrant spaces, which had been expertly decorated at the hand of my mother, felt like I was intruding on a space where I did not belong.

Upstairs, my bedroom was unrecognizable. Throughout my 14 years living on Hickory Road, I had moved the furniture countless times and always left behind a mess to clean up at an unspecified later date. Walking through it then, it sat empty. The once tan walls with a red pennant border that my father had painstakingly painted had been erased with a fresh coat of daisy yellow. My Grandfather's rosary no longer hung on the curtain rod alongside the curtains. The closet looked unusually large without the overflow of trinkets that had always filled the small space. The sudden urge to leave my mark and indicate to anyone who saw that I once lived at 48 Hickory Road hit. I ran to the car, in search of anything that I could use to write any future inhabitant a message. Under the seat, next to an empty gum wrapper and a lonely nickel sat a pen. I ran back upstairs, avoiding my parents questioning looks – afraid that they would deny my hopes to sign my name. I had already decided that the inside of the small closet's door frame would be where I left my mark. A simple signature was all that I left behind: "Colin Latch 2001-2015." Satisfied with my work, I turned and left the unfamiliar space which was no longer my own.

Leaving home and moving on made me sad for the past, yet enthusiastic about the future. As we drove away, I reflected on the years I spent living at 48 Hickory Road and hoped that I would find the same happiness wherever I ended up. All while counting the bumps in the road.

Honorable Mention—First-Year Writing

Create an argument related to an aspect of education based on research and your personal experience.

— Professor Gail D. Rosen

Marshall Nisselbaum
The Perils of Gifted Education

When the term "gifted" is brought up, what comes to mind? Does the image of a wickedly smart, confident student who answers each and every one of their teacher's questions without hesitation appear? Or does "gifted" conjure up a stressed, burnt-out drug abuser? While the former may be true in some cases, as everyone seems to know someone like that, the latter is surprisingly common. This is because oftentimes gifted education doesn't work. Those who aren't enriched by these enrichment programs face stress, stigma, stereotypes, expectations, mental health problems, and drug problems. What good programs exist are few and far between because of unbalanced, biased admissions, varying legislation both nationally and globally, and the need for more individualized gifted supplementation. According to the United States Department of Education, about six percent of U.S. students were enrolled in gifted and talented programs during the 2011-2012 school year ("Frequently Asked Questions about Gifted Education"). If these issues aren't rectified, we may inadvertently leave our best and brightest behind.

I have a personal connection to this topic because I am a product of early gifted education. In my elementary school in New York City, I was placed into the Talented and Gifted program ("T.A.G."), for a few years, most notably 4th and 5th grades. Every so often, I would be pulled from my normal classes and, together with the other gifted students, complete thinking exercises intended to stimulate our minds. Time may have clouded my judgement, but I remember these feeling much more like art projects, which they very well may have been due to my elementary school's intertwined relationship with the Guggenheim Museum of Art. Despite their best efforts, T.A.G. ultimately harmed my development instead of boosting it. Growing up "gifted" meant I never felt like I had to learn the same habits as normal students, like studying or note-taking. Combining that with all the class time I missed in the gifted classroom makes for a shaky foundation that affects me to this day. I know my story is not unique and data will clearly demonstrate the dismal state of these programs and their students worldwide.

Gifted education programs fail gifted students because of how people perceive gifted students, both positively and negatively. Stereotypes play a huge role in a gifted student's life, beginning first with being selected for gifted programs. Often, teachers are not trained to recognize the minute variations in gifted students and will select candidates based on generalized and subjective ideas (Baudson et al). These expectations in turn influence student performance and negative perceptions of gifted students, which can be especially damning (Baudson et al). In a study published in *Gifted Child Quarterly* in 2016, 246 teachers in Germany rated fake students, both gifted and average, on characteristics such as intelligence and social ability. The researchers found that the teachers overall assumed that the gifted students were smarter, which empirical data supports, but also more antisocial and less well-adjusted to life, which empirical data does not support (Baudson et al). While gifted students may not be as awkward and socially inept as our image of them tends to be, teachers certainly think so and these biases adversely affect gifted students under their guidance. For example, a teacher may withhold support from a gifted student because they think he or she can function without it, or they may overly smother an otherwise functional gifted child if they believe gifted students need to be coddled.

Gifted education also fails students because of how burnt out and listless many gifted students become. Underachievement among gifted students is a pervasive problem, partly because it is tricky to quantify and even trickier to define. Definitions of "underachievement" vary based on the time since the definition was published and the factors used to create it. The most common definition of underachievement is a "discrepancy between potential and performance" (Reis); in other words, it is when a student's output based on grades and schoolwork is lower than their anticipated output based on what they are believed to be capable of, and this is the definition that this argument will use. Research shows that many gifted students perform below expectations because they lack academic goals and they do not appreciate schoolwork. In one study published in 2003 from the journal *Gifted Child Quarterly*, profiles of over 150 high school students were taken based on their academic self-perceptions, goals, and attitudes towards teachers and school. The researchers found that gifted underachievers tended to lack motivation; they had more negative feelings towards education than gifted high achievers and they lacked ambition in academics (McCoach). Gifted underachievers were also more heterogeneous in their characteristics than the relatively similar high achievers studied (McCoach). The problem of gifted underachievement, therefore, lies in gifted education. These programs lack the ability to inspire students in their current state. Without the support necessary to develop an idea of what they want to be doing with their lives, many gifted children will flounder in academics despite their intelligence. These same researchers argued that gifted programs need to help students discover the intrinsic and extrinsic benefits and help foster setting goals (McCoach), which will encourage gifted students to succeed and narrow the discrepancy.

Gifted students are also prone to drug and alcohol abuse, due to both peer pressure, stress, and mental health disorders. The American Academy of Pediatrics asserts that gifted teenagers exhibit higher rates of anxiety and depression than their peers and that teens with "genius-level IQs are at an extremely high risk of abusing drugs" ("Gifted Students"). It is not surprising, then, that many gifted students turn to drugs as a way to cope. In 2011, a group of researchers tested this idea by examining alcohol use in gifted and non-gifted students and published their research in the journal *Gifted Child Quarterly*. Using a sample size of 300 seventh graders, their research concluded that while gifted students did not try alcohol at a specifically higher rate than their non-gifted peers, the gifted students may have been partial to pressures and a "peer context", both of which encouraged substance abuse (Peairs). While researchers may debate over the exact rates and figures of gifted students using drugs, the mention of a peer context promoting alcohol is more worrying. Gifted education needs to be supportive of its students rather than harmful. If gifted students are abusing drugs to cope with the programs or the pressures of being gifted, or if even the culture of gifted education is triggering substance abuse issues, then the goal of gifted education as an enriching supplement has failed.

Lastly, if you have managed to find a gifted program that is enriching, supportive, fosters ambition and drive, and discourages drug use, consider yourself lucky. Quality gifted education does exist, but it is few and far between because of a distinct lack of guidance for administrators and a lack of opportunity for students. Ideas about how to run gifted programs and where to get the money for them vary between schools, cities, states, and even nations. There is no global standard, and foreign nations struggle just as much with this issue as the United States does. A study conducted in England and published in 2012 in the *British Educational Research Journal* found that many teachers nationally had difficulty interpreting and administering the country's gifted and talented policy and could not easily identify students as gifted and talented (Koshy). In the United States, there is only one federal program that provides for gifted education: the Jacob K. Javits Gifted and Talented Students Education Act, which received only 12 million dollars in federal funds in 2017. Common Core standards have also been exposed for not adequately providing for gifted students in their curricula ("Frequently Asked Questions about Gifted Education"). Without federal standards for gifted education, the quality of programs will vary wildly and potentially in ways that negatively affect minority and lower income groups. Gifted education programs have a history of appearing "elitist"; since they generally depend on leeway in local budgets and donations from parents or communities, gifted programs tend to be most common and highest quality in more well-off neighborhoods, which are generally white and Asian ("Myths about Gifted Education"). Gifted status doesn't favor any particular race or national origin, so this uneven spread is detrimental to otherwise prosperous lower-income students. This diversity problem is coming to a head in New York City, where I grew up and had my experience with gifted programs. Just this past summer, Mayor Bill de Blasio was approached with a slew of reforms for the city's public school system, in particular a provision which would eliminate all gifted and talented programs from the city that Schools Chancellor Richard Carranza supports (Shapiro).

New York City is incredibly diverse, and Carranza worries that a program that benefits only a portion of the student populace is harming the remainder. Clearly, the global problem of how to fairly and effectively implement gifted education has to be solved before the students can reap any sort of benefit.

The idea of gifted education is novel and purposeful: support students who are more advanced than their peers and fuel their higher intellects. However, in practice, this novelty wears off and the problems become apparent. Stereotypes, both positive and negative, unfairly shape how gifted students develop. Chronic underachievement in the programs can be attributed to faulty administration and a lack of effective support. Widespread stress and depression leads to a culture of drugs and alcohol. Even the best gifted programs that exhibit few or none of these issues may only be available to certain students who can afford them. As a gifted student myself, I experienced all of these and more during my time in my elementary school's program. The students of this world need gifted programs that work and right now, they aren't getting them. Gifted education must not interfere with regular classes, but at the same time must provide more challenge and rigor than the system can alone. It must encourage students to be introspective, to find what they want to accomplish within themselves and make that their motivation to succeed. It must find ways to mitigate stress and distress, so gifted students do not become gifted addicts. And perhaps most importantly of all, it must be uniform and available to all students who need it. Until these changes are made, gifted students will continue to suffer.

Works Cited

Baudson, Tanja Gabriele, and Franzis Preckel. "Teachers' Conceptions of Gifted and Average-Ability Students on Achievement-Relevant Dimensions." *Gifted Child Quarterly*, vol. 60, no. 3, 30 Apr. 2016, pp. 212–225., doi:10.1177/0016986216647115.

"Frequently Asked Questions about Gifted Education." *Frequently Asked Questions about Gifted Education | National Association for Gifted Children*, National Association for Gifted Children, www.nagc.org/resources-publications/resources/frequently-asked-questions-about-gifted-education.

"Gifted Students." *HealthyChildren.org*, American Academy of Pediatrics, 2 Nov. 2009, www.healthychildren.org/English/ages-stages/teen/school/Pages/Gifted-Students.aspx.

Koshy, Valsa, and Catrin Pinheiro-Torres. "'Are We Being De-Gifted, Miss?' Primary School Gifted and Talented Co-Ordinators' Responses to the Gifted and Talented Education Policy in England." *British Educational Research Journal*, vol. 39, no. 6, 15 Oct. 2012, pp. 953–978., doi:10.1002/berj.3021. https://onlinelibrary-wiley-com.ezproxy2.library.drexel.edu/doi/full/10.1002/berj.3021

Mccoach, D. Betsy, and Del Siegle. "Factors That Differentiate Underachieving Gifted Students From High-Achieving Gifted Students." *Gifted Child Quarterly*, vol. 47, no. 2, 1 Apr. 2003, pp. 144–154., doi:10.1177/001698620304700205.

"Myths about Gifted Students." *Myths about Gifted Students | National Association for Gifted Children*, www.nagc.org/myths-about-gifted-students.

Peairs, Kristen F, et al. "Academic Giftedness and Alcohol Use in Early Adolescence." *The Gifted Child Quarterly*, U.S. National Library of Medicine, 1 Apr. 2011, www.ncbi.nlm.nih.gov/pmc/articles/PMC3177422/.

Reis, Sally M., and D. Betsy Mccoach. "The Underachievement of Gifted Students: What Do We Know and Where Do We Go?" *Gifted Child Quarterly*, vol. 44, no. 3, 2000, pp. 152–170., doi:10.1177/001698620004400302.

Shapiro, Eliza, and Jeffery C. Mays. "De Blasio Weighs Eliminating Gifted Programs in New York." *The New York Times*, The New York Times, 27 Aug. 2019, www.nytimes.com/2019/08/27/nyregion/de-blasio-gifted-talented-nyc.html.

Honorable Mention—First-Year Writing

Using the guidelines in the "Profiles" chapter in *The Norton Field Guide*, write a profile of an interesting person, place, or event. You will be required to interview someone, go somewhere, and/or participate in a live event.

— Dr. Christopher Nielson

Kalahne Serpanchy
Involuntary Disguises

On Halloween night, we dress up. We clothe ourselves in the costumes of monsters, celebrities, kings and queens, creatures of the Earth and beyond. We roam the streets in packs and gather in living room covens to celebrate in disguise. It is so rare that we are given the opportunity to shuck our skins and prance about in anonymity, that it failed to occur to me that I might meet someone unguarded and bare on a night devoted to cloak and trickery.

Dane looked ordinary; like any man I might meet on any night of the week. No camouflage: no charade. We laughed, we talked, and we smiled. I watch Dane get up and bounce lankily down the hallway, headed to the washroom.

"Where did Dane go?" someone asked. "They went to wash their hands."

I realized then that Dane had, in fact, been wearing a costume, and likely wore a costume every day of their life.

Dane is gender-fluid, or gender non-binary. They use they/them pronouns, and their gender identity fluctuates between man, woman, and somewhere in between. Identity is fickle, and when I sat down to ask Dane about theirs, it took some probing to uncover what they believed to be the catalyst of their realization regarding their gender-fluidity. A moment came to mind, and they bashfully leaned in to tell me about the partner they had when they were sixteen years old. Dane's long, light brown hair tumbled in front of their far-away eyes as they recounted the epiphany they underwent at the behest of this partner. Their partner was also questioning their gender identity at the time and together, the two of them explored what it meant to be divorced from the concept of the gender binary, or the idea that the only inhabitable states are man or woman. Dane and their partner have since gone their separate ways, but the experience and everything they learned from it stuck. Though they now feel comfortable in their self-identification, Dane still faces challenges in regards to how other people interact with their gender, and in turn how that interaction makes them feel.

As we sat in the dining hall, discussing who we are and how we act, I brought up the topic of presentation. Dane let me know that they also identify as transgender and suffered from gender dysphoria, which is a deep pain and discomfort that can stem from a feeling of the body not lining up with the brain.

As someone who identifies as non-binary but does not experience dysphoria the same way, I was curious to know how Dane balanced drifting between the gender they were assigned at birth and the opposite in such a way as to not activate their dysphoria. What they relayed to me was that it can often be a struggle. On certain days their dysphoria can peak, and there isn't a clear way of winning the battle when it does. Mostly what it comes down to for them is asking themselves questions, such as how they can present themselves in a way that best embodies how they feel.

This attempt to present one's gender identity on the outside, so as to be recognized as a preferred gender, is referred to as gender expression. For people like Dane and myself, gender expression is a complex game fraught with pitfalls and trap doors. As an occupant of the space in between man and woman, Dane often feels like someone who is pretending to be one or the other when they try to present themselves in a way that feels true to them. When they shared this feeling with me, I immediately let them know how familiar I found that experience to be. It can be hard to reconcile the inadequacies we feel about the way we present, and no permanent shape change or physical alteration can fully remedy this due to our equal perceived inadequacies on the opposite side of the gender spectrum.

Dane related to me the sensation of being a performer who has dressed up and is imitating a person of their desired gender, and that impression can be dehumanizing when it feels like there is no space for those who exist outside or in the middle of the gender binary. This is particularly true in cases where Dane has been misgendered, or perceived and identified as the wrong gender by the people around them. It is frustratingly common for non-binary people to get misgendered, as their outward expression can lean too heavily to a given side of the gender spectrum, or be androgynous to the point of people making a decision about their identity on their behalf. Dane, with their pained blue eyes, elaborated that they are frequently misgendered due to their inability to reject one side of the spectrum or the other. They are both, they feel like both, and this intertwinement is irrevocable. I looked at Dane, and took in their faint stubble and slender but angular jawline. They spoke quietly, and moved in a delicate but nervous fashion. It was clear to me the distress they felt from these interactions, wherein they were forced into a box they had tried so hard to evade.

This isolation weighed heavy on them. I pushed forward, my small hand on their large one, and asked if they could tell me about things they felt they'd had to surrender to embrace their gender-fluid identity. The response was sorrowful. They told me about their struggles with gendered spaces, specifically with public washrooms. The disconnect between their image of themselves, their personhood, and their perception by others resulted in an exclusion from places that should be accessible to them. I asked them how they healed the divide between how they felt and how they were perceived, and their reply took purchase in my heart.

"They don't know; only you know. And that's ok."

Dane wears costumes. Not on purpose, not by any choice of their own. The eyes of others drape them, veil them in the robes of an identity that cannot fit. Still, they walk freely in the light of their own love and self-acceptance. They wanted to leave me with the sentiment that the only thing that can be done in the face of isolation, rejection, and dysphoria is to trust in themselves and their identity. Though I met them on a night of disguises, I am so glad I got the chance to talk to them about their true self.

Honorable Mention—First-Year Writing
Write a profile.

— Professor Cassandra Hirsch

Ibim Sobiharry
Hustler's Paradise

Okay people, are we set? Yes? Alright then onwards we go. I will be your guide through this madness of a marketplace. Mind you, this is unlike any other marketplace you have ever been in. If you would like to leave, please do so now; leaving any time later could be incredibly hazardous to your wellbeing. This place is not for the lily-livered or faint-hearted. When David in the Bible spoke of "the valley of the shadow of death" he was almost certainly speaking of this place. At the same time this is also "the land of milk and honey." Ladies and gentlemen, as we enter this market make sure to guard your wallets, guard your personal belongings, guard your bodies. And, above all else, guard your faith, sanity, and morality.

The first thing that hits you is the noise; the glamour of hundreds of thousands of souls buying and selling, trading and begging, and shouting and yelling. That's how you know you have arrived in the market. If you look around you, you will no doubt notice the colors and the dirt. These are things you will find everywhere in this market; the dirt however will come in different forms and in varying degrees. Notice the smell, the strong overpowering smell of pastry sellers with puff-puff and donuts and roadside cooks forcing you to pay attention to their various meats and stews. In the course of this trip, we will encounter different scents all the time with something begging to be noticed. That is the nature of the market and the people of the market. Within the multitude there are individuals and groups of individuals that will just not go unnoticed. Mind the mud all over the floor. These are just the dirtier parts of the market. You can see the rickety stalls of some traders right next to the buildings that house others? That is how it is over this market; this is a market of extremes, the extremely rich right next to the extremely poor. Constantly there are people tugging on your clothes to "come and buy these jeans" or "see this fine belt I have for you." In the market everybody wants you. A strong will and foreknowledge of your purpose are essential to not be swayed by the waves of people offering you 101 things at once. Many people come and end up spending all their time and money and leaving with things they don't need or even want.

The vendors at this market often have several "boys" scouring the streets looking for customers, essentially anybody. In my opinion, these are some of the best and most relentless marketers the world over. Never have I seen a group of people so devoted to their hustle. First off they approach you and hit you with the "feel-good" move by saying "fine boy, fine girl, angel, my colour etc." If you are ever feeling down just step into the market and you are definitely getting a compliment. Then they quickly offer their product to you promising to have all the varieties you could dream about. If you display even the slightest hesitation or interest, they are convinced you are hooked and will do almost anything in their power to reel you in. If by some witchcraft they do not have the specific product that you need, rest assured that one "boy" is going to scour the market for that exact design or the closest possible to it. Not because they value you or your time, but because there is a strong bond and money lust in the market. The "boy" knows that as he gives you that referral, he's going to get his cut. That's the funny thing about the market, it's every man for himself, but amongst the poorer it's not quite dog-eat-dog as it is with the richer.

It is rare that two customers get the same item for the exact same price. There is obviously a price range but the exact price has many variables to it. The vendors have an impeccable sense for detecting foreigners, people from the upper classes that have never been poor, and recently relocated Nigerian a.k.a JJD (Johnny Just Drop). For this class of people, the quoted prices are two to four times inflated so if you find yourself within this class, start negotiations at a fourth of the quoted price. To an extent, you can say everybody is trying to cheat you but understand they are just trying to make more money like everyone else. After all, man must eat and provide. Sometimes the paths we take to reach our petty goals are so extreme and who are these vendors to do anything different? In the market it's all about packaging. The container is the difference between a $5000 and a $50 coat. Truthfully, the quality may have some part to play but it's mostly the branding. In the market it's all glitz and glam and flashing lights. Everything is made up, painted over, it's all just props. All packaging affects the product's price: the nature of the shop, the presence of an air conditioner, seating space, down to how to vendors are dressed.

All prices are negotiable but watch yourself, asking below a certain unspoken threshold can result in insults and curses even down to your 4th generation to be evoked on you. And when these insults and curses come, I beg of you to hold yourself or as they say in pidgin *"no go do pass yourself."* Returning the insults could be fatal to your health. *"Nobody get mind pass person wey no get shishi to lose"* meaning nobody is bolder than people without anything to lose which is the case with many "boys."

Due to the raw size and human population of the market, it is often subject to political ventures. Recently, a part of the market has been demolished and rebuilt in order for some elitist governor to brag or *"raise shoulder"* and use it as a talking point at a political rally. When these shopping complexes go up it is usually an incredibly violent and corrupt process. Many vendors and "boys" are brutalized by state police and their products destroyed without as little as a second thought. Worst off are the food vendors you saw closer to the street. Usually the old ladies are beaten and their foodstuffs are stolen or destroyed on sight. Additionally, rent in the complex is too expensive for most vendors to realistically afford. The cost to sell in the complex or close to it is ridiculously high but the curious fact is that these complexes still get filled up. That's where the corrupt nature of these buildings come in, many store owners have relationships with corrupt officials or some illegal source of money and need to put up a legal front. To make matters worse, these buildings are poorly constructed and maintained so officials can pocket money budgeted to construction and maintenance.

Above all the problems and issues in this market, there is one thing that remains true. The market always smiles at the end of the day. No matter how many times it is ravaged, raped, beaten and broken down, in the words of Maya Angelou, "still they rise". I believe market dwellers have found the secret to life because for them there is always a reason to dance and *"flenjo."* Maybe it's in celebrating the small victories, or appreciating life more or maybe not taking life too seriously all the time. Don't be fooled by the laughter and music you hear in the market. Living here is for the strong. Life is tough for both the rich and the poor. While their sufferings are not the same, they are comparable. You can survive anywhere if you survive here and you have not been anywhere if you haven't been here. Welcome to the market. This market is the city of Lagos, Nigeria, a hustler's paradise.

Honorable Mention—First-Year Writing

The purpose of this assignment is to write a paper built around your own primary research. Choose a topic that interests you and figure out a way to use primary research to explore it. Remember that you can generate primary research in many ways.

— Professor Henry Israeli

Renae Tingling
Sleepless Nights of a University Student

When can we say we've had "enough" sleep? Does the amount of sleep someone gets in a night make a difference? Is getting enough sleep even worth it? According to Newton's first law of motion, a body in motion will stay in motion unless acted upon by an opposing external force. The human body experiences this opposing force in the form of tiredness, slowly approaching as our day comes to an end. For most college students, their days are jam-packed with an infinite number of responsibilities, ranging from exam preparations and homework assignments to managing student organizations and completing chores. Much like myself, many students find themselves trapped in a cycle of work with rest on the back burner.

As a first-year student, I took on a list of new and exciting ventures during my first week. As the weeks progressed, the announcement of midterms marked the end of the adjustment period. I found myself adding more tasks to my to-do list than I was marking off, while time ran shorter by the day. Surrendering a portion of my sleeping hours to my work was involuntary. Even though I felt satisfied having completed my assignments, the lack of sleep did not go unnoticed by my body. My body's demand for compensation resulted in me waking up at some ungodly hour the following Saturday afternoon. This hadn't been common practice for me, which made me wonder if the same could be said for other students. Is this something that most college students perpetually struggle with? If so, why? Apart from just waking up later than usual, how does it affect their lives as students, if at all? It's best if we start by figuring out what the big deal is about sleep.

Sleep plays a crucial role in the maintenance of an individual's overall health and wellness. A good and consistent quantity and quality of sleep can help with the regulation of physiological processes (Kabrita 189-96) such as cardiovascular activity and glucose regulation (Cheng). For students, sleep is like our very own pot of gold in some sense. It is essential for effective processing of information (Kabrita 189-96), memorization and proper immune function (Carter 315). Worley (758-63) makes reference to statements made by Dr. David F. Dinges, PhD, Professor of Psychology and Chief of the Division of

Sleep and Chronobiology in the Department of Psychiatry at the University of Pennsylvania School of Medicine:

> We know, for example, that sleep is critical for waking cognition—that is, for the ability to think clearly, to be vigilant and alert, and sustain attention. We also know that memories are consolidated during sleep, and that sleep serves a key role in emotional regulation.

So, what exactly is a good quality of sleep? Some would argue that it's almost entirely subjective. Some students find taking short and frequent naps is a much more effective way of getting all their hours in, while others couldn't disagree more. For the average person, the target should be around seven to seven and a half hours of uninterrupted sleep (Worley 758-63). Lichtenstein (790) refers to a list of recommended sleeping hours issued by the National Sleep Foundation. In this, young adults are recommended to have a total of seven to nine hours of sleep with no fewer than six and no more than ten. Anything below six hours and you've reached the danger zone. Sleep deficiency can have a severe and lasting impact on a student's academic performance. A poor quality of sleep can greatly impact our decision-making process (Pilcher 284), short- and long-term cognitive ability, and our processing of emotional memory (Worley 758-63). This can not only lead to a decline in academic performance but can also be a catalyst for future mental health issues (Hyder).

Ask any university student and they would probably agree with the phrase "Sleep is a privilege." There are countless factors at play during a student's academic journey that can heavily disrupt their sleep schedules. Habitual procrastination is a major cause of increased stress among university students (Sirois), which may result in developed health issues such as insomnia (difficulty falling and/or staying asleep). A study conducted by G. Suna and A. Ayaz (S131-2) found that though consumption of most caffeinated beverages had no correlation to poor quality of sleep, coffee was the exception. Students with a poor sleep quality consumed a notably larger amount of coffee than those with a good sleep quality. Prolonged internet usage and cigarette smoking are other behavioral factors that can eat away at students' precious hours of sleep. This brings into question those factors that exist beyond the control of the student. Who better to ask than the students themselves?

A total of 33 students participated in this survey, ranging from freshman to pre-junior year. The questionnaire collected information pertaining to participants' class level, sleep patterns, and factors that may disrupt their sleep schedule and how that affects them academically. Most students reported sleeping for the recommended number of hours (7 – 9) either a few times or not at all (80%). Behavioral influences, like prolonged internet usage and late-night studying for upcoming tests/exams, showed prevalence among the sample group. In the case of external influences, many students reported that disruptive roommates and outside noise hindered them from sleeping. Some students also pointed out that trying to complete assignments before their fast-approaching deadlines caused heavy stress and prevented them from getting more hours of sleep. Very few placed the blame on social activities. With habitual and external factors such as these, it is understandable that a low quality of sleep can lead to low academic success (Carter 315). Consequently, many students found it difficult to be attentive and involved during lectures (87%), successfully complete an exam (56%), and maintain their involvement in student organizations (65%) after a night of little to no sleep. Approximately half of the participants reported that they rely or have relied on medication and/or caffeinated beverages to feel alert during the day. About halfway through my experiment, I didn't mind the thought of having a cup of coffee myself.

I'll admit, getting out of bed at 5 was a bit of a challenge, especially after sleeping for a total of four and a half hours. It wasn't by chance that by the start of the first day, I had already reached my quota of embarrassing absent-minded mistakes after having pressed the wrong button on the elevator and wandering into the wrong classroom. This unusual behavior is due to the effect that lack of sleep had on my level of self-control (Pilcher 284) and alertness (Worley 758-63). This can greatly throw off a person's decision-making process.

By the second day, getting half of a night's worth of sleep took a greater toll on me. Most of the day's lectures had managed to slip right past me. Too often to count, I found myself opening eyes I hadn't even realized were closed. What little attention span I had left went to counting down the minutes until the end of each session. Now, we can all agree that conducting an experiment like this during the exam period would not be the wisest thing to do. Knowing this, I was prepared to add this to my list of mistakes. Funnily enough, my lack of sleep did not have its way with the quiz I took that day. In that moment, the effects of my sleep deprivation seemingly vanished. It was as though my brain ensured that I was able to place all my efforts into not failing Math. Sadly, those effects came back sometime afterwards and with a vengeance. I became so demotivated to do just about anything afterwards that even having dinner with friends seemed like too much of a task. I was completely against the idea of preparing for upcoming lectures and exams and used how tired I felt as an excuse. This drives home the notion that sleep deprivation can have serious psychological impacts such as weakening our ability to concentrate on academic material (Kabrita 189-96).

Oddly enough, I felt a lot less tired on the third day. Though I still felt somewhat tired, it was as if my body was getting used to the of sleep I was getting. By the end of the day, my experiment came to a close, allowing me a well-deserved night's rest. What took me by surprise was how exhausted I felt the following morning after a full eight hours of rest. I initially expected to feel well-rested having given myself the chance to get the recommended amount of sleep. I felt as I had on the first morning of the experiment, even though I had double the amount of sleep time. Thankfully, a few days of seven to eight hours of sleep afterwards was enough to get me back on track. I was able to focus on discussions during lectures and more motivated to attend club meetings and study with friends for whatever the next exam would be. It was surprising to discover just how much greatly each day was affected by the amount of sleep I got several nights before. It wasn't too hard for me to imagine the damaging effects that poor sleep habits would have long-term.

Sleep is a beautiful thing; my experiment is a testament to this. Many of us see it as the easiest and most convenient thing to sacrifice on our journey to academic success. How ironic is it that, as we continue to undermine its significance, sleep can potentially determine whether we achieve that success. It should be mentioned that students often find themselves in situations where valuable hours of sleep are stolen from them by circumstances beyond their control. Whether deliberate or unintentional, lost sleep can take a lot more than bargained for. If I had to speak on something I took from research, it would be that we as students have fallen for the misconception that less sleep is the only way to stay on top of everything. As a result, we tend to make everything a priority except ourselves. We place getting those extra hours of studying above resting the brain that has to take the exam the following day. At the end of the day, the benefits of getting a good night's rest are limitless, so ask yourself this: Do I get enough sleep?

Works Cited

Carter, Briana, et al. "An Analysis of the Sleep Quality of Undergraduate Students." *College Student Journal*, vol. 50, no. 3, 2016, p. 315. Gale Academic Onefile, Accessed 11 Nov. 2019. Web.

Cheng, Shu Hui, et al. "A Study on the Sleep Quality of Incoming University Students." *Psychiatry Research*, Elsevier, 18 Feb. 2012. Web.

G. Suna, and A. Ayaz,. "Relationship Between Caffeinated Beverages and Sleep Quality in University Students." *Clinical Nutrition*, Elsevier, vol. 37(1), 2018, pp. S131-S132. Web.

Kabrita, Colette S., and Theresa Hajjar-Muça A. "Sex-Specific Sleep Patterns among University Students in Lebanon: Impact on Depression and Academic Performance." *Nature and Science of Sleep,* vol. 8, 2016, pp. 189-196. Accessed 11 November 2019. Web.

Lichtenstein, Gary R. "The Importance of Sleep." *Gastroenterology & Hepatology* vol. 11,12 2015, Millennium Medical Publishing, p. 790. Accessed 11 November 2019. Web.

Mirghani, Hyder Osman, et al. "Good Sleep Quality is Associated with Better Academic Performance among Sudanese Medical Students." *BMC Research Notes*, vol. 8, no. 702, 2015. Gale Academic Onefile, Accessed 11 Nov. 2019. Web.

Pilcher, June J et al. "Interactions Between Sleep Habits and Self-control." *Frontiers in Human Neuroscience*, Leonhard Schilbach, ed. vol. 9, Frontiers Media S.A., pp. 284. 11 May. 2015. Web.

Sirois, F. M., van Eerde, W., and Argiropoulou, M. I. "Is Procrastination Related to Sleep Quality? Testing an Application of the Procrastination–Health Model." *Cogent Psychology*. 2015. Accessed 11 November 2019. Web.

Worley, Susan L. "The Extraordinary Importance of Sleep: The Detrimental Effects of Inadequate Sleep on Health and Public Safety Drive an Explosion of Sleep Research." *P&T: a peer-reviewed journal for formulary management* vol. 43, 12 2018, pp. 758-763. Web

Honorable Mention—First-Year Writing

Write a profile of an interesting person, place, or event. You will be required to interview someone, go somewhere, and/or participate in a live event.

— Dr. Sheila Sandapen

Najifa Zaman
Dancing in The Rain

Tap tap tap, the drizzling rain danced on top of the tin roof of the two-story house. Inside, everyone sat around the fireplace with various roasted nuts and hot masala chai, chatting so loud that the sounds of the rain were completely drowned out. Almost twenty people, but no one seemed to notice that she was missing, no one noticed the thundering laugh and dorky stories of the youngest daughter were missing; she was gone from their mind just like the sounds of the rain.

The bells of her silver anklets played against beautiful pale ankles; rainbow-colored bangles jingled loudly on her hands as she tightened the strings of her skirt against her slim waist. A clumsy smile bloomed on her face as rain fell through the open window on to her small figure. She carefully climbed out the window of her room, silently making sure no one was around to catch her, and ran towards the path to a beautiful clearing that had become a special place. The clanking sound of her silver jewelry and swish of her knee-length hair almost made her look like a flying angel, the sounds of her bells grew as she quickened her pace when she got a glimpse of the green clearing in front of her. To one anyone else this would have been quite foolish, walking out in the rain when it was this cold, walking out in the monsoon rain without an umbrella but to her, the rain was heaven, it was her own heaven, which made her completely immune to the cold. She ran to the middle of the field as she hummed to her favorite sound, the sound of her anklets and the rain. Her delicate hands moved with so much grace that it could put any goddess to shame. Each movement of her hands moved with the rhythm of the rain, which would then be followed by a twirl that would make her white skirt expand so much around her that it almost made all of her legs underneath visible if not for her tights. Each of her movements were done with so much precision and so much passion that it could take the breath away from anyone who was willing to watch, but no one was watching, no one was there, it was only her, the rain and sounds of her anklets. Each and every curve of her hands flowed with so much ease, each gesture contained a bliss that almost made her forget about everything wrong with her life. She almost forgot that this was forbidden and that she was currently playing with fire. If she were to be caught, she would be doomed. Dancing was a sin. Her family made sure she knew, they made sure to remind her of the consequence every time it rained, and she danced. It was a blessing that it didn't rain much until monsoon.

After an incense stick of time—a mere thirty minutes—she realized that she overstayed her welcome. She ran while hastily collecting her sandals from where she had randomly thrown them under a magnolia tree. As dread overcame her entire figure, she thought of everything, everything that she forgot while dancing. She was born and raised in a religiously strict family where dancing was an unforgivable sin, and leaving the house without anyone accompanying her was an even bigger one. If she was caught, she knew she would have no say in the punishment, she knows she will submit, she will bow down like the angel that she is. Reaching the back windows of her room, she hurriedly yet carefully climbed into her room and relief washed over her as she realized that a search party hadn't been sent for her.

The four months-long monsoon season was coming to an end. It was almost the end of September, she was twenty, the perfect age. The monsoon season makes life hard for everyone, but for her, these rainy months were the only time she knew she was safe from judging eyes of her neighbors and from the thing that she hates the most in the world: proposals; marriage proposals. The father that looks at his beautiful daughter with so much love shining in his eyes that it seemed almost impossible for him to punish his daughter like that, it seemed as if he would never cage his beautiful angel like that. Angels were meant to fly, she thought. Angels have wings, so why couldn't she just fly away? Why couldn't she just dance to her heart's content? Why was she stuck here, under the supervision of her five older brothers and a village chief of a father?

He was an average-looking boy almost six years older than her. She had yet to utter a single word to him, but she could it feel it, the acceptance of her family had for the young man in the ugly black suit. This is not what she wanted, she thought as he slipped the simple gold wedding band onto her ring finger, and at that very moment, she felt as if her wings were being ripped away from her. At that very moment, she heard a distant sound, a pair of dancing anklets falling apart.

The day was finally here. The red and gold wedding dress fit her body like Cinderella's glass slipper, the dozens of red gold bangles on her arms perfectly matched with her dress, while the gold crown on her head mimicked a halo. Almost every visible part of her body was adorned with beautiful exotic gold pieces. She looked like a goddess. The gasps of the guests were loud and clearly heard by her as she walked past them on a flowered path to her husband whose name she had already forgotten.

It was the last rain of that year's monsoon; it was beautiful, but it was too heavy to dance in. It almost looked almost as if the sky was crying, crying with her, crying for her. Knowing that her wedding was just two weeks away, knowing that she had nothing to lose she walked out of the house again, but this time through the front door and with an umbrella. Everyone was shouting at her to stop walking, to come back home, that it was almost her wedding, that she will catch a cold, but she was numb. She kept walking until she arrived at that clearing again. She tried to hum her song again, she tried to remember the tune and the words of her favorite song, but she couldn't remember anything, yet she kept on trying and trying. Finally, her legs gave out and she fell on her knees. It was so cold, her tears blending in with the rain, making her look like a lunatic who was laughing by herself in the rain. She cried, she cried as her brothers cut off her wings, she cried as her family replaced her white dress with a bright red wedding robe, she cried as she made vows to a stranger, she cried as the bells of the anklets broke off and pried through her heart.

"I cried," she told me, "I cried until I couldn't anymore. Do you know why I danced in the rain?" my aunt asked me.

"No." I said.

"It's because no one saw me, no one heard me, it was just me, my anklets, and the rain." She told me this as she tied her anklets on her ankles and walked out in the rain with her newly-formed wings.

Drexel Publishing Group

Essays

Introduction

Researching, thinking, and writing are at the core of the College of Arts and Sciences. In every field, students must be able to find and evaluate the best evidence and information on a topic. Students must be able to form original ideas, and then write with a fresh approach.

The following essays were selected from student submissions to the Drexel Publishing Group Essay Contest. The contest was judged by faculty from a wide range of disciplines in the College of Arts and Sciences. The essays in this section of *The 33rd* explore diverse topics such as climate change, genetic modification, education, gender roles, and literature. These student writers demonstrate originality, skill, and passion, and do so in a variety of disciplines in the arts and sciences.

To honor the stylistic requirements of each field, we have reproduced the essays and articles in their original forms.

—*The Editors*

First Place—Humanities

Sanjana Ramanathan
The Story of Philomela in Eliot's *The Waste Land*

The mythological story of Philomela is used by T.S. Eliot in his poem *The Waste Land* to represent the ignorance of modern life. Philomela and her association with the nightingale act as symbols for the endurance of story. In the hellish setting of modern life that Eliot paints throughout the poem, the allusions he makes become a connection to what he considers a more classically educated time. The repetition of the nightingale's song in *The Waste Land*, surrounded by Eliot's lamentations for lost culture, becomes an echo of a forgotten past. Like Philomela using her tapestry to tell the story of her rape, Eliot weaves the princess of Athens' story and its symbolism through *The Waste Land*.

The story of Philomela, contained in Book VI of Ovid's *Metamorphoses*, is a tragic one. Tereus, the king of Thrace, marries Procne, princess of Athens. The marriage is ill-fated from the start, as many divine beings choose not to attend the wedding. After five years of marriage, Procne misses her sister Philomela, and asks her husband to escort Philomela from Athens to Thrace. Tereus obliges but is overcome with lust at the first sight of Philomela. Tereus rapes Philomela and then hacks off her tongue when she threatens to expose him.

Unable to speak, the only way Philomela is able to convey her story is by weaving the events into a tapestry, which she then sends to her sister. After receiving the tapestry depicting Philomela's rape, Procne retrieves her sister and they plot revenge against Tereus. Procne kills her and Tereus' son, Itys, and chops his body to pieces, which she then boils and serves to Tereus. After he finishes the meal, Procne and Philomela reveal its true contents by presenting Itys' severed head. Enraged, Tereus chase the sisters with an axe. Philomela and Procne flee, praying to the gods in desperation; their pleas are answered, and the gods turn Procne into a swallow and Philomela into a nightingale (Ovid lines 412-677).

The story of Philomela's rape is mostly explicitly referred to in the second part of *The Waste Land*. The section, titled "A Game of Chess," opens with the description of the elaborately furnished room of a lavish woman. On the wall hangs an artwork depicting Philomela's story, a tragic and seemingly out-of-place scene to display among the luxurious surroundings; it is described in lines 97 to 103:

> Above the antique mantel was displayed
>
> As though a window gave upon the sylvan scene
>
> The change of Philomel, by the barbarous king

> So rudely forced; yet there the nightingale
>
> Filled all the desert with inviolable voice
>
> And still she cried, and still the world pursues,
>
> "Jug Jug" to dirty ears.

The contrasting imagery plays into Eliot's criticism of modern life, in which the upper class uses what is considered "high culture" to flag themselves as being superior, while their actual understanding is shallow. This is a message prevalent in Eliot's work, even outside of *The Waste Land*. For example, in his poem *The Love Song of J. Alfred Prufrock*, the narrator expresses contempt for the banality of modern conversations, in which topics like the Renaissance are considered high culture but used shallowly without real understanding.

Eliot uses Philomela's connection to the nightingale as a recurring motif for the struggle of expression. The nightingale continues its cries, yet its persistence is futile; the message is lost on the "dirty ears" (line 103) of people who are unaware to the suffering behind it. Instead, the nightingale's "Jug Jug" (line 103) is taken for its colloquial meaning, a "crude joking reference to sexual intercourse" (Reeves 56). Eliot uses the reduction of the nightingale's cry to criticize the loss of classical knowledge. A painting of Philomela's pivotal change hangs in the room of a rich woman, but how much of the princess' story is really known to the house's inhabitants? Eliot implies that works like Ovid's *Metamorphoses* are used to indicate cultural superiority, while the actual story fades from knowledge.

The next stanza begins by saying that "other withered stumps of time / Were told upon the walls" (lines 104-105), referring to the scene of Philomela's change and other classical depictions of art hanging in the lavish room. Describing these pieces as "withered stumps of time" (line 104) serves a double purpose. The first is a direct reference to Tereus cutting out Philomela's tongue, leaving behind a stump. On a metaphorical level, the meaning of these pieces has decayed in modern times. As modern people can only speak shallowly on these topics, their words would be just as meaningful if nothing were said at all.

Eliot's use of the shortened name "Philomel" is likely inspired by Shakespeare, who is referenced often in *The Waste Land*. Shakespeare likely shortened the name so it would better fit the meter, and he used the name as a representation of female characters who are suffering in his works (Harriman-Smith). Though Eliot does not have Shakespeare's restrictions of poetic rhythm, he uses "Philomel" similarly: as a symbol for those suffering in silence, due to their stories not being passed on.

The nightingale reappears in the third section of the poem, titled "The Fire Sermon," on lines 203-206:

> Twit twit twit

Jug jug jug jug jug jug

So rudely forc'd

Tereu

The nightingale's cry repeats in the poem like an echo of the past. The birdsong's rhythmic melody is a connection between music and modernity, especially in this section of the piece. "The Fire Sermon," more often than other sections, uses pieces of popular songs and references to music from the past and present to show the degradation of culture.

The stanza before the nightingale's return ends with the following line: "*Et O ces voix d'enfants, chantant dans la coupole!*" (line 202). It translates to "And oh those children's voices, singing in the dome!" It comes from the work of French poet Paul Verlaine's, "Parsifal," in which a knight of King Arthur has to resist sexual temptation in order to drink from the Holy Grail. Eliot's characters sing this line as they wash their feet in the Thames, which has become polluted as a result of modern life. He removes the original line from the context of "Parsifal," whose protagonist was a symbol of hope and renewal, and instead uses it to represent the opposite: modern people giving in to temptation and, rather than drinking from the holy grail, are left instead to soak in filth.

Following this stanza with the nightingale's cry and emphasizing King Tereus' name (shortened here to "Tereu" [line 206]) is significant, as the tragedy of Philomela is set in motion when the king gives in to his own temptation. In this context, the repetition of "jug jug" becomes a warning to modern people, one that goes unheard because those same people are ignorant of Philomela's tale. The song of the nightingale becomes a reflection of the lost past in the cultural ignorance of modernity.

The "Fire Sermon" ends with a description of a man and woman having sex, though it is dispassionate and loveless. The superficiality of this meeting is, in Eliot's eyes, a reflection of the modern world. After the man leaves, the woman "puts a record on the gramophone" (line 256), playing popular music of the time. The nightingale's song, imbued with deeper meaning, is a contrast to the record, which represents popular culture. The modern woman is passive about her sexual experience and becomes a contradiction to Philomela's perseverance.

In critiquing this aspect of modernity, however, Eliot seemingly contradicts himself throughout the poem. His portrayal of modern people using cultural milestones devoid of context is reflected in how Eliot himself references work: taking the words of others and using them without their original meaning. He takes lines from Shakespeare, Verlaine, and other authors and uses them in *The Waste Land*, then expresses contempt for the modern public mimicking classical education. In most of his references, Eliot strips cultural lines of their context and fits the words to meet his own meaning.

This makes it significant that Eliot has provided context, however little, of Philomela's story within the poem. Although critiquing the lack of cultural knowledge in modern day, Eliot himself keeps Philomela's story alive, giving the context of her rape "so rudely forc'd" (line 100) at the hands of the "barbarous king" (line 99) even when the characters of the poem can't understand the bird's cry. This small addition sets Philomela's story apart from the other allusions he makes, which are usually removed entirely from their original context in the poem itself. Eliot, while weaving *The Waste Land*, made the choice to convey Philomela's tale to the modern people who would read his work.

Although Eliot's depiction of life and reality in *The Waste Land* is dispiriting, Philomela's story almost serves as a silver lining. Despite the erasure of her story in modern times, her voice remains "inviolable" (line 101) through the nightingale's song. Eliot despairs over the public forgetting the culture of the past yet chooses to preserve Philomela's story using *The Waste Land*. Philomela exemplifies the importance of a story's survival; without her persistence, her story would have been lost when Tereus took her tongue from her. Eliot, in his use of Philomela as a motif, both critiques modern life and expresses hope that the stories and culture thought to be lost can still find a way to survive.

Works Cited

Eliot, T. S. "The Love Song of J. Alfred Prufrock." *The Waste Land and Other Poems*. New York, N.Y., U.S.A: Penguin Books, 1998.

Eliot, T. S. "The Waste Land." *The Waste Land and Other Poems*. New York, N.Y., U.S.A: Penguin Books, 1998.

Harriman-Smith, James. "Word of the Day: Philomel." Open Literature, 15 Oct. 2011, openliterature.net/2011/10/15/word-of-the-day-philomel/.

Ovid. "Metamorphoses." *Metamorphoses*, Book 6, Brookes More, Ed., 1922, www.perseus.tufts.edu/hopper/text?doc=Perseus:text:1999.02.0028:book=6:card=412.

Reeves, Gareth. T. S. Eliot's *The Waste Land*. Routledge, 29 Sept. 2017.

Second Place—Humanities

Priya Dudhat

Flight as Escape or Confrontation; Mercy the Unspoken Wish of the Novel's Population

In the foreword of *Song of Solomon*, Toni Morrison expresses mercy and flight as two terms "central to the narrative: flight as escape or confrontation; mercy the unspoken wish of the novel's population" (xiii). Both terms are intertwined as, without flight, or freeing oneself from limitations, one cannot obtain mercy-- which Morrison defines as the attainment of anything the white world restricts from the black community, whether it is freedom, the community, or unity-- and vice versa. Morrison introduces and connects the two concepts through the characters Robert Smith, Jake, Pilate, and Milkman, for each character attains freedom or relief through either mercy or flight. Morrison begins and ends the novel with a plea for mercy and an attempt at flight, both of which highlight what the characters lack-- a life free from suffering and true freedom. By bookending the novel in this manner, Morrison helps readers better understand the purpose of Milkman's quest both for him and for his community.

Morrison first introduces the connection between mercy and flight with Robert Smith, whose leap off of Mercy Hospital symbolizes a call for mercy and freedom from suffering. Morrison specifically states that Mr. Smith leaps into the air after seeing the rose petals. The rose petals symbolize conformity or a lack of independence, for Magdalena uses the petals to silence herself and keep herself in her role of being a proper, dutiful daughter. Morrison also describes the petals as a "smothering death of dry roses," using descriptive words with negative connotations to highlight the suffocating nature of the roses, especially through the noun "smothering" (199). Robert Smith sees these petals, which distract the audience's attention from his call for mercy to "the bits of red flashing around," and he recognizes their fixation on the roses instead of his flight (5). Despite Smith's wearing "wide blue silk wings" and standing on the edge of Mercy Hospital, no one pays attention to him and, instead, focuses on the petals, highlighting their inability to be free, as they ignore the freedom Smith's flight represents (5). So, he then jumps to demand "a cessation of things as they are," such as the community's conforming to their societal role as inferior to whites, instead of freeing themselves from those roles and gaining mercy (xiii). And, following his leap and death, the townsfolk gain a bit of mercy, for Milkman is then born into the hospital-- now known as No-Mercy hospital due to the realization, after Mr. Smith's flight, that they do not have mercy-- as the first colored baby. His birth expresses, for the colored community, an increase in power and relief from suffering from discrimination, also known as mercy. So, Mr. Smith's leap results from the lack of independence blacks have in relation to the racial hierarchy, which the rose petals symbolize, but his flight represents "a radical gesture demanding change" (xiii). All in all, Robert Smith's leap brings "change" in the form of mercy for the community, since the color barriers that once restrict them decrease, proving that flight allows one to obtain mercy.

Although the two characters are distant in terms of chronology and geography, Morrison links Jake to Robert Smith through the motif of flight, for Jake refuses to bind to the racial hierarchies and instead, soars above those restrictions. Before Jake dies protecting his property, he gets "blown off a fence five feet into the air" (140). While his time airborne does not last long, he flies, nevertheless. Jake's ability to fly results from his independence and self-sufficiency. In his community, he owns one of the biggest plots of land, named "Lincoln's Heaven," which contains "a fortune in oak and pine," "a stream, full of fish," a "four-stall hog pen," and a "big barn," all of which are located "in the heart of a valley" and near mountains with "deer and wild turkey" (51). The description of food, animals, agriculture, and vast land express the idea of self-sufficiency-- that Jake has the power to provide for himself and his family independent of others' help. Additionally, the name "Lincoln's Heaven" conveys Jake's possession of power and his emancipation from racial struggles. Although Jake soon loses the right to his property to the Butlers, for his illiteracy causes him to sign off his land, he does not conform and give up his property. Instead, he sits on the fence armed, waiting for the Butlers to appear. His protecting the property conveys defiance, for he rebels against the whites' rule. Because Jake dismisses the Butlers' influence and risks his life for everything he once earned, Jake demonstrates his courage and power that allows him to become independent from racial hierarchies. His independence and courage cause Jake to fly "five feet into the air," despite losing his property and facing death, as he does not allow blacks' so-called inferiority to whites to bind him, allowing him to fly freely.

While Jake's narrative solely expresses the concept of flight, Pilate's story highlights the idea of mercy, especially through Hagar's funeral scene; Pilate wishes mercy for Hagar, but because of her authority, she manages to provoke mercy in the townsfolk as well. During Hagar's service, Pilate first shouts "Mercy! as though it were a command" (316). This command prompts the winos "who dared not enter the room" to begin sobbing, for the desperation and authority in Pilate's voice reaches them, forcing them to sympathize for both Hagar and Pilate. The winos' lack of sympathy beforehand demonstrates that the townsfolk are disconnected from each other, as they deemphasize the importance of community by physically and emotionally separating themselves from the service. However, Pilate's shouting, "Mercy!" brings the townsfolk and Hagar together, suggesting that mercy stems from unity. Throughout the era during and after slavery, white supremacy destroyed the cohesiveness of the black community. By regaining this sense of togetherness that Pilate's shouting promotes, the community acquires relief from their suffering, of a loss of unity, and obtains mercy. Despite Pilate's singing and crying out for mercy, the nerve of the townsfolk "failed them" and their "glances would climb no higher than the long black fingers at her side," displaying their emotional detachment from each other once again (319). Additionally, when she leans in and tells them, "My baby girl," Morrison describes Pilate's statement as "words tossed like stones into a silent canyon" (319). Comparing the townsfolk to a "silent canyon" highlights their apathy during the sermon, especially since they refuse to meet Pilate's eyes as if they fear relating to her. By emphasizing the lack of emotion the townsfolk display throughout the sermon, Morrison expresses that the townsfolk lack unity. It is not until Pilate yells, "And she was *loved!*" that the townsfolk unify and earn a degree of mercy. Pilate's exclamation causes a wino to drop his wine, "spurting emerald glass and jungle-red wine everywhere" (319). Both the glass shattering and the "jungle-red wine everywhere" convey a dramatic change or realization, for the glass cannot be restored to its original state and the red wine stains everything-- representing community's inability to go back to the way things were-disconnected. This realization would not occur without Pilate's call for mercy and declaration of love, for her cries snap the townsfolk out of their apathetic lives and force them to sympathize with Hagar and Pilate, proving that mercy stems from unity, community, and love-- three concepts that the white world limits.

Lastly, Morrison connects the concept of flight to the motif of mercy through Milkman's leap during his final confrontation with Guitar, conveying that mercy leads to flight, the inverse of what Mr. Smith's leap expresses. Morrison explains in the foreword that "Mercy touches, turns, and returns to Guitar at the end of the book, and moves him to make it his own final gift to his former friend" (xiii). His "final gift" to Milkman is the mending of their friendship. Earlier, Milkman and Guitar's differences in beliefs regarding their racial identities divide them, as they represent two extremes of the Civil Rights era-- a lack of action and an aggressive, militaristic fight for freedom, respectively. Morrison displays the two characters' disconnection when Guitar reveals his involvement in the Seven Days to Milkman; Milkman then states that he himself could be a target, and Guitar responds with, "We don't off Negroes," emphasizing *Negroes*, not "Milkman" (161). Guitar's separating "Milkman" from "Negroes" highlights the two men's detachment from each other, for Guitar's behavior revolves around protecting the black community-- as his participation in the Seven Days demonstrates-- yet Guitar excludes Milkman from that community. But, during their final confrontation, Guitar fortifies their relationship, for Guitar calls Milkman his "main man," reinforcing the strength of their friendship, and even puts down his gun (337). The gun signifies Guitar's aggressive approach to obtaining freedom, which Milkman challenges-- so by putting the gun down and, instead, intimately confronting Milkman, Guitar puts aside the issues that divide them, allowing Milkman to acquire mercy through their unification.

Additionally, the connection, unity, and freedom that both Guitar and Pilate offer Milkman in the final scene allows him to fly. Guitar's act of mercy by forgoing his gun and engaging in combat, instead of shooting him on the spot, gives Milkman the opportunity to fly. More importantly, Milkman manages to fly due to Pilate's inspiring him. For example, when Milkman leaps, Morrison describes him "as fleet and bright as a lodestar" (337). His comparison to a "lodestar" alludes to the scene when Pilate's earring "blazed like a star," during Hagar's service, "Out of the total blackness of her clothes" (317). By the earring's shining against the darkness, Morrison expresses hope and unity, which comes from the connectedness and love the earring represents-- as the earring symbolizes the Dead family's history, such as Jake Dead's writing Pilate's name-- and the fact that the light chases away the darkness. The comparison of the earring to a "star" also displays unity, as the stars are the same across the world, and freedom-- referring to when African Americans used stars to guide them to freedom during and after slavery, such as the North Star. So, the symbol of the "star" represents mercy, as it provides hope, unity, and independence-- all of which the black community lack because of white oppression. So, by alluding to these three concepts that Pilate's earring presents, Morrison conveys that Milkman attains the same kind of power and mercy the earring offers, one that stems from freedom and family, which gives him the ability to fly freely like a "lodestar." All in all, the unity and freedom, or mercy, that Guitar and the allusion to Pilate's earring give Milkman allow him to finally fly.

In conclusion, Morrison introduces and connects the concept of mercy and flight through Mr. Smith, Jake, Pilate, and Milkman, demonstrating that both flight and mercy stem from unity and the freedom from the sufferings caused by white supremacy. By bookending the novel with the two attempts at flight, one expecting Milkman's birth and the other anticipating his death or immortality, Morrison hopes to highlight the purpose of Milkman's journey. Although Milkman's birth results from the product of mercy and flight, he is unable to fly until the final scene due to his inability to connect to his racial and familial history. It is not until Milkman retraces his familial roots and builds stronger relationships with others that he obtains mercy and the power to fly. Milkman's journey serves as a model for the rest of the community; his journey's end result- his connection with his family and community-- frees Milkman from what prevents him to fly and attain mercy, demonstrating that members of the African-American community must reconnect with their heritage and culture to obtain the power to soar above racial limitations and gain mercy.

Works Cited

Morrison, Toni. *Song of Solomon*. New York, Random House US, 2007.

Honorable Mention—Humanities

María José Garcia
Haunted Houses and the Subjugation of Women

Haunted house stories encapsulate the perfect combination between entertainment and societal criticism. These stories, with eerie hallways, lonely rooms, and inexplicable events, grasp the readers' attention with an extensive use of the senses and profound ambiguity. However, behind flashes of lightning and whispering voices, these tales touch upon timeless societal problems. "The Fall of the House of Usher" by Edgar Allan Poe, and "A Visit" by Shirley Jackson delve into the oppression of women and how, through the centuries, the perception of an oppressive environment seemingly differs, but the overall core remains the same. The idea of women being presented briefly during a story as a supportive element to drive the plot rather than as a well-rounded character is not an uncommon practice. However, to assure a woman's brief appearance always correlates to their lack of power within a story alludes to a limited analysis on the piece being read. The roles of women in Poe's and Jackson's stories and the environments where they live in greatly differ; however, they demonstrate how it is not necessary to live in a dreary, calamitous environment with no option or voice in order to be oppressed.

In "The Fall of the House of Usher" by Edgar Allan Poe, Lady Madeline, the only woman in the story, is briefly introduced by the narrator as Roderick Usher's sister. Described as a woman with a disease that has "baffled the skill of her physicians," she is referred to as "a gradual wasting away of the person" (Poe 94). During the entire story, she never speaks and is only mentioned in order to highlight how "her decease...would leave [Roderick] (the hopeless and the frail) the last of the ancient race of the Ushers" (Poe 92). Madeline is ultimately declared dead by her brother and the male narrator and is buried, only to appear at the end of the story to claim her brother's life and her own. At first glance, Madeline is seemingly a frail and sick woman that causes the deterioration of her brother's mind and ultimately claims his life. Even though she has a physical ailment, Roderick is presented as the victim. His mental health deteriorates as her disease progresses, and the entire story focuses on the narrator attempting to improve Roderick's spirits. Dawn Keetley, in their article about pregnancy, reproduction, and woman subjugation, highlights how Roderick and the narrator are unable to perceive Madeline as a whole individual. Madeline is subsumed into Roderick's being as if she is part of him and has no need to tell her own story (Keetley 4). Her only obvious duty is to complete Roderick and carry on the Usher family line.

Despite her brief, voiceless appearances in the story and despite being mistakenly declared dead and buried in the house by her brother and the male narrator, Madeline holds power within the story. She inspires the same dread in the narrator that the house does, alluding to a strong presence. When she "dies", Roderick's mental state rapidly deteriorates, which contradicts the notion that Madeline, a woman, was dependent on him. Rather, when Madeline appears at the end of the story she presents "evidence of some bitter struggle upon every portion of her emaciated frame," symbolizing the will to fight and resist the oppression she was subjected to. As her brother dies, "a victim to the terrors he had anticipated," Madeline dies, bringing the house of Usher to the ultimate collapse as well as her family line (Poe 133).

Written in the early nineteenth century, "The Fall of the House of Usher" has some distinct symbolism regarding Madeline's brief but powerful appearances in the story to the roles of women of the time. Bridget Hill, in her article about ideas of female perfection, delves into how a woman's role in the eighteenth century was "to listen rather than to speak." Their roles were expected to be those of "... industrious, sober and humble servants and labourers content to endure the sufferings..." (Hill 17). Madeline's lack of dialogue and the perception that her illness was in direct correlation with Roderick's rapid mental decline indicates that the eighteenth-century mentality bled into the new century. In fact, "the image of the perfect [nineteenth-century] lady...became the image of the disabled lady, the female invalid" (Duffin 26). The amount of solely female diseases skyrocketed during this period.

Lorna Duffin, in the book *The Nineteenth-Century Woman: Her Cultural and Physical World*, describes how "the image of the woman as an invalid, as weak, delicate and perpetually prone to illness" was promoted by physicians. Based on social anthropology and historical material, Madeline's ailment "baffled her physicians" just like many women in the nineteenth century (Poe 94). Nineteenth-century doctors contributed to sexual differentiation, discrimination, and disability, as well as justified the social inequalities imposed by sex (Duffin 26-27). Roderick was often perceived as being anxious and irritable, common symptoms of hysteria, yet it was Madeline's condition that rendered her useless (Tasca 114). That entrapment within her bed and her house symbolizes how often medical theories were used to oppress and "to reinforce the social prescription of appropriate behaviour for women..." (Duffin 28). In fact, the early nineteenth century laid the groundwork for the twentieth century family structure and the role of women within it (Keetley 10).

"A Visit" by Shirley Jackson, on the other hand, seemingly provides us a very different tale. Margaret, the narrator, is a girl that visits her friend, Carla Montague's house. At first glance, the family and their life seem very proper, traditional, and beautiful. Proper to the aristocracy connoted in their last name, their house is bewitching, almost resembling a castle. Margaret is awed by the "lavish grounds" and "curving staircases" (Jackson 414). She even points out that she "... never saw anything so lovely" (Jackson 415). Though imposing, the house is described with very feminine attributes such as "graceful" and "curving." The most striking feature of the house are the tapestries, which Carla points out have been made "...by [her] grandmamas and [her] great-grandmamas and [her] great-great-grandmamas" (Jackson 417). Unlike

Madeline in "The Fall of the House of Usher," the protagonists are women. In fact, most of the characters are women and the readers are exposed to their perspectives in the entire story. However, as the story progresses, Margaret learns that her environment is not as safe and as lovely as she once thought. By the end of the story, she is trapped. As Carla points out, "[they] should be models of stillness" (Jackson 452).

Unlike Madeline in "The Fall of the House of Usher," Margaret goes willingly into the house and enjoys exploring the grounds. However, under the beautiful, ornate place, the house has sinister underpinnings. Maura Rose Calderone, in her piece analyzing the dark architecture of women's gothic fiction, remarks how the house draws female characters and confines them (Calderone 46). Instead of being two separate entities, the females and the house are one. For example, Mrs. Montague is described as a tall, thin woman in "pale green and pale blue," and later the room in which she, Margaret, and Carla are standing is described as "pale green and pale blue," with tall windows (Calderone 47). This symbolizes how the women are forever trapped and immortalized in the house. Reality is so distorted that "it was so difficult for [Margaret] to tell what was in it and what was not, and how far in any direction she might easily move" (Jackson 419). Despite how beautiful the house was, the sense of loss, entrapment and oppression is subtly interwoven with "the perfect grace of the house" (Jackson 444). By the end of the story, her illusion of safety and perfection is foreshadowed when she revisits a mosaic of a girl she saw when she first arrives to the house and notices a missing tile that resembles a tear. The description, "Margaret-- Who Died for Love," foreshadows the eventual confinement Margaret will suffer at the end when Carla's mother immortalizes her and adds her image to one of the tapestries.

Margaret seeing the missing tile is the first time she notices a flaw in the household. Even Carla's brother, towards the end of the tale, criticizes the house's imperfect condition and points out the "broken statue by the lake," a badly worn carpet, and, most alarmingly, "a crack in solid stone" outside the conservatory window (Jackson 447). These conditions demonstrate how women in the twentieth century had different conditions of entrapment and oppression than those in the prior century. Rather than living in blatant conditions that violated their human rights, they were presented with a faux sense of security, love, and beauty. Unlike "The Fall of the House of Usher," there are no male counterparts exerting a patriarchal command that represses their voice and wishes. Instead, they are consumed and suffocated by the household chores, that through generations, have shifted from imposed to expected.

While the captain, Carla's brother, and Paul, a figment of Margaret's imagination, can leave and are able to clearly see the flaws of a seemingly perfect environment, all the women are unable to notice any change and in fact await a male companion in order to exert a sign of independence. Though Carla's brother rarely visits, she repeats several times in the story how "when [her] brother comes again, [they] shall have a musical evening, and perhaps he will take [them] boating on the river," despite having no obstacle of doing so alone (Jackson 420, 451). This symbolizes how the twentieth-century woman was independent and autonomous at first glance but was constantly oppressed by societal expectations such as approval, love, and tradition. Paul even points out that they could never replace anything from the house, instead add to it just like generations of women before them did. Alice Kessler-Harris, in her work *In Pursuit of Equity: Women, Men, and the Quest for Economic Citizenship in 20th-Century America*, points out how women, despite having financial independence and the right to vote, were still subjected to an archaic family structure. "The normal order of family life properly subsumed women within its boundaries, rendering their needs and desires as well as rights and obligations secondary to those of husbands and children" (Kessler-Harris 3). The independence, needs, and desires of the Montague women, true to twentieth-century women, were kept on a tight leash by the obligations they had to maintain the house in optimal standards.

In fact, just like the women in her story, Shirley Jackson, the author of "A Visit," is the epitome of a twentieth-century woman. Zoe Heller, in her biography about Shirley Jackson, delves into the intricacies of Jackson's life and how her experiences translated into the genesis of proto-feminist literature. Jackson was often criticized by her family because of her weight and lack of female charm despite being her family's main source of income. Despite being able to work and write her stories, she felt patronized and oppressed in her role as a faculty wife (Heller 2). "Jackson did the cooking, the cleaning, the grocery shopping, and the child-rearing; [her husband] sat at his desk, pondering the state of American letters and occasionally yelling at his wife to come and refill the ink in his pen" (Heller 2). Shirley, like Margaret and other twentieth-century women enthralled by a seemingly beautiful environment, willingly sought acceptance and refuge, only to discover that, just like Madeline in "The Fall of the House of Usher," there is a creeping evil wanting to oppress her within the household. "The hope of an alternative, happier life proves illusory" (Heller 3). The hope of a safe and loving future proves to be nothing but an illusion since they must compromise their independence, needs, and desires for a mediocre semblance of acceptance.

Poe, in "The Fall of the House of Usher," has dramatic scenes of rebellion, freedom, and shock, while Jackson has a more subtle way of introducing the idea of entrapment. Nevertheless, both houses, despite their different appearances, represent women being oppressed by either a current patriarchal society or their own belief (stemmed from centuries of systematic oppression) of what women's role in society should be. Madeline represents a nineteenth-century woman that was physically restrained and kept voiceless due to a patriarchal society that limited women's independence. Margaret, on the other hand, represents a twentieth-century woman that was "pressured by the media and the commercial culture to deny her personal and intellectual interests and subsume her identity into her husband's" (Heller 4). These stories and these characters demonstrate how a house can represent "a place of warmth and security and also one of imprisonment and catastrophe" (Heller 4). Unlike Madeline, Margaret is not restrained by societal pressure or a patriarchal figure; instead, she is trapped in centuries of expectations women have been forced to achieve and have gradually adopted as a norm. These works, despite being written in different centuries, touch upon themes and symbols, such as women's role in society, that resonate through generations. As the twenty-first century progresses, I wonder what new shape and shade women's oppression will evolve to.

Works Cited

Calderone, Maura Rose. "The Lady of the House: The Dark Architecture of Women's Gothic Fiction." *The Journal of the Honors Program, Marywood University*, 2006, pp. 33–59., http://www.marywood.edu/dotAsset/122092.pdf.

Duffin, Lorna. "The Conspicuous Consumptive: Woman as an Invalid." *The Nineteenth-Century Woman: Her Cultural and Physical World.* vol. 13., pp. 26-40., Taylor and Francis, Hoboken, 2012, doi:10.4324/9780203104118.

Heller, Zoe. "Haunted Houses." *The New Yorker* Oct 17 2016: 90. ProQuest. 28 Jan. 2020.

Hill, Bridget. "Part 1: Ideas of Female Perfection." *Eighteenth-Century Women: An Anthology.* vol. 21., pp. 16–24., Routledge, London; New York; 2013; 2012; doi:10.4324/9780203104071.

Jackson, Shirley. "A Visit." *American Supernatural Tales*, Penguin Books, 2007, pp. 400–446.

Keetley, Dawn. "Pregnant Women and Envious Men in "Morella," "Berenice," "Ligeia," and "The Fall of the House of Usher."" *Poe Studies*, vol. 38, no. 1-2, 2005, pp. 1-16.

Kessler-Harris, Alice. *In Pursuit of Equity: Women, Men, and the Quest for Economic Citizenship in 20th-Century America.* Pp. 1-8 Oxford University Press, USA, US, 2001; 2003.

Poe, Edgar A. "The Fall of the House of Usher." *American Supernatural Tales*, Penguin Books, 2007, pp. 92–123.

Tasca, Cecilia, et al. "Women and Hysteria in the History of Mental Health." *Clinical Practice and Epidemiology in Mental Health: CP & EMH*, Bentham Open, 2012, www.ncbi.nlm.nih.gov/pmc/articles/PMC3480686/.

First Place—Social Sciences

Jillian D'Souza
Cross Cultural Comparison of Gender Roles: Prevalence of Gender Roles in Indian Versus Indian American Culture

Gender roles are a significant part of many cultures. They restrict the way that both males and females behave and define the interactions between individuals of every sex (Arasa et al., 2016). These roles are most influenced by the socio-cultural norms of a specific community and are traditionally oppressive of women. Recently, women in certain parts of the world have transcended these confines and are assuming new gender roles. This includes holding full time jobs and assuming equal status to their male colleagues. Due to their ramifications, gender roles affect how families, economies, and societies function (Arasa et al., 2016). For this reason, it is important to analyze the types of gender roles present in a culture. One country that has been known to have stringent gender roles is India (Suar, & Gochhayat, 2014). Although their culture is shifting towards a more equal perspective, it is apparent that gender roles are still limiting. Traditionally, gender roles in India confine women to homemaking activities, while men assume roles that are meant to provide for the family. Moreover, women are thought of as inferior and are subject to their husbands' control (Ramu, 1987). Although gender roles are evolving in India, with women receiving the right to own property and obtain an education, they are still expected to fulfill these marital roles. Comparing them to their Indian American counterparts shows some of the subtle similarities, as well as the stark differences in the value of gender roles. It is shown that more accultured Indian American families are likely to support more egalitarian views. Therefore, while still apparent in both cultures, the emphasis on traditional gender roles is more prevalent in Indian culture in comparison to Indian American culture.

Overall, Indian American culture is more likely to support equality between sexes than its Indian counterpart. This support of equality in turn encourages a more modern definition of gender roles. Patel and Parmentier (2005) conducted a study that analyzed female engineering students who attended several different colleges and organizations across India. They obtained students' opinions on female employment in the engineering industry. It was shown that as economical needs and modernization become a priority, traditional gender roles become redefined in such a way that supports equality. Although India has begun to follow this model with women gaining equal rights in a political context, there are still evident discrepancies in a cultural context. Despite being a democratic nation, India was ranked higher than Saudi Arabi and Kuwait in terms of inequalities between men and women (Patel et al, 2005). These inequalities are further supported by Indian culture, which has a preference for men. This preference is shown in the male/female illiteracy gap, the wage gap, and the disparities in management positions between females and males in India. The average Indian woman earns only around 60% of what men of the same qualifications earn, and women only hold 3% of management positions. Furthermore, women that live in North India are more likely to be subjected to marital castes and practices such as female infanticide, child marriage and dowry. These practices that target women and the discrepancies that exist between the two sexes show the inequality that is caused by the traditional gender roles found in India. On the other hand, a survey was conducted where 46 Indian American families from the tristate area responded to three questionnaires that determined their attitudes towards women, dating, and mental health disorders. It stated that while women in both populations tend to have more egalitarian views, Indian American culture supports these views more overall (Dasgupta, 1998). A country whose culture supports equality has a greater influence on individual beliefs. Furthermore, a culture that supports women's egalitarian views is one that is more likely to possess empowered females. Dasgupta states that first generation Indian American women, more often than not, believe that moving to America liberated them from some of the oppressive beliefs they experienced in India (Dasgupta, 1998). These women believe that much of the oppression they faced was caused by the inequality between males and females in India. Indian American women that have experienced both cultures tend to believe that equality is more widespread in America than it was in India. Therefore, Indian Americans tend to support more egalitarian views than Indians, which leads to less perpetuation of traditional gender roles.

Indian American spouses that have lived in the U.S. for longer are more likely to share an equal responsibility in homemaking activities. A study was conducted whose aim was to analyze decision making on fertility choices among women and their relatives. It used the data from a 2002 survey of women aged 15 to 39 from Madhya Pradesh, India. It found that Indian women are more likely to put more emphasis on their husband's and family's opinion on their fertility choices than their own (Macquarrie, & Edmeades, 2015). This means that they prioritize the wishes of their family over their own. This is most likely due to the widespread idea that women have to obey their spouse. Moreover, this further displays the inequality between women and men in Indian and their home and family related decisions. A qualitative investigation was conducted that looked at age, how long lived in the US, marital status, education, family structure, place of birth and living situation for each participant (Mann et al., 2017). The goal of this study was to explore how gender roles of Indian American women are affected by acculturation and reproductive variables. It showed that in the U.S., women are more likely to share an equal role in fertility decisions and homemaking activities. In America, because males and females usually both provide a source of income, household work is more evenly shared. Like their Indian counterparts, however, mothers-in-law are also a main influence on homemaking decisions. Despite this similarity, it was found that women who were more bi-culturally integrated put less emphasis on their extended family's opinion. This shift accounted for lower stress levels among the women and a more equal sharing of responsibilities. This assimilation into U.S. culture often leaves women, as well as men, with more egalitarian views towards gender roles and women's rights. This in and of itself defies traditional gender roles.

Women that live in America are more likely to seek out higher education and carry out a more independent life. These actions stray away from traditional gender roles and are shown to cause conflicts between Indian American women and their families back in India. In India, education seems to be less of a priority than marriage for women and their families (Maertens, 2013). As a result, the education gender gap in India is significant and grows as the education level increases. A study that analyzed data collected from three villages in rural India found that women are less likely to be allowed to pursue education overall. This creates a distinct gap between males and females in their ability to achieve goals and gain access to opportunities. This study found that 39% of girls were allowed to get an education and only 8% of those girls were expected to get a higher education. Meartens (2013) states that this is most likely due to traditional gender roles that encourage males to provide for their families. As a result, males have more access to educational prospects. This responsibility obligates males to take care of financial responsibilities and obtain a higher education or a job that provides money. In America, the more acculturated Indian American women are, the more likely they are to seek a higher education (Mann, Roberts, & Montgomery, 2017). This acquirement of a higher education, paired with sharing of household responsibilities between spouses, goes against traditional gender roles that confine women to homemaking jobs. Women that live in America are more likely to seek an education and put their careers on a similar level to their familial responsibilities. For these reasons, Indian Americans are more likely to follow modern gender roles rather than the ones carried on by their Indian family members.

Therefore, traditional gender roles play a more important role in Indian culture than they do in Indian American culture. They are rooted in a long history that confines women to marital practices that entail inequality for them. Furthermore, they limit men to primary breadwinner roles. Traditional gender roles hinder educational prospects, create unequal home environments, and support inequality between the sexes. Although they still affect the way that Indian American parents care for their children, it is shown that the more acculturated an individual is, the more likely their views are to be egalitarian on various subjects (Mann et al., 2017). While traditional gender roles are thought to have been rooted in a time where women had to obey men, society in and of itself has progressed far beyond that. This is an age where women are achieving innovation and prosperity independently. Women and men are demanding equal freedoms and responsibilities all around the world. Whether or not traditional gender roles are relevant in a culture, it is important that countries start recognizing the capabilities that both women and men have. In countries like India, where women are slowly starting to gain equality not only politically but also culturally, the traditional gender roles that confined both males and females are likely to start disappearing. The institution of modern gender roles may lead to a prosperous society in which the economy, government, and other sectors flourish.

Works Cited

Arasa, J. N., Echterhoff, W., Heinecke-Muller, M., Kariuki, P. W., Mwiti, G. K., & Quiser-Pohl, C. (2016). "Gender Roles with Regard to Family and Work from a National and a Cross-cultural Perspective." *Adaption for the Use of European-African Human Resources Management*, 1, 122-129.

Dasgupta, S. D. (1998). "Gender Roles and Cultural Continuity in the Asian Indian Immigrant Community in the U.S." *Sex Roles*, 38(11-12), 953-974.

Macquarrie, K. L. D., Edmeades, J. (2015). "Whose Fertility Preferences Matter? Women, Husband, In-laws, and Abortion in Madhya Pradesh, India." *Population Research and Policy Review* 34(4), 615-636. doi:10.1007/s11113-015-9364-y.

Maertens, A. (2013). "Social Norms and Aspirations: Age of Marriage and Education in Rural India." *World Development*, 47, 1-15. https://doi org.ezproxy2.library.drexel.edu/10.1016/j.worlddev.2013.01.027

Mann, S. K., Roberts, L. R., Montgomery, S. (2017). "Conflicting Cultural Values, Gender Roles, Attitudes, and Acculturation: Exploring the Context of Reproductive and Mental Health of Asian-Indian Immigrant Women in the U.S." *Issues in Mental Health Nursing*, 38(4),301-309. https://doi-org.ezproxy2.library.drexel.edu/10.1080/01612840.2017.1283376

Patel, R., Parmentier, M. J. C. (2005). "The Persistence of Traditional Gender Roles in the Informational technology Sector: A Study of Female Engineers in India." *Information Technologies and International Development*, 2(3), 29-46.

Ramu, G. N. (1987). "Indian Husbands: Their Role in Perceptions and Performance in Single and Dual Earner Families." *National Council on Family Relations*, 49(4), 903-915.

Suar, D., Gochhayat, J., (2014). "Influence of Biological Sex and Gender Roles on Ethicality." *Journal of Business Ethics*, 134(2), 199-208. https://doi.org/10.1007/s10551-014-2424-0

Second Place—Social Sciences

Megan Peng
The Culture of Education

  Hidden influencers can often be the most impactful developmental factors in education. Consider the role of culture in shaping education. To see this effect, look no further than how cultural parenting habits result in American "helicopter parents," Chinese "tiger parents," or a more supportive, background role for Finnish parents. The same desire for a successful child becomes adapted to suit the expectations of each respective culture. These differing cultural styles also produce different approaches when it comes to how a nation teaches generations of students, and manifest in other aspects such as peer pressure and the emotional levels of students. I have experienced both "helicopter parenting" and "tiger parenting" in a mix of American academic culture and Chinese parenting culture, so I would like to delve deeper into how these different cultures produce success in their respective societies. Additionally, considering the sheer number of standardized tests I have endured, I am also interested to see how these tests can affect the academic success of students and their toll on students' emotional levels. Overall, I hope to discover if any cultural practice maximizes success within students, in both emotional and academic terms, and why they appear to be more beneficial.

  From the time American students are young, standardized tests loom over each lesson plan. I took my first state standardized test in third grade before I knew what standards were being tested, nor even cared enough to know how this test could affect my future. Because these test results are used as an assessment for academic progress and can determine a teacher's salary, as was the case in my school, teachers are pressured to shape their lessons around concepts that do not even assess students' knowledge past the surface level (Mulholland). So why do students continue to take these tests? The short answer: it is cemented in American culture. America likes nothing more than a competition to prove worth, and the tests' numerical scores provide an easy metric to judge students on. However, when faced with test scores that rank only average on the international scale, our competitive spirit realizes that something must change (Serino). Unfortunately, this action takes the form of more tests to make sure students are improving academically, which means more information to be learned in the same period. This increase translates to an aversion of "deeper learning," where students take the time to truly understand the material and its applications instead of cramming all the material needed to achieve a specific score on a test (Mehta). Instead, students push themselves to the top percentiles of these test scores, assuming higher scores equate beating the competition and a higher chance at success.

  Upon closer examination, students may not be the only ones placing pressure on themselves to succeed. In American culture, a common trend amongst parents is to constantly monitor the actions and successes of their children—if unsatisfactory, parents will intervene. Parents who do not subscribe to this idea of "helicoptering" over their children are viewed as strange, defying the norm (Vinson). Despite good intentions, this hovering only constricts students, with the parent blaming others for the failures of their child instead of addressing the issue. For example, one parent called my school to complain about how much extra credit students received, arguing that it inflated grades and made her daughter's grades look worse. The ideology that success is achieved by beating down the competition has established itself as an American cornerstone, carrying over to areas like education. As a result, students are pushed to be the best in everything at the price of mental health, from standardized test scores to extracurricular awards. With many of my peers, if you were not first, you were last. The American dogma is that success and financial stability are created from a good college education and that is only achieved with scores that are high enough for admittance into higher education. All this pressure cumulates to immense stress in students, as the American Psychology Association reports that teenagers now experience more stress than adults, especially during the school year (Bethune). Holistically, the American approach of standardized testing and constant competition result in both poor academic performance and mental health. These issues often stem from the focus of education. When the educational mindset shifts from blaming the competition for personal failures to looking at the competition for ways to improve, it produces a system like China's educational structure, with potentially more successful results.

A common stereotype is that Asian children are academic geniuses who all become successful. While this does not apply to every person, a study shows that students in Beijing, China often outperform American students on math tests (Chen and Uttal). This perceived prosperity is not limited to geographic boundaries, highlighting the idea that culture produces this success. Asian communities present in the United States have often been labeled the "model minority" as proof that through perseverance, one can achieve success in any society (Chang and Au). Due to this harmful stereotype, success is the baseline for Asian American students, not the end goal. These expectations are not only found in society, but more specifically, family. Those students from Beijing who scored higher had parents who reported lower satisfaction rates than the American students who performed more poorly (Chen and Uttal). Achievements are dismissed because they are expected, and students work themselves to a point of burnout. During senior year, everyone assumed that I would only apply to Ivy League universities, due to my ethnicity. They overlooked my extracurricular achievements because they were expected, and I felt the pressure to do more and more until I became mentally and physically exhausted, coupled with the stress American students face. Part of my actions was fueled by my "tiger parents," who were taught that success meant financial stability, and success was best achieved through being first in academics (Cheah et al.). However, unlike my situation, parents are not the biggest stressors in China. Instead, students fear the single test that will determine their future: *gaokao*.

Gaokao is known as the college entrance exam and serves as one of the only metrics that college admission is based upon. Naturally, this creates immense pressure on both students and parents, since college is the gateway to academic achievement. Students religiously attend cram schools to prepare, pushing their bodies to exhaustion (Pinghui). However, this effort may pay off. If a student can score high enough, their future success is secured. For the less lucky, however, the gate to opportunity has been closed—temporarily. As per Chinese culture, there is always room for self-improvement and to learn from mistakes, and students will retake the exam year after year until they succeed. Contrast this to the American habit of "helicopter" parents complaining, and the answer to why Chinese students outperform American students is uncovered.

Like China, standardized tests are rare in Finland, but in contrast, little pressure is placed on the college entrance exam – Finnish students are simply not worried about attending college (Walker). In contrast to the American and Chinese parenting styles that can result in high stress levels, Finnish parents are laxer about their involvement in constantly pushing students to succeed. In Finland, the principle that education is not competition forms the basis of the schooling system, positing that it is a field where everyone should have an equal chance to succeed (Hancock). Compare this to America's cultural belief that everything is a competition. Seemingly contradictory to the expected results, Finnish students rank among the top performers in the world with some of the highest levels of happiness as well (Anderson). Unlike their American and Chinese counterparts, Finnish students take as long as they need to complete their degrees. This slower pace trickles down to elementary schools, where a recess break is mandated, following the Finnish cultural values that a child's only responsibility is to play and that children learn best through play (Doyle). I experienced this perspective in an American preschool, where piecing together anatomy sculptures has allowed me to remember specific body parts to this day.

However, this hands-on learning is not the new norm. Finland is still "teaching to the test," formatting its curriculum around the goals of the PISA test. These recent changes have left Finnish parents very confused and inclined to complain about the unfamiliar, accentuated by a lower involvement of parents in children's educations when compared to "helicoptering" or "tiger" parents (Strauss). In a broader scope, Finland's education model is difficult to cross-apply to countries like the United States and China. For one, Finland has a much smaller population of 5.3 million, compared to America's 318 million and China's 1.3 billion (Shumer). This makes state-funding schools much easier and teachers can undergo a much more rigorous education to reach their position. Furthermore, America has a much greater variation in wealth and diversity, and China's rapidly increasing population cannot be sustained by a slow-growing education sector.

Both ends of the spectrum of educational approaches work well in certain aspects. For example, both a lack of pressure and extreme pressure can produce successful students. These pressures arise from a parenting culture that is ingrained into the larger mindset of the country. However, when a middle-ground is attempted like in the U.S., where extreme pressure to succeed meets no pressure to adapt from failure, both aspects fail—trying to balance pressure, stress, and achievement are so heavily focused on that it is easy to lose grasp of all three.

Overall, the most beneficial type of educational culture is situational. Some traits like aggressive tiger parenting can work well in producing academic results but also cause high stress in some cultures. But when executed in other cultures in the form of "helicopter parents," this only creates stress with little academic achievement. Success is relative to the surrounding culture. What may be considered successful in one country, can be considered average in another. Therefore, it is hard to judge success as an objective goal without its contextualizing standards. In the end, the definitively positive approach is to let students become comfortable with learning from their mistakes and growing into their success, rather than pushing them into situations of ephemeral prosperity. It can be better to let students be students of both their failures and formal education, just as the happiest children are those who can simply be children.

Works Cited

Anderson, Jenny. "The World's Largest Assessment of Teenage Students Suggests Happiness Is Crucial to Learning." *Quartz*, Uzabase, April 19 2017.

Bethune, Sophie. "Teen Stress Rivals That of Adults." *Monitor on Psychology*, vol. 45, no. 4, 2014.

Chang, Benji and Wayne Au. "You're Asian, How Could You Fail Math." *Unmasking the myth of the model minority. Rethinking Schools*, vol. 22, no. 2, 2007, pp. 15-18.

Cheah, Charissa et al. "Understanding "Tiger Parenting" through the Perceptions of Chinese Immigrant Mothers: Can Chinese and Us Parenting Coexist?" *Asian American Journal of Psychology*, vol. 4, no. 1, 2013, p. 30.

Chen, Chuansheng and David H Uttal. "Cultural Values, Parents' Beliefs, and Children's Achievement in the United States and China." *Human Development*, vol. 31, no. 6, 1988, pp. 351-358.

Doyle, William. "Op-Ed: Why Finland Has the Best Schools." *Los Angeles Times*, Los Angeles Times, March 18 2016.

Hancock, Lynell. "Why Are Finland's Schools Successful?" *Smithsonian*, Smithsonian Institution, September 1 2011.

Mehta, Jal. "In Search of Deeper Learning : The Quest to Remake the American High School." *Harvard University Press*, 2019.

Mulholland, Quinn. "The Case against Standardized Testing." Harvard Political Review, May 14 2015. *Harvard*

University.

Pinghui, Zhuang. "Gaokao: How One Exam Can Set the Course of a Student's Life in China." *South China Morning Post*, June 8 2017.

Serino, Louis. "What International Test Scores Reveal About American Education." *The Brookings Institution*, 2017.

Shumer, Robert. "Finland Not an Apt Educational Model for U.S. Schools." *Star Tribune*, Star Tribune, July 11 2014.

Strauss, Valerie. "What Finland Is Really Doing to Improve Its Acclaimed Schools." *The Washington Post*, The Washington Post, August 30 2019.

Vinson, Kathleen. "Hovering Too Close: The Ramifications of Helicopter Parenting in Higher Education." *Ga. St. UL Rev.*, vol. 29, 2012, p. 423.

Walker, Timothy. "American High School Students Inspired by Less Stressed Finnish Teens." *Taught By Finland*, 2015.

Honorable Mention—Social Sciences

Steven Zhao
The Different Effects of Parental Expectations

Whether we love or hate them, our parents play a huge role in all aspects of our lives. This is especially prevalent during the shaping of our education. But how much should parents be curating their child's education? Does setting lots of expectations help children meet them, or does it potentially discourage them from going towards those expectations? I want to determine the effects of a strict predetermined education from parents, as well as how parental expectations and support affect their children's success in life. These factors might also affect life or career satisfaction and motivations. I find this topic important, because my parents have been a huge factor in my education up until even college. While I think that in a simple direct way, parental expectations can cause students to achieve better grades, I want to examine the different ways parents do this and the long-term effects on their children.

This topic is something I have often reflected upon over the years, and more recently now that I have started college. During my years in middle school and high school, my parents always had the idea that I would go into some sort of medical profession, because it offers a stable and well-paying job. My education was then focused on the math and sciences. In high school, I took the highest level of biology, and math up to the AP calculus course. I didn't really protest this career that was forced onto me due to my own goody two-shoes nature and knowing that it was for my own good. Looking back, I realize I was locked out of exploring my own interests and developing my own career aspirations. In high school I lacked any real interests in subjects. If you were to ask me about chemistry, I wouldn't say that I hated it, but I also couldn't say that I particularly enjoyed it either. In this sense, parental expectations didn't hinder my financial or career success possibilities but stunted my own development as a person.

Parental expectations can cover a wide range of things. Some parents, such as my own, set very high standards for me to achieve, while other parents might be lax and leave that up to their children to discover. Some parents sadly might even have low expectations for their children (Almroth). Additionally, it might also depend if the children receive those expectations well, or if they even have the same expectations as their parents. In a study done in the education system of Sweden, students in 6th-8th grade and their parents were given a series of questionnaires. The questions were things like "how far they would like their child to go in school" (Almroth). Some questions pertained to expectations while others were for aspirations. Different answers were considered high or low types of responses, and also determined parental warmth, as well as democratic parenting through the child surveys. Children's academic performance were measured from their 7th-8th grade grades. For high expectations, they found that academic grades and parental warmth were greater, while emotional and conduct problems were low. For the children of parents with low expectations, they "were associated with increased odds of high/very high externalizing symptoms" (Almroth), which makes children with parents who have low expectations more likely to have emotional and conduct problems. As someone with high-expectation parents, I can agree that my academic success was definitely helped by high expectations, which forced me to do better in my academics. I also didn't have any emotional problems controlling or conducting myself properly at that age. My experiences though don't line up with increased parental warmth. While I wouldn't say that my parents treated my coldly, they had some strictness, and increase academic performance wasn't the result of my parents being very warm and pleasant often. The benefits and detriments of high and low expectations seem clear in terms of academic success and mental/physical problems, but parental warmth seems like a more individual factor.

Another angle from which you could explore parental expectations is from students who go into college undecided. In this instance, while there might be parental expectations to do well in school or get a stable job, there are no preset conditions for any particular career path or profession. Most of the expectations and pressure, as well as career path, are up to the student to decide. But does going into college with more options than a defined path benefit students, or is it a detriment? One study examined students who had gone into college with a level of uncertainty as to what exactly they wanted to do in their future careers. Annual surveys were given out over a ten-year period up to the 12th grade. These surveys asked these students about their career aspirations. Eight years after the survey, follow up interviews were conducted. One thing found was that "youth who are uncertain at age 16 are especially likely to be uncertain 10 years later" (Staff). At age 26, at the very end of the entire process, those who still "express uncertain occupational ambitions" (Staff) had lower wages. It seems that, while there is a possibility for students to utilize uncertainty as role exploration in a positive manner, consistently, a lot of students are unable to do this and instead the uncertainty becomes a detriment that follows them through their lives. Some scholars have the notion that they missed "out on some of what college had to offer by sticking to predetermined scripts" (Bruni) and by doing so were unable to learn from their mistakes. While this is the case, most adolescents don't seem to benefit from going through college with no guidance and problems don't become a learning experience. My parents set expectations and career choice, and if anything, gave me the basics to understand what my goals should be, and which types of fields would be good for me to pursue. I feel that as someone with a level of maturity and guidance, I could take advantage of role exploration. But a large majority of people don't have the same experiences that I have and are unable to turn uncertainty into a positive factor.

An additional factor to consider is the biological nature of the adolescent brain during a time of decision making and change. Technically, at the age of

18 one considers themselves an adult, but the brain is still in development, with parts like the prefrontal cortex "not reaching full development until approximately age 25-30" (Timbrell). According to a study tried to analyze why nursing students continued to have difficulty with the curriculum, "Adolescents are also more likely to react impulsively and emotionally to certain situations as the emotional centers of the brain dominate the underdeveloped neurons" (Timbrell). Giving adolescents the option to choose their career paths could result in an impulsive decision that is not ideal. During this stage there can also be stress and anxiety due to "feeling overwhelmed and under-prepared" (Timbrell) in the transition to adult life. Some parental guidance and expectations could then have a positive impact in lowering stress due to uncertainty and avoiding potentially bad decisions. Reflecting back, while I may not have fully enjoyed the path that my parents had for me, I don't really have any worry that I won't be able to find a good job or career due to the structure that they had set up. The parental expectations dissipated the long-term stress that could have occurred.

The goals and notions of success parents set up for their children also can have different effects on career satisfaction and overall outlook on one's profession. A lot of parents push for their children to become doctors or lawyers, most of the time for the job stability and the large income. This doesn't mean that their children will develop a real passion and enjoy their life work. In a study that surveyed medical students in Australia, parental influence on their choice to study medicine was surveyed as well as many other factors, such as career attitudes and well-being. They found that those whose parents had heavy expectations and valued "medicine for its prestige and less value of its opportunity for service" (Griffin) were more unsure about their choice to study medicine after being the program for a period of time. They also found that those students also had higher burnout at the end of the five-year period and were also more likely to have "more negative attitudes to medicine" (Griffin). Interestingly though grades were unaffected by these expectations. Taking on the long journey to becoming a doctor isn't something that would be easy for someone without any real passion for doing so. The entire process will seem like a huge mountain of work and frustration instead of something you enjoy due to the nature of the profession. I can relate to that feeling of ambivalence, and not having any real connections to what you're studying other than the monetary reward at the end of it all. It seems that if parental expectations are very high, but none of those expectations fulfill any sort of personal passion or interest, then those expectations can have negative impacts on things like attitude and career enjoyment.

Parental expectations play a large part in children's education and careers, in negative and positive ways. Across the board, high expectations have a positive influence on grades as in most of the studies, students' grades increased, or at least did not drop. When it came to factors like career attitudes, high expectations started to cause negative effects. All the studies in some way reported that low or the absence of expectations caused negative effects across the board. Going into this essay, I very much wanted to write about parental expectations in a negative light, but after doing the research and reflecting on my own experience, I can say that while parental expectations didn't set me up perfectly, they definitely had a huge positive impact that gives me an advantage in whatever I choose to pursue.

Works Cited

Almroth, Melody, et al. "Academic Expectations and Mental Health in Adolescence: A Longitudinal Study Involving Parents' and their Children's Perspectives." *Journal of Adolescent Health*, vol. 64, no. 6, 2019, pp. 783-789. http://tinyurl.com/yyxvhxqa.

Bruni, Frank. "How to Get the Most Out of College." *New York Times*, New York, 2018. http://tinyurl.com/yxdaolju.

Griffin, Barbara, and Wendy Hu. "Parental Career Expectations: Effect on Medical Students' Career Attitudes Over Time." *Medical Education*, vol. 53, no. 6, 2019, pp. 584-592. http://tinyurl.com/yxjl2p4e.

Staff, Jeremy, et al. "Uncertainty in Early Occupational Aspirations: Role Exploration or Aimlessness?" *Social Forces*, vol. 89, no. 2, 2010, pp. 659–683. JSTOR www.jstor.org/stable/40984551.

Timbrell, Jessica, and Holly Relouw. "Exploring the Disconnect between Developmental Stage and Academic Expectations: Implications for Nursing Education." *Nurse Education Today*, vol. 82, 2019, pp. 74-78. http://tinyurl.com/yxt4bves

First Place—Zelda Provenzano Endowed STEM Writing Award

Lee Feinman
Geoengineering: The Climate Change Solution

For a world facing an existential crisis, "the time to repair the roof is when the sun is shining." John F. Kennedy advised his Congress, his nation, and the world with these strong words in the heat of the Cold War in 1961. At the time, the threat to humanity had been human conflict and the prospect of nuclear war. Fifty-nine years later, we still live under a shadow that is a product of human conflict, but a new one: an uninhabitable global climate. We have learned from this looming shadow how we put ourselves in this dangerous spot, but also how to get out of it. The time to repair our planet is now.

Scientists have been reiterating that anthropogenic environmental stresses on our global ecosystem are causing an approach to an inhabitable earth's tipping point. If we continue to damage our ecosystems, we will soon reach a point where no change in current practices will reverse or halt the slide to an unlivable planet. Assuming scientists have made a proper prognosis, Earth will not be able to fix itself like it has so many times in the past. What will we do, as humans? The answer to that question, and my argument in this paper, is that we must geoengineer and we must start now. I write this paper because I have a passion for our planet and all things associated; moreover, I write this paper because geoengineering is not being done—its future needs a compelling argument. I hope to make such an argument.

Geoengineering, in premise, uses synthetic systems and substances to make an uninhabitable environment inhabitable. It is a reaction science to the study of climate change in environmental science, and it encompasses two research factors: the science of reconditioning what have become large-scale environmental impacts, and the ethics and governance regarding this synthetic solution to climate change. Geoengineering our planet is analogous to certain surgeries for humans, wherein a chain smoker receiving lung surgery can be compared to humanity, who has caused an environmental situation that could have been avoided. The 'surgery' that a geoengineer may perform on the planet could range from injecting sun-blocking particles into the upper sky to cool down the troposphere to designing machines that suck up CO_2 just like all the cut-down trees used to be able to do (Caldeira et al. 241-250, 237-238). And just as a surgeon must consider the ethical components of her practices, such as a treatment decision disagreement or the inevitability of medical errors, the practice of geoengineering must also be done with the ethical consideration of possible unknown negative reactions. A commonly discussed example of geoengineering is solar geoengineering by sulfur dioxide injection. By injecting sun-reflecting particles into the stratosphere, a smaller amount of sunlight would reach the lower atmosphere—this happens naturally when volcanos erupt. Like sitting under a tree on a sunny day, less sunlight yields cooler temperatures. As mentioned though, there are potential dangers to this practice: atmospheric sulfur dioxide could lend itself to dangerous ozone depletion depending on its concentration, just like too much anesthesia can be neurotoxic. Cooling down the planet could cause unpredictable novel climates in some areas, just as a surgical operation could lead to an unrelated infection. Because of these possible outcomes, ethical considerations of geoengineering must always be made.

Even though the global ecosystem may not have reached its tipping point, some damages to specific environments are irreversible. Ocean acidification is a clear example. If we were to hypothetically halt all emission of CO_2 across the planet, the oceans would continue to acidify until the global system reaches an equilibrium. Such equilibrium will not happen for a very long time; therefore, the decreases in oceanic biodiversity, global fish supply—on which a significant portion of the human population depends for primary nutrition—and aquatic ecosystem services will continue long after our habits are changed (Darton 7:35-8:15). This fact is strong support for advancements in geoengineering, considering the resistance to change of both the human social system and nature's biotic/abiotic mechanisms.

Those in opposition do not want us to geoengineer; they would rather see us mitigate our problems by decreasing emissions and using more sustainable infrastructure. Although being a more favorable solution in a system where time is not a factor, the probability that mitigation alone solves this grandiose problem before we meet the said tipping point is slim to none. Many who fear the dangers of geoengineering are now admitting that it may be the only workable solution (Barrett 46). It must be understood that there no longer exists a this-or-that choice when it comes to saving our future. Mitigations now could lead to an easier planet to geoengineer, but they will not eradicate climate problems that will get worse with time. By arguing against geoengineering's "side-effects," one is arguing against a necessary evil. With that in mind, by tabling research in geoengineering, we are making matters worse for ourselves. An environment that is past its buffering capacity turns into a positive feedback loop. We are facing cancer of the environment and we are currently at a stage lower than what it could be tomorrow. Kennedy would say to repair the roof now, fix the destruction of the global ecosystem now. Stopping all CO_2 emissions now is not possible; therefore, it is clear a different approach is needed.

An argument against geoengineering was exposed in research done by Environmental Science, Policy, and Management experts Jane Flegal and colleagues, who focus on the ethics and social issues of geoengineering. They reported a public survey in which "Pidgeon et al found that 'outdoor research (in geoengineering) opens up additional questions around safety and risks, both for humans and for the environment. Some participants raise concerns about uncertainty and control'" (qtd. 2.3). The thing being time and time again civilization has given the go-ahead on huge decisions even when it was aware that many outcomes of that decision were unknown. One may raise the point that the implementation of fossil fuels was an immature, rash decision resulting in a horrible outcome which can now be compared to the unknowns of geoengineering. To that, I counter by stating the lack of rectitude and plentiful ignorance had by those leading the industrial revolution. As studies of environmental degradation show, seldom do our understandings of the earth get marked off like a checklist; rather, our findings lead us to more questions, more systems to examine. Though we may not be learning at a rate one may wish, we are, however, becoming less and less ignorant. From both a social and physical science point of view, this point must be stressed when discussing whether we should advance in geoengineering. We do not know what the secondary effects of geoengineering will be just yet, but if we can reasonably prove that it will have a net positive result for humanity, then we can be honest with one another in recognizing the setbacks we may face along the way. For the patient battling lung cancer, chemotherapy will run its course, but chemotherapy is needed.

To expand on the aforementioned counterargument, conversations—thus perceived risks—of geoengineering far exceed the work done. The Harvard Geoengineering Research Program published its findings on funding for geoengineering in the years spanning from 2008 to 2018. In those ten years, only around $50 million in funding has been granted (Necheles et al.). This amount averages $5 million a year. To put that into perspective, the United States Department of Energy has appropriated $562 million for Fossil Energy Research & Development alone for the fiscal year 2020 (United States, Dept. of Energy, FY 2020 Congressional Budget Request). Those who prefer taking the route of mitigation to solve our environmental crisis believe we can outcompete the US's $562 million investment in future fossil energy production.

Moreover, the desperate strategies of the fossil fuel industry to exhaust all methods of oil, natural gas, and coal extraction have blazed possible trails for geoengineers to follow. Enhanced Oil Recovery (EOR) is a process by which CO_2 gas is collected, transported, and pumped into an underground oil reservoir to decrease the viscosity of the oil and initiate oil movement toward a well, causing roughly 10 to 30% more oil produced than conventional methods (Alvarado pp. 15-16). One of the greater challenges that geoengineers face, and thus an argument for those against geoengineering, is the sequestration of carbon. Carbon sequestration is the transformation of carbon from the gaseous phase to the solid phase wherein it causes no harm. The most recognizable occurrence of carbon sequestration is in photosynthesis where a tree, per se, brings in CO_2 and uses it to make sugars. Many argue that creating the technology needed to sequester carbon at any significant level is too ambitious a feat. Despite this, however, EOR is already being implemented and can be used as a strong counterargument to this concern. To reiterate, there currently exists the necessary infrastructure to first, collect carbon dioxide; second, transport it to a desired and specific location; and, lastly, store it. To say that this technology is too ambitious is incorrect. On the other hand, to say this technology is very confusing, very expensive, and very difficult is correct.

But let the fact be known that if the market proves it is interested in difficult technology, as seen by what the oil industry has been capable of, then the technology can very well be implemented. If the fossil fuel industry has taught us anything beneficial, it is this. Like big-oil folk say, "if there's a well, there's a way." We need to understand what is possible if the global consumer's interest is in mind. Allow geoengineering to be our liquid gold... and so much more.

The inevitability of a climate crisis is clear to most, but sadly not to all. Governments all over the planet may be implementing monetary investments toward green energy, but it is clear there remains a commitment to the use of fossil fuels; therefore, successful full-scale mitigation of environmental degradation is unrealistic. There is a solution to this problem, though, and it needs not unanimous global consent to change daily life habits. It requires the backing of the most important stakeholder: you. We must proceed with geoengineering. Look outside, the sun is still shining.

Works Cited

Alvarado, Vladimir Manrique, Eduardo. (2010). *Enhanced Oil Recovery - Field Planning and Development Strategies*. (pp. 16, 83, 84). Elsevier. Retrieved from app.knovel.com/hotlink/toc/id: kpEORFPDS1/enhanced-oil-recovery/enhanced-oil-recovery. Accessed 17 Feb. 2020.

Barrett, Scott. "The Incredible Economics of Geoengineering." *Environmental and Resource Economics*, vol. 39, no. 1, 2008, pp. 45-54. ProQuest, DOI: 10.1007/s10640-007-9174-8. Accessed 5 Feb. 2020.

Caldeira, Ken, et al. "The Science of Geoengineering." PDF ed., Annu. Rev. *Earth Planet*. Sci., 2013.

Darton, Richard. "Lecture: Geoengineering - Fantasy or Feasible Future?" *University of Oxford*, Video ed. Viewed 5 Feb. 2020.

Flegal, Jane, et al. "What Do People Think When They Think about Solar Geoengineering? A Review of Empirical Social Science Literature, and Prospects for Future Research." *Earth's Future*, vol. 4, no. 11, 2016, pp. 536–542., doi:10.1002/2016ef000461. Accessed 5 Feb. 2020.

Necheles, Ella, et al. "Funding for Solar Geoengineering from 2008 to 2018." *Harvard Solar Geoengineering Research Program Blog*, Harvard University, 13 Nov. 2018, geoengineering.environment.harvard.edu/blog/funding-solar-geoengineering. Accessed 20 Feb. 2020.

United States, Congress [END_NAMES2], House, Department of Energy. *Department of Energy FY 2020 Congressional Budget Request*. Government Publishing Office, Mar. 2019. Accessed 20 Feb. 2020.

Honorable Mention— Zelda Provenzano Endowed STEM Writing Award

Meghan Mohnot

Genetic Modification: The Future of Curing Disease?

Genetic modification, while a relatively new technology, has already gained attention in the genetic world. In the past, the technology has been used on plants and animals, leading to major improvements in the quality and production of goods (Ross). As genetic modification technology advances, research says that it may be able to cure thousands of genetic diseases. In fact, this treatment has already been tested on certain individuals. This is significant because it can be safer, quicker, and more accurate than other cures for diseases, proving to be a revolutionary step in the world of science (Fernandez). A technology called ADC may even reduce side-effects involved with the treatment of certain diseases because it can target specific genes causing the disease (Armitage). However, there are many who are concerned with the potential long-term effects of this technology. It is associated with its own risks and complications and should be utilized with caution (Ross).

The most well-known version of genome editing for human cells is called CRISPR Cas-9. Through this system, genes can be removed or replaced in order to prevent the occurence of certain genetic diseases (Ross). It was developed based on the natural editing system of bacteria. In this process, a piece of RNA and a guide sequence binds to a targeted DNA segment and Cas-9. Once the RNA recognizes the DNA, the Cas-9 enzyme cuts the DNA at a certain spot. Then, researchers can alter the DNA or delete genes (What Are). The use of genetic modification for diseases is currently highly controversial, with the general consensus being that it should not be done without proper research.

There has been significant research done to determine which diseases could be cured or prevented through CRISPR. Somatic genetic modification, or manipulation in an existing person is gaining support because unlike germline genetic modification, or manipulation in an embryo, egg, or sperm, it will most likely not cause effects on other cells or future generations (Licholai). There are more than 10,000 diseases which lead back to a genetic mutation that have the potential to be removed (CRISPR/Cas-9). For example, Sickle-Cell Anemia and Beta-Thalassemia, which are disorders that reduce the amount of oxygen being transported to the brain, are caused by single base-pair mutations which can be removed through CRISPR. This is an example of a toxic loss of function disease (Fernandez). According to the National Academy of Sciences of the USA, a study has been done which provided proof of positive effects of CRISPR on various blood disorders. A group of researchers modified bone marrow and progenitor cells in order to elevate the amount of hemoglobin in the body, which can increase the amount of oxygen that β-Thalassemia and Sickle Cell Disease cause the lack of (Ye). The technology may also be used for toxic gain of function diseases, such as for transthyretin, a disease which causes proteins to clump together contributing to aggregates (Fernandez). It could possibly be a candidate for genetic modification because the disease is mostly produced in the liver, making it easier for nonviral vectors to modify targeted cells (German). Blindness has the potential to be cured as well, because many forms of blindness are caused by a specific mutation which could possibly be removed by CRISPR. Editas Medicine and CRISPR therapy are working together currently to research the effects of CRISPR on a common cause of childhood blindness, Leber Congenital Amaurosis (Fernandez). Columbia University and University of Iowa scientists have even used CRISPR on a patient for the purposes of curing Retinitis Pigmentosa, an inherited blindness condition (CRISPR Used). Muscular Dystrophy, which causes muscle weakness, is a candidate for CRISPR because it is heritable and does not have any other effective cures (German). Other diseases that could be cured include Cystic Fibrosis, AIDS/HIV, and Huntington's Disease, all of which are currently being extensively researched (Fernandez).

Perhaps the most exciting is CRISPR's potential to treat cancer. Cells can be modified to remove proteins that tumors bind to and then instruct cancer cells not to attack the body. This treatment is significant because cancer cells mimic human cells, making them invisible and hard to combat. The CRISPR technology is able to seek out these cancer cells, unlike any other cancer treatment utilized before (Fernandez). For example, Chemotherapy works by attacking cancer cells, but also ends up attacking healthy human cells, making the procedure prone to side-effects. CRISPR, on the other hand, can target a specific gene, which may be a more favorable option (Armitage). Results of the first study using CRISPR for cancer in the United States were released in November 2019. The data is positive and shows the potential of CRISPR for fighting cancer cells. The study was done mostly to check whether or not the procedure was safe rather than effective. Dr. Edward Stadtmauer, a Professor of Oncology at the University of Pennsylvania, who was heavily involved in this study, believes that CRISPR has the potential of becoming an effective cure in the future (Stein). If CRISPR is able to cure cancer, it will transform the health of the human population.

While many believe that CRISPR should be utilized, many also believe that CRISPR should either be avoided or that it should be used only with proper research and testing due to complications and risks involved. Within the two kinds of genetic modification, somatic genetic modification involves manipulating genes in an existing person, while germline genetic modification manipulates genes in embryos, sperms, or eggs. Somatic genetic modification can be categorized into two types, removing the gene from the body and altering it before putting it back in, and doing injections in the body to turn genes on or off (Licholai). While the somatic genetic modification is likely to be safe to use, germline genetic modification is highly controversial because of the risks it involves (Human Genetic). In fact, embryo genetic editing is illegal in multiple countries (What Are). It is also prohibited by a "binding international treaty of the Council of Europe" (Human Genetic). Despite this, a Chinese researcher experimented with CRISPR on human embryos in 2018 (Ross). The scientist, He Jiankui, edited the genes of twin girls, who then faced public scrutiny because of experimentation without proper research done (Human Genetic). He was then placed on house arrest for a period of time (Ross). China in particular is moving extremely fast in the direction of genome editing, while other countries have been taking more precautions. The main concern with embryo editing is that it may cause problems in the genetic system. Humans are not fully aware of how the body works and CRISPR may create mutations we never knew of before. Any gene manipulated in the embryo would appear in every cell of the person who developed from it, and could be passed along to future generations. It is unknown what consequences this could potentially cause (Human Genetic). Along with this, genetic drive may cause problems. When genes are manipulated, those genes may be passed on to other organisms, in turn bringing those genes into the environment. There are also concerns that CRISPR might cause cells to lose their ability to fight or be damaged in other ways (Licholai). Mosaicism, or the state having cells with different genotypes may also develop through gene editing. However, it can be prevented if gene editing is done before cell division begins in an embryo (German).

Embryo editing does come with ethical challenges as well, as people believe that the more advanced the technology becomes, it could start being used for the purpose of designer babies, or embryos whose traits such as eye color, intelligence, height, etc are manipulated through gene editing. Designer babies raise concerns such as the limitation of human diversity. (What Are). They may also cause a negative effect on the gene pool, and may create new social classes and contribute to natural selection (Minchin). The use of CRISPR on diseases, if established, may end up being expensive, which means only the wealthy will be able to afford the treatment, creating an advantage for only certain people (What Are). However, the use of CRISPR to cure diseases may be more significant than these concerns. Despite any possible risks, there was a case of successful embryo genome editing in 2017, when CRISPR was used on an embryo to fix a mutation that causes a heart defect (Licholai).

Based on research currently being done on CRISPR, the use of the technology is proving to be a positive advancement. Thousands of diseases have the potential to be solved by CRISPR which excites many researchers and scientists. The technology is known to be more accurate and effective than other cures because CRISPR can target specific cells (Ross). However, it should be utilized with caution. This is because genome editing can cause unknown consequences to future generations and other organisms, and it may create new mutations and damage to cells. The former director of the National Institute of Health has placed restrictions on the use until more research is done. Inventors and patent-holders of CRISPR have also put in restrictions in order to make sure any steps taken are safe (Licholai). Overall, CRISPR may be an effective cure for many diseases in the future, but should be researched extensively before any steps are taken.

Works Cited

Armitage, Hanae. "Scientists Zero In On Cancer Treatments Using CRISPR." *Stanford Medicine*. 26 August 2019.

Couzin-Frankel, Jennifer. "Cutting-Edge CRISPR Gene Editing Appears Safe In Three Cancer Patients." 6 February 2020.

"CRISPR/Cas-9." *CRISPR Therapeutics*.

"CRISPR Used To Repair Blindness-Causing Genetic Defect In Patient-Derived Stem Cells." *Columbia University Medical Center*. 27 January 2016.

Fernandez, Clara Rodriguez. "7 Diseases CRISPR Technology Could Cure." *LabioTech*. 23 July 2019.

German, David M.; Mitalipoc, Shoukhrat; Mishra, Anusha; Kaul, Sanjiv. "Therapeutic Genome Editing in Cardiovascular Diseases." *PMC. NCBI*. 25 February 2019.

Licholai, Greg. "Is CRISPR Worth the Risk?" Yale Insights. 21 August 2018. *Human Genetic Modification Center For Genetics and Society*.

Minchin, Steve. "The Pros and Cons Of Having a Designer Baby." *Explore Biotech*. 11 August 2019.

Ross, Rachel. "What Is Genetic Modification?" *Live Science*. 1 February 2019.

Stein, Rob. "CRISPR Approach To Fighting Cancer Called 'Promising' In 1st Safety Test." *NPR*. 6 November 2019.

"What Are Genome Editing and CRISPR-Cas9?" *Genetics Home Reference*. 11 February 2020.

Ye, Lin; Wang Jiaming; Tan Yuting; Beyer, Ashley I.; Xie Fei; Muench, Marcus O.; Wai Kan, Yuet. "Genome Editing Using CRISPR-Cas9 To Create The HPFH Genotype In HSPCs: An Approach For Treating Sickle Cell Disease And β-Thalassemia." *PNAS*. 20 September 2016.

Drexel Publishing Group

Creative Writing

Introduction

The following creative works were selected by faculty judges from student submissions (of creative nonfiction, fiction, humor, op-ed, and poetry) to the Drexel Publishing Group Creative Writing Contest.

These pieces engage with issues of culture, mental illness, current controversies, and personal struggles. They are as varied and diverse as the students who wrote them. You may marvel at the insight, compassion, humor, and humanity these writers possess. These writers are brave and generous in their desire to share their work. Please enjoy the writing they shared.

—The Editors

First Place—Creative Nonfiction

Sara Beinish
Cut Ties

My favorite pair of shoes I own are slippers. A dark brown suede on the outside and lined with white fur on the inside. The bottoms are charcoal black, and although I've had them for nearly a year, they are fairly clean. A bow of long, tan ribbon once was perched on top of the tongue of each shoe but were cut off months ago.

I have suffered from Major Depressive Disorder since I was thirteen. Since my diagnosis, I have seen upwards of 10 therapists (my phone contacts app is practically a yellow pages for New Jersey psychotherapists), tried all kinds of medications (I can basically explain the scientific workings of selective serotonin reuptake inhibitors), had genetic testing, attended various types of group therapy... none of which worked. Eventually, my psychiatrist came to the conclusion that I have a rare type of depression: "Treatment Resistant Depression." He explained that my body does not respond to medications or psychotherapy treatments. So as the months came and went, it did not come as a surprise that my condition only seemed to worsen. By my senior year of high school, I was absent so frequently and falling so far behind in my classes, I was no longer on track to graduate high school. The mailbox next to my front door had become routinely stuffed with letters detailing the school's attendance policy and how I was in violation of it.

"Montclair High School requires a student has no more than five absences per quarter," the letters read.

"Yeah, try making it to seven classes a day when you can't even make it to the kitchen for meals," I thought. My ever supportive and positive mother tried continuously to encourage me out of bed and to school, but more often than not, the weight of my illness won the battle.

Around winter break, my depression had worsened to the point that I had stopped taking care of myself altogether and could hardly force myself out of my house. My teeth and hair had gone unbrushed for days, I hadn't stepped in my shower in well over a week, and the few days I actually did go to school, I wore the same gray sweatpants and sweatshirt. After a few long weeks and dozens of walk-in visits with my student assistance counselor, it became clear to the people close to me that my life was in danger.

One particularly rough morning, I had an emergency visit with my school counselor. After a few hours in his office, he insisted a parent pick me up and take me straight to my doctor. That night, my psychiatrist declared that for my own safety I was to be hospitalized immediately. Post category 5 shockwave landing, my family and I began to plan.

Both of my parents had taken off work to be with me the following day (and frankly many times the following month). We investigated the best hospitals for treating mental illness in the area. We checked with insurance providers, consulted online packing lists, and reached out to family friends who had gone through similar experiences. The main thing we gathered from our research was that I was to bring only comfortable clothing. However, for the safety of the patients, clothing was to have no drawstrings. My mother, father, and I spent that entire February afternoon silently pulling all the ties out of my sweatshirts and sweatpants. They even helped me muster up the courage to go out to a few shops in town, and bought a brand-new pair of brown, fuzzy slippers.

Two days later, my parents drove me to the hospital we had found and agreed upon. I was ushered by nurses and technicians from stark white room to stark white room and filled out questionnaire after questionnaire. Each room smelled even more of latex and cleaning supplies than the last. My parents and I said our long, tearful goodbyes before I was led through a labyrinth of white halls to where I would be staying. Vulnerable and afraid in nothing but a thin hospital gown and my new slippers, I kept my eyes on the ground ahead of me. It wasn't until we had reached the locked, heavy double doors to my wing when the technician I was following looked down and frowned.

"Oh, no. The ribbons on your shoes are a safety hazard," she explained. "I'm afraid we'll have to remove the bows or confiscate the shoes entirely."

So I waited as the perfectly tied bows were cut off my brand-new slippers.

Everything in the hospital was focused around the safety of the patients, so the rooms resembled a mix of a prison cell and a college dormitory. The walls of the room I shared with another girl were a white cinderblock, and the windows were sealed shut and blocked by metal bars. It consisted of two twin beds, two desks, two chairs, some cubbies, and no door. All of the furniture was firmly bolted to the ground. The bathroom was almost worse—for the valid fear of the patients being able to hang themselves, we had no shower curtain or bathroom door, just another cinder block wall that blocked the view from the hallway. I was given a composition notebook for journaling and a pencil about three inches in length, the point of which was only lightly sharpened and no eraser.

The time I spent in the hospital felt like a dream. My wing consisted of 16 teenage girls, each more tormented by mental illness than the last. Each morning, we were woken at eight and had our vitals taken. We were then escorted to breakfast as a group and then to our activities for the day. From art therapy to music therapy to journaling to processing groups, I was kept fairly occupied. In our remaining free time, we had no choice but to stay in the locked wing in either the lounge or our bedrooms. I felt like a child: an absurd number of naps, constantly supervised, next to no say in how I spent my day, with only books and coloring for entertainment.

Initially, I made no effort to engage whatsoever. I felt as if I had nothing in common with the other girls—after all, I was the oldest of the group and the only one there to have gone to the hospital voluntarily. My heart sunk when I found out every other patient was there as a consequence of a failed suicide attempt. I spent my time alone in my room reading and avoiding speaking to other patients. During calling hours, I begged my parents to bring me more to read. I tore through the novels of Phillip Roth and the short stories of Kurt Vonnegut in a matter of days. I'd read and then reread and then reread again the letters from my friends and boyfriend informing me of who got into what college and who was in what piece for the dance company show. The single fluorescent light above my bed remained on at practically all hours, so I could read and write whenever I pleased. Overall, I kept to myself the first few days.

My assigned roommate encouraged me to join the other patients a number of times. "You should come to the lounge. We're about to play cards," she said on multiple occasions. Each time I smiled politely and said I was fine where I was.

Around the third or fourth day I was there, I began to notice a shift. I had started to make my bed each morning and arrange the photos my parents had brought during visiting hours on my desk so my dog's face could be seen from the first step walking in the door. After my showers, I put my hair into two neat french braids that fell down my back. I even began to match my fuzzy socks to my sweatshirt each morning. Slowly, I became more active in group therapy sessions and often contributed to the discussions. I spent more and more time in the lounge working on puzzles with the other older girls and even began to form relationships with them. I even began to notice myself laughing at a joke one of them had told every now and then. By the end of the week, I was seated at the table in the lounge with all the girls' focus on me as I explained how to play BananaGrams. Slowly but surely, I caught glimpses of the girl I once was beginning to reemerge.

Nearly a year later, I still don't know what exactly caused this shift. I assume it to be a combination of many elements. My support system of phenomenal parents, a devoted best friend, and a loving boyfriend that I'm still with today were the foundation of it all. The doctors adjusted my medications, which undoubtedly had a large impact. Meeting girls around my age who struggled in the same ways I did truly made me feel less isolated and lonely. Having time away from the stressors of my competitive high school and the college application process and my various extracurricular responsibilities definitely contributed to my growth. At the hospital, I learned to treat depression like any other ailment and that there is no shame in asking for help. One of the therapists once told me, "You wouldn't be embarrassed or ashamed if you had broken your leg. Mental illnesses need proper treatment, too: professional help, a crutch or two, and time to recover."

Today, I don't think much of the hospital. Having progressed so much since last February, very little of my life now reminds me of my life then. I no longer struggle with getting dressed each morning or having to make my bed. This time last year, I would have never thought that I'd be attending college away from home. I still journal as often as I can. I slowly drifted from relying on communication with the girls from my wing for comfort during the occasional bad day. I've threaded all the drawstrings back in my hoodies. I placed my journals and letters from friends and artwork from those eight days and seven nights in a box in my attic back in New Jersey. I even began to open up and tell close friends and family about my time there. Overall, I have erased all signs of the hospital from my daily life. Every morning, however, as I make breakfast in my suite overlooking the Philadelphia skyline, the cut off bows on my slippers, remind me of how far I have come.

Second Place(tie)—Creative Nonfiction

Yasemin Dayi
The Good, The Bad, The Evil

Many people say that money is the root of all evil. This phrase is often regarded as a universal truth. I have not found this to be the case. I have been rich, and I have been poor, and I know exactly what struggles come with each set of circumstances. The root of all evil is greed. My father is a brilliant businessman and his success brought my family great wealth once, but his greed took him down a path that would leave our family with nothing, and with him sitting in a federal prison cell for over six years.

My father, Kenny, built an incredibly successful sneaker business and quickly became one of the largest clothing liquidators in the country. This business was my whole life ever since I was a child, and my father groomed me to become a sneaker genius while I was still in elementary school. I learned the history of sneakers, how to price, photograph, list, and ship merchandise. I learned how to micromanage a million-dollar business just as much as my father because I was with him constantly. I was a sponge in my most impressionable years and these skills were going to help me build my own empire. My father had the wildest sneaker collection anyone could dream of in warehouses over 12,000 square feet. I always had the hottest fashion, from Gucci to True Religion, even as a child.

He taught me business. He taught me how to make money on a maximum scale. Business is all I know. Making money is all I know. I was taught money over everything and everyone. The sneakers weren't his only form of income, though. He was still my dad and he took me wherever there was money to be made and lessons to be learned. He would take me everywhere like an accessory, from top secret business meetings, to lunch dates, to meeting "uncles" in the slums of Baltimore and Paterson. I was his "roll dog." I was the DJ in long car rides.

I remember riding around in his Rolls Royce Ghost like it was nothing. He bought cars like it was nobody's business. My favorite was his 2013 BMW M3- hard-top convertible, blood red interior, wrapped in matte black, with his clothing brand plastered in red decals around the car. When I first saw the top go down, I knew it was my dream car. As soon as I stepped out of the car, he handed me the keys and said, "This is YOUR car. I'm going to teach you how to drive in it and you will take your test in this car and this car only." He had turned me into a real-life Veruca Salt, getting anything I wanted (although maybe a little less obnoxious). But it was a short-lived dream.

A lot of things will go over your head as a child. Sometimes you will see or hear things you do not quite understand, but they will be burned in your memory, only to realize many years later that things were not what they seemed. One of many activities, one that was relatively common, was counting money. Since I was eight years old this was a bonding time for my father and me. Kenny used to tell me, "Make all the bills face the same way in these stacks. When you're done, count out 20 bills and make stacks." Music would be blasting, we would be singing songs and talking about what new shoes we wanted. The focus of the task was never how much money was there; it was always prepping the money for the money counter. It was practicing my counting skills; it was the sheer action of helping my father with anything and everything because that is who I look up to the most, without question. The amount of money flew over my head completely. Millions of dollars went through the money counter. This was all normal to me. Never for a second did I ever question it. Why did we have so much money? Where was it coming from? It was all normal. This was an everyday thing for us, something we thought would never go away.

Looking back now, I can see what I was exposed to. One of my favorite things to do was to vacuum-seal Kenny's marijuana for packaging. As a kid, I had no idea what it was. I just knew I liked the smell of it; earthy, musky, a very distinct and strong smell. To be quite honest, I don't even recall calling it anything. It was always, "Can you help me vacuum seal this?" At 11 years old I had seen more strains of marijuana than any medical marijuana dispensary employee. I was in the presence of a master-grower and marijuana producer, a true kingpin. There I was, completely oblivious to the fact that my father was a major drug trafficker.

Once I started getting older, I became less oblivious and more curious. I asked questions, but only to myself. I knew it was safer to keep my thoughts to myself because if my father realized I was becoming curious, he would stop keeping me involved, and that was my biggest fear. It was a fear of missing out. It was a fear of not learning everything I could. Why did my dad have three phones? Why did he go to California every other week? Why did I have so many "uncles?" Why were so many people in and out of my house? I started putting the pieces together when I was about 13 years old. I made connections from the rap music I listened to, as well as watching *Breaking Bad*. But by then it was too late…

Tuesday, January 15, 2013. I woke up to the sound of banging at five a.m. The blue and red lights filled my room through the windows. "Not again," I said to myself. This wasn't my first rodeo. In fact, the DEA raided my house twice before, but this time was different. I heard my mother yelling, trying to wake up, and more importantly warn, my groggy father. The first thought in my head was to hide my MacBook. I had just gotten this one, and the last time I hid it they didn't find it, so I put it in my usual hiding spot between my bed frame and my purple painted wall in the corner. Before I could even get out of bed, I heard the front door get kicked in. My Pitbull, Zoey, was barking like crazy, Feds were yelling at my mother downstairs, my brother was screaming in his room confused as to what was going on. The booming of the DEA agents' heavy boots stomped up the steps. I'll never forget how rudely I was woken up and grabbed out of my bed. All of us were forced to sit on the living room couch. My poor grandmother from Turkey was here for vacation and almost had a stroke because of all the shock and commotion. But there was one person absent on the couch. The star of the show, Kenny. I watched the police put my father into handcuffs and usher him out of our house. The last words he spoke to us as a free man came out of his mouth, painfully: "I love you Yaz," Only me.

The two weeks that followed were the worst in my life. We lost our huge house, our cars, our dog, and most importantly our money. In the government's eyes, everything, from the clothes in my closet to our house, was paid with "drug money" so we deserved nothing. How were his children to know it was all wrong? Why did we have to suffer as well? My father was always my idol and he had literally given me everything I had ever wanted. He made us rich, but the $10 million dollar per year eBay and Amazon business was not enough money for my father. He needed to maximize profits. Seneca the Younger (circa 5 B.C –A.D. 65) famously said, "It is not the man who has too little, but the man who craves more, that is poor." His greed made him crave more and we all had to suffer.

My father is still in federal prison. My mom, brother, and I live in a two-bedroom apartment, where my mother sleeps on the couch just so me and my brother can have our own room. My mother is working two jobs, at Bank of America and Marshalls, to make ends meet. Her paycheck isn't enough though, and we need state help, such as food stamps and free lunch at school, to live. I was always taught to make money, yet it became impossible to do that on my own. I had no startup money, I had no product, and I still had to go to school. I had to step into my father's shoes and take care of my household, but most importantly, my little brother. I felt trapped to be blessed with such a business mindset with no way to utilize it. This was our family's fresh start, but we were in prison with him.

Second Place (tie)—Creative Nonfiction

Sana'i Parker
The Signs of Disruption

If there's one thing above all that I have found fascinating about the Drexel University campus, it would be the "busy" feeling that it gives off to its fellow inhabitants and I. Day after day, the unremitting flow of human traffic that navigates the sidewalks of this urban environment feels like it belongs in an ever-churning machine. Mornings were always hasty, as the swarms of individuals all poured out their dorms to traverse to their class on time. Vehicles would fill up the roads, amassing us at intersections, and forcing the daring souls on boards and bikes to weave in and out between them. In between common hours, the "machine" would switch on and off, getting packed for a short span of time and then subsequently emptying upon that strike of the hour.

It was one of those numbingly normal days for me and the thousands of other hopeful souls scuttling about the campus. I spent the blissful October morning going to and from class, with not enough sleep and too much on my mind, like most students. Throughout class, nothing filled my head but the thought of the comfortable haven that was my dorm room, where I could relax for hours before embarking upon my next task. Leaving my lecture, I felt a sense of relief that I could finally get a taste of relaxation and sleepy laxity. That was, until I came into view of the signs.

Across my view, on the corner of 33rd and Market Street, stood impediments in the way of my view of the proceeding sidewalk I was so accustomed to seeing. Bold, black cardboard signs were posted up in the air, filled with contrasting colors and words that I could not yet see. As I got closer, their picture became clearer: flame-filled messages were plastered on them. These signs, attached to their respective posts, came down to meet with the hands of estranged individuals. Right from a glance, those people felt like interlopers, immediate disturbances in the usual flow of student traffic.

The contents of the signs were fiery, both literal and figuratively. At just a glance, I could make out statements threatening hellfire and damnation to homosexuals and Muslims, calling out women and labeling them as whores, and mocking transgenders. Reading these sharp, succinct declarations of extreme temperature, I felt an initial sense of unease. Being a Muslim myself, seeing a sign denouncing my own religion was already a massive red flag for me. A clear chill meets me, as I approach earshot of a bellowing voice: one of the people, standing near the sign-holders, is shouting through a megaphone. Though the business of the street drowns out some of his words, the first few I hear pierce through: "There's too many homos on this campus!" the person speaks in brash exclamation. And such was the very beginning.

This cluster of protestors, officially known as the Key of David Christian Center, is a nondenominational group of self-labeled Christians, who have gained their popularity through demeaning demonstrations such as what I experienced. Led by self-proclaimed "pastor" Aden Rusfeldt, this group spends much of its time traveling to public areas around the Philadelphia area, rousing local passersby and accumulating antagonized crowds of people who shout, swear, and swing back at them. This past October, I had the experience of witnessing one of their demonstrations for the first time on Drexel's campus. Having never experienced the likes of it before, that day's turn of events left me shocked, bewildered, and confused. However, I was ultimately able to learn a very important lesson that day about displaying my identity and fighting with silence.

As I first stood there, watching, and listening in on the spews of the group, I had the sudden sense to run away. *Escape*, my mind demanded of me. Just from scanning the few messages they had raised high in the air, and hearing their short, offensive exclamations, I knew that there would be no benefits to my being there. Still, I watched in and listened, as the gathering of us students continued to grow. Over the hours, waves of witnesses came and went, many of which deciding to stick around like myself. Time and time again, someone on the megaphone would shout something offensive and drastic. At one point, the group even had a child who looked just short of fourteen years old stand up and "preach." For someone that age, the snobby profanity that exited his mouth was startling to us all. Bothered, we knew we had to try to retaliate.

By this point in time, the crowd evolved from just bystanders, to counter-protestors, directly opposing Aden and his followers. I witnessed students make satirical signs of their own and play loud, eccentric music to counter the clamor of the megaphone. Some of them began dancing together, kissing, and waving pride flags to contest Aden's soulless demonstration. One student even went so far as to strip and stand in front of them, proudly topless. And yet, even with all these efforts, those few interlopers remained steadfast; unmoved, unfazed, untethered, and with no intention of leaving anytime soon. Many students gave up soon after, continuing to go about their days. Confused, I stopped one of them, asking him why they were all leaving. He simply responded, "Why shouldn't I? They're just toying with us. I should've ignored them and kept walking."

For most of the event, I kept my interactions with the demonstrators to a minimum, as I didn't want to rile myself up by directly debating with them. However, upon seeing many of my peers challenge them, and see others give up, I decided to make a few comments. On their sign, I noticed how one of the signs included the censored word "m*****bators". Since every other slur was clearly printed on their signs, I found it funny to see that out of all them, *this* word was censored. Jokingly, I pointed to the word and asked, "What's that word?". Dumbfounded, he just stared at me in response, seeing what I was pointing to. I smiled. "Could you explain what it is to me, or read it aloud?", I say sarcastically. It felt like I had finally got him in a corner and shut him up. But then, he hit me with a stern, surprising response. "Can you not read?" he replied, "You're black, so you need to get an education."

Upon hearing that, I felt frozen in time, unable to resume my normal day as continuous, outrageous events that unfolded before my eyes and ears. *Breathe*, I told myself. I wasn't angry, or even remotely insulted by what that person said, but rather confused by what their purpose in that pointing out about me. And I wasn't the only one who had to endure that sort of dialogue. One of my Hispanic friends was continuously called a Mexican, even though he was from Puerto Rico. Girls in tight pants or skirts were called whores and sluts, unfit for college education, and only good for cooking. Jewish students were called out, being mocked with the stereotype of being cheap. It seemed like every color, creed, or background was targeted. Despite all these events that continued to ignite and boil my insides, I still had no incentive to leave as many students did. I did not want them to win, as I felt that their goal was to make us offended until we could no longer stand our ground. I felt that nothing could push me over the edge.

After about two hours of being there, a few fellow Muslim students, some of whom I knew, approached Aden, regarding one of the signs that mocked Islam. Impatient about my lack of accomplishment, I decided to join them, and we jointly demanded that he take all the signs down and leave. We questioned his seeming hatred towards us and how he planned to get anything accomplished if he was just blindly insulting. Annoyed by our presence, Aden flared at us and proceeded to do something none of us expected. He reached into his bag, pulling out the Holy Quran. With a mocking smirk, eyes covered by his dark sunglasses, he tears the Holy Book to shreds, and then stomps the remains on the ground.

The look on my friends' faces were horrified; it was as if he had directly ripped a piece of their souls and shrouded them with anguish. I was beyond disgusted by this, and I felt like I had just swallowed molten liquid, which slowly ate away at my steaming insides. Up to that point, I felt confident in my ability to not be broken, but this nullified everything. Right before I was about to retaliate, one of my friends flung himself at Aden. Almost instinctually, the officers stationed around the group held him back, as he was crying. As I looked once again towards Aden, I saw nothing but a smug look on his face. It was unbelievable, and many in the crowd who also witnessed it felt repulsive. However, the police forced all of us to immediately leave the premises. By the time I came back, they had begun to pack up and quickly leave, as their warrant to be there expired.

I spent a good while after the whole ordeal wondering about those demonstrators and what exactly they were trying to accomplish. Sure, I was angry, but more so puzzled about their direct hate towards my religion, the LGBTQ community, and other groups who did absolutely nothing to provoke them. It seemed like almost every group in existence had some problem in their eyes. Looking up their website afterwards, I found that they claim to be "preaching to rebuke sin and sinners and save their souls." I'm pretty sure threatening hell and calling everyone demeaning slurs wouldn't be the best idea of persuasion or salvation.

Still perplexed, I decided to gain outside perspectives on the situation, by speaking to a few students on campus. Some felt that Aden and his group came just solely to attack us and elevate themselves on a pedestal of superiority. Others felt that the entire situation was one giant inside joke to them, which us students just always took seriously. It wasn't until I spoke with my RA, Almas, that I began to piece together their underlying intentions. Since she was also Muslim, I told her about the events that transpired during my standoff with Aden. "I'm so sorry you had to go through that," she told me. "It's crazy, because when I was a Freshman, my RA told me to pay them no mind." Having this discussion with her, it finally clicked to me. I was reminded of what I was told from someone who walked away that day: that he should've ignored them.

Aden's amassing of crowds, many of us pissed off, confused, and appalled by their demonstration, is exactly the amount of chaos they hope to create. The vast array of diverse individuals, each with an aspect of them that is pointed out by Aden as something inherently wrong, all come together to witness and try and defend themselves and others. Some take it all as satire, some get defensive and debate, and some even get so heated that it ends in a physical altercation. It's these altercations that they use against us. They take them to courts for lawsuit and win cases by justifying them as an expression of "free speech." Using their cameras to record everything, they flip the perspective to make us seem like the perpetrators. When I stood there, as a witness to the event, I noticed how many Drexel police were stationed around the protestors. In hindsight, I now see that they weren't there to protect the group but were there to protect us from their scheme.

Looking back on my experience with Aden and his following, I am gladder than ever that I was not emotionally charged enough to do something rash. Had I stayed any longer, I knew that I would've probably went over the edge, acting exactly how they wanted me to. Their polarizing comments on my race and my religion, while offensive and wrong, were nothing more than triggers, meant to trip me up and keep me around. Realizing that now, I still wondered why so many of us, including myself, wasted hours of our time standing amongst their presence. Presenting this question to my fellow peers, I got a handful of responses. "I just found the situation funny," one of my friends said. "I wanted to waste their time." I also got answers such as "It was just so much of a shock," or "I wanted to stand up for us." Regardless of their different responses, they all were connected in a way: that Aden and his protest was a distraction, one that threw us off from our normal routine.

The Key of David Christian Center is not a group that we can battle and get rid of physically as students. Like they said at the end of their demonstration that day, they'll be back again and again, spewing the same senselessness.

Because of the country we live in, their outward protests that denounce and slander the diverse population of our campus will always be protected under the guise of the First Amendment's "free speech." However, they are only as strong as the amount of attention they receive. Because of their interruption in our daily routines, they were able to get under our skin, wasting our time with their pointless banter. If we all continued walking and ignoring them, following the regularly flowing machine of our respective journeys, they would have been the ones to waste *their* time.

Their attack on me for being an African American and Muslim in this country was hurtful, shocking, and unforgettable, but it taught me something. All of us students come from a diverse number of backgrounds, and that's why they single us out. That's why they target universities and public spaces, because they know it can be easy to call out traits or characteristics that give each one of us identity. So, the next time I see Aden and his crew on this campus, reading his signs calling out my religion, and hearing the megaphone bellow aimless insults, I'll smile and keep walking along my way. By continuing to be proud of my individuality and not giving in to their tempts of disturbance, I know that I will have won. By remaining silent, I will speak louder than any of their megaphone-holders. I will shine outward, confident in the traits that define the unique person that I am, and unfazed by those protestors who tried so hard to strip it from me.

First Place—Fiction

Ferishta (Freshta) Rahmani
Mass

I feel the pebbles from the road digging into the soles of my feet through my paper-thin shoes. Ota Jan[1] promised that we only had a little more to go, but then again, he also promised me new shoes. I look over at my brother's feet and wonder if he's thinking the same thing, but his sheer normalcy tells me how accustomed he's become to our situation.

The wind picks up and I shield my eyes from the dust about to hit my face. The wind persists like a bad cough and I pull my scarf around my face and wrap it the way Modar Jan[2] taught me to when these sorts of things happened.

Ota Jan heard about how Kaka[3] Rahman's family was visiting and how they were from America. As soon as he found out, he told us to put on our best shoes and clothes and asked us to bring him his black vest, the one that had the forty afghanis in it.

Forty afghanis is not a lot—definitely not enough for a new pair of sandals—but it *is* enough to bring a small gift to the Americans.

I dream about America whenever we take these kinds of trips, letting my mind drift off to a place where I can escape to. Ota Jan was always telling me about how they lived in a land where the grass was green and the skies were pink, but the skyscrapers that they had were shinier than anything Afghanistan's ever seen. He used to sing a little song about the country to me—something he did only when he was truly happy—as a lullaby.

I love to picture myself there, standing underneath a skyscraper that Ota told me was called the "Empire State Building," smiling and waving to my reflection in the shiny, shiny metal. Ota Jan thinks that someone will be able to help us. *Him.*

He makes us walk several miles each time, trying to convince us that this person will be different. But most of the time, it's himself he's trying to convince.

"No, no, bacha jan[4], this person will help, he rambles on, gripping our hands while we cross the street, dodging death amongst the speeding cars. "They will. And when they do, I can finally buy you the new shoes I promised you, and we will have dishes with chicken and lamb and oh! You all will grow tall, and big, and strong—strong enough to beat your old man." He'd laugh at the end with the kind of laugh that sounds genuine. But I know my father. His laughter is forced, and I think deep down he realizes that there's no hope for any of us.

---
1 Father
2 Mother
3 Uncle
4 Dear child

I ignore the pebbles, telling myself that we only have a few more minutes to go; soon we'll see Kaka Rahman's yellow house at the end of the wide alley, and I'll see kids racing and playing around and maybe I'll join them. Maybe, this time, I won't have to deal with the Americans staring. But it's useless; everyone stares.

I don't even have to follow my father's large footprints anymore; I've been to Kaka Rahman's house so many times that its location is etched into my muscle memory. I make a small prayer in the four seconds I have before we reach the front door, asking for this visit to be the last one. Asking for Father to be helped.

He raps on the door loudly, and I hear a dog barking on the other side. A girl who looks only a couple of years older than me peeks her head out, but I don't recognize her. She must be one of the Americans, then. An *Amreekoiy*[5]. She lets us inside when Kaka tells her to shut the door, then leads us past the gates into the space outside the living room. We take our shoes off and I long for a chance to freshen up before I take a step inside.

From a quick eye sweep over myself, I notice that my feet and nails are dusty from all the streetwalking. I look down upon my dress and see the tiny tear in the collar and the hole in the sleeve that Mother never had a chance to fix. I try my best to smooth out my scarf and tuck in the few strands of hair that escaped while I was running, and I walk inside after my father and brother, greeting Kaka Rahman as soon as I enter.

The audible gasp I hear doesn't take me by surprise—in fact, I relax after I hear it. It assures me that there won't be any polite ignorance as we had the humility to endure multiple times before. The lady opens the door behind her and calls her kids, telling them something in English. They pile in one by one, four girls in total, and begin to stare as I had predicted.

"How long have you had this?" The lady asks my father while she pulls out a large telephone. She paces around him and winces appropriately at parts of the story.

Her camera zooms in.

He tries to stay still during the recording, but I can see his pinky start to twitch as slight perspiration makes his forehead look shiny and his breath hitches when he speaks. I grab his hand to stop the shaking.

He has a mass on his right eye double the size of his fist.

When it's time to go, my father is nearly in tears and can´t stop thanking the lady, who promised to send him to India for surgery. She asked for merely a prayer in return, and my father raises his hands to the sky, pleading to God for a special spot in heaven for the woman and her family. We bid everyone goodbye.

---

5 American

Father starts humming on the way home, and suddenly, I no longer feel the pebble.

*Originally published in Johns Hopkins Center for Talented Youth, Imagine Magazine (2017)

Second Place—Fiction

Samantha Nicole Johnson
Show and Tell

The room was purple, then white, then yellow. It flashed pink next before it lit up red and orange. Photos wilted against the walls as the room glowed brighter. Clothes and shoes slowly reduced to ash. The smoke billowed around her like thunderclouds. More and more, the room glowed a dark red. She looked up at the ceiling as the black clouds filled up the space. The tears continued to roll down her face, around her tightened smile and drip from her chin. The room was red and orange and black. Then it was no more.

Ori blinked at the ceiling. The room was quiet, the sounds of Soul City traffic echoing through the windows. On the 15th floor of the Medical Care Office, Ori sat across her therapist, Dr. Rei Drum. She'd been going to him for the past eight months, each meeting starting in uneasy silence. It was eleven o'clock in the morning. Ori shifted her weight in the chair. The doctor watched as the girl stared out the window, her reflection slightly blurred against the old windowpane. Dr. Drum tapped away at his tablet before leaning back into his chair.

"Tell me about this last time."

Ori didn't budge. He was the twelfth therapist in the city to have asked her that question. He was the first, however, to remain as her therapist past the three-month mark. She had tried to explain her illness before. Ori had no recollection of how she started fires. For her, the match didn't exist until the flames had already begun stripping the room of its memories.

It started off as little sparks; the first time it happened, she somehow lit the firebox of her family's fireplace when she was seven. In a matter of months, however, the fires grew worse. She had hoped someone had the answer to why she kept setting things on fire, or how she could stop doing it. Her therapists were all confident they could solve her "textbook pyromania" case. She was, too. They had her meditate at first, to see if maybe if it was a behavioral issue. Then came the pills and the heavy drugs. Nothing worked, and each solution resulted in one more fire. One by one, they came to the conclusion that it was in fact *not* a textbook case, and not a case they were eager to solve. After almost two years of unanswered questions and failed solutions, Ori stopped searching for answers, using her time in therapy to listen to the city's sounds.

Dr. Drum cleared his throat. He shuffled in his chair for a second before propping his elbows on his knees, his hands clasped together in silent prayer. Ori shifted her attention to him.

"Ori, for the past eight months, we've been trying to explore the origin of your pyromania through conventional methods. I think it's time to look at other options."

Ori sat up in her seat. "What are you saying?"

"Well, I think I'm starting to understand a bit more about your situation. In the past, my colleagues have maintained that this is a behavioral issue. It seems to me that there's something more to it, quite possibly innate. I want to try a new method. I think it'll help make this process better," he said.

Ori hummed. Taking that as a positive sign, Dr. Drum stood up and shuffled back to his desk. He fumbled with his drawers before pulling a black box out of one of them, and slamming the drawer shut. He shuffled back to his chair.

"This, this right here is the Ninpo 100. She's the latest memory device designed by Med Care."

He pulled the sides of the box up. Inside was a metallic blue pair of goggles. Next to the goggles was a small tablet with various buttons on its side. Beneath it, a thumb-sized disc of the same color. He gently pushed the box closer for Ori to see.

"The Ninpo 100 is designed to help those unable to talk about trauma. Think of it like the VR sets from the 21st century. You'll show me your memory, rather than having to tell me. The goggles will find your memory and project it through the lenses. You'll, in a sense, be brought back to that memory, where you can take some time to address the parts that triggered you. We'll take this nice and slow, and eventually you'll be fixed." He gestured at the disc. "This is to monitor your neural responses, in case you get over excited or anything. The monitor is for me. I will be watching you, ensuring that the system is working, and ensuring that you go through the treatment properly. I have a mic as well to communicate to you, but I doubt that will be used a lot."

Ori watched the man silently. His eyes lit up as he talked about the device, his voice firm but with a childish tinge. It was funny, but unsettling. She looked down at the box, at the shiny blue gadgets.

"I don't know," she mused, "seems a bit intrusive."

Dr. Drum sensed Ori's hesitation and put the goggles on her lap.

"It doesn't hurt to try, Ori."

Ori picked up the goggles and slipped them over her face. They fit perfectly. Dr. Drum leaned over to connect the disc to her temple and fumbled with its settings until a blue light flashed. He guided Ori to a lounger by the window and had her lie down. The monitor flashed a blank white screen before showing a control panel with Ori's picture and data on the left side. Dr. Drum fumbled with the equipment one more time, before taking a step back.

"Well, you're ready to go. I'll count down from five, when I get to one, you'll feel a slight pull. Don't panic, go with it. After that, what happens inside is up to you. And remember, I'm right out here, making sure that everything is fine as you go through this process."

Ori nodded her head in understanding. She closed her eyes and steadied her breathing. *Five...four...three...two...one...*

***

Memories of smoke and flames jumbled together as Ori was pulled into her subconscious. Some images repeated themselves: the shining firetrucks and the burly firemen racing towards the torched house. Splashes of reds and blues and police officers waiting behind yellow caution tapes. The tears. The endless tears of her now estranged family as they stared at their burning home. Her smile. Her mother grabbing for her, screaming *"how could you?"* when she's burned down their home, how could she keep living when all she's done is destroy their lives. She remembered all these moments and all the feelings that came from them. Ori's heart sank as she saw her family's image dematerialize, their looks of terror and disgust fixated on her. Before she could stop herself, Ori found herself shouting at her fading family that she didn't mean to start those fires. More memories appeared and disappeared, folding on top of one another like an accordion. Each memory was more emotionally painful than the last, the following image materializing quicker than before. Suddenly, the images were everywhere one mass of colors swirling around Ori. They jostled her around, pulling and pushing her until finally the memories swelled around and pulled her into a deep darkness.

Dr. Drum watched intently as Ori laid there, motionless. On the top right corner of the screen, "ACTIVE" flashed on and off. On the monitor, Ori's memories blurred by. The therapist pressed a few buttons, and the room glowed a faint blue. Dr. Drum scrunched his face. With a few more taps to the monitor, the Ninpo 100 was ready to begin the simulation.

"Come on Ori, let's see what you can do."

Dr. Drum hit "START." Ori's body jerked to the right, like a puppet on strings. In the simulation, she stood there for a bit, suspended in darkness. And then, she moved.

***

Ori woke up in a heavy daze. The pull was much harder than she expected, her subconscious body stinging with pain. Her eyes slowly adjusted to the low lighting of her surroundings. From first glance, she could make out a window in the corner, soft white light seeping through. The space was a small cube, the walls a faint lavender. On the right corner was a twin-sized bed; a ragged stuffed toy rested on the pillow. A closet claimed another corner of the room, a desk claimed a third. As Ori's eyes continued to adjust, a buzzing rang throughout the room.

"Ah Ori, hello! Oh good, you're in one piece," Dr. Drum chimed. *"Everything is as realistic as it'll get, so walk around a bit, get acquainted."*

Ori stood up and slowly paced around the room. She walked over to the bed and picked up the stuffed animal, gently worn but greatly loved. She picked up some of her old clothes—a dull yellow jacket, a pair of jeans too small for her now. She smiled at her favorite pair of shoes thrown haphazardly by the closet, a bright blue pair of Jordans. She recalled some of her favorite memories in the little room, all the times she used to play pretend, jump from her bed into her clumpy pile of laundry. Ori chuckled. *"I was asleep at this point,"* she thought. Her bedroom alarm read three o'clock. In the real world, the monitor read half past noon. She noticed a floor-length mirror standing by the window. Hesitant at first, Ori shuffled over to the mirror.

Staring back at her was a little light-skinned girl with dull brown eyes. Dark coils sprang from her head and down to her shoulders, cupping the sides of her face. Her arms and legs were skinny, the nightgown she had on too boxy for her petite frame. She couldn't have been older than eleven. Ori tilted her head, and the girl did the same. Arm extended, Ori reached for the mirror, and the girl reached for Ori. Ori's fingers gently stroked the mirror, connecting with the girl's.

Dr. Drum chimed in again. "We are in the most delicate part of your subconscious now. Based off my readings, this is your most traumatic memory. While your current body is biologically seventeen, we've found it best to recreate you back to the age of the incident. Right now, you're looking at you at ten."

Ah, she thought, *this is ten-year-old me.* She overlooked Drum's use of "we," transfixed with her younger image. It was hard to imagine that was her at ten. The constant fires left no photo unscathed, and her family chose not to retake any family portraits. The buzzing returned.

"What exactly am I looking for?"

"Well, we're looking to see how this fire started. It looks like this one was the catalyst that led you to spiral and lose control. We want to get to the root of the problem, so we can potentially work on avoiding triggers."

Satisfied with the answer, Ori nodded her head and kept walking around her childhood room. As she walked by the bedroom door, Ori heard a voice from outside the room. It was slurred and gruff, using a combination of grunts and curses to complete a sentence. Ori didn't recall this from her memory, but the voice made her stiffen. It had been ten years since she heard that voice, and it sent a wave of terror over her. His gruff voice was followed by a softer voice.

"We need to get rid of her, Sharon. She's a freak."

"She's my daughter, Ryan. You promised you'd take care of this whole family."

"Yeah, before I realized she's a xxxking psycho. She's trying to kill us. And I won't let that happen."

"What are you going to do?" Sharon's voice wavered.

"End of the week, she's going away." There was a silence.

"For fxxx's sake, Sharon, I'm not gonna kill her. But we can't put her up for adoption, she's too old and we'll look suspicious. I know a guy; he takes care of these things." Her stepfather grunted again. "I don't know why you're asking; you've been looking up boarding schools since the first fire!"

Ori clutched the sides of her head, pulling her coils tightly around her face. Her breathing turned haggard; her eyes lost focus of the room. *Go away,* she thought, *make it go away.* She squeezed her eyes shut, rocking back and forth on the floor.

***

Ori opened her eyes to a sight she had seen many times before. Her lavender room was ablaze. The fire stretched across the floor, snaking its way up the walls. She turned her head to the right, only to see the closet already burning away. She looked around and watched the last pieces of her life go up in smoke. More and more, the room glowed a dark red. She looked up at the ceiling as the black clouds filled up the space. She knew what would happen next: the firefighters would burst through the bedroom door. One would run to her frozen body, scooping her in two arms and rushing back out the doorway, down the stairs and out the house. Ori pulled herself off the floor and dusted off her pants. She turned towards the bedroom door and waited. No one came.

Confused, she looked around the room. Everything was burning much faster now. The lavender walls were replaced with flames and soot. In the beginning, the flames didn't feel real, but as seconds passed on, the room grew hotter, and the flames grew more uncontrollable. Ori shuffled to the door, unsure of what was happening. *This is not my memory,* she thought. "Dr. Drum!" She yelled over the roar of the fire. "Something's wrong!"

Dr. Drum buzzed in, "What's wrong?"

"This—I wasn't here for this. The firefighter should have come and pick me up by now!"

The room filled with silence for a moment before Dr. Drum spoke again. "I think we've finally discovered what's really going on with you. Ori, I think your current emotions and your past are overwhelming the Ninpo 100. You're creating real fires! Ori—I think you're a pyrokinetic, not a pyromaniac."

Silence engulfed the room again.

"Huh?" Ori said, "Pyrokinetic? That's not possible."

Dr. Drum hummed. "You're manipulating what you feel and making it into fires. I couldn't tell you if fire is the only thing you can manipulate, but Ori, you've got your answer!"

Ori shook her head in frustration. "Make them stop!! I can't get out!" From inside the simulation, Ori scratched away at the door unsuccessfully. She tried to pry it open, but the door was firmly shut. She ran over to the window and tried to pull it open. No luck. Ori shuffled back from the window, watching the flames overcome the curtains. The smoke increased more, throwing Ori into a coughing spell.

The buzzing from Dr. Drum's mic grew louder, the doctor's voice coming through rushed and excited, "You can't leave yet! We're making progress! This is the beginning!"

"Please, *please* just get me out of here, I—I can't breathe." The smoke drowned Ori in a sea of darkness. She slowly slumped to the ground, tears streaming down her face.

"Alright Ori. You can do this; we just need to practice more. I'll ask to extend your session time, and to extend your deadline. Just say 'End Ninpo' and you'll be pulled out."

Ori didn't respond.

"Ori. Say 'End Ninpo' and get out. Now."

"End..."

She looked back into the mirror. The little girl was still there, watching Ori cough up smoke and blood. Ori stared at her younger self. The dullness in her gaze was gone, replaced with a glowing shimmer. Taking one last look at the ceiling, Ori watched as flames and smoke engulfed her room whole. The flames danced on her skin, singeing her legs, her arms, and her face. The smoke clogged her lungs, weighing them down like boulders. She feebly gasped for what little air there was left. Her vision blurred. *I want this to be my end,* she thought.

She closed her eyes.

***

Dr. Drum watched the monitor. The red-orange glow of the fire colored the screen, the smoke darkening the corners. The young woman's gasps could be heard through the speakers. Dr. Drum muted the volume and put the monitor on his desk. He stood at his desk in silence for a minute, before grabbing his tablet again and tapping away.

Log 923: Patient OL17, Trauma Memory Simulation: House Fire. Patient initially capable of recognizing manifestation of ability. While Ninpo 100 made trauma reenactment realistic, patient's ability forced overstimulation, causing real events and increased pain reception. System malfunction made it impossible to control ability and perform extraction. Patient OL17 suffocated and burned to death in Ninpo; unable to continue. Status: Brain Dead.

Dr. Drum saved his notes and closed out of the file. He reached over to his desk phone and dialed a number. "Carla dear, please have a clean-up crew come to my office and remove Patient OL17. If she has any living relatives, send a notice that, after careful consideration, she's been assigned and relocated to the asylum indefinitely, for further *treatment*." He hung up and let out a disappointed sigh.

"*Tsk*, another failure." He checked the monitor, now black, before looking at the limp body on his lounger. "Well Ori," he said dismissively, "I'm afraid this concludes your mandated therapy sessions. Thank you for sharing, this was a *very* telling experience."

Three men shuffled into Dr. Drum's office moments after, all clad in black. Dr. Drum gestured to Ori and turned to face the window. With a silent nod, they picked up Ori's unresponsive body and carried her away, the sounds of Soul City traffic echoing below.

Honorable Mention—Fiction

Luis Cruz
La Llorona: The Weeping Woman

The village square was lavishly decorated for the festivities. *Cempasúchiles* were placed around and on top of the well that lay in the center of the square. *Papel picado* hung across each street as candles were lit among the *ofrendas*. The *alfeñiques* were brightly colored and arranged on every windowsill. The band played their instruments while the women danced to the music. As beautiful as everything was, nothing was more beautiful than Maria. She glided around the village square barefoot, her embroidered white dress flowing around her as she twirled around. Her long, wavy raven hair bounced with each step she took. Every man stopped in their tracks to watch her dance including many Spanish noblemen, though none other than Alejandro de la Cruz was bold enough to do anything other than admire her.

"*¿Quien es esa mujer hermosa?*" Alejandro asked one villager, fixated on Maria.

"Her name is Maria, *Señor*."

Maria continued to dance, coyly denying the men brave enough to ask to be her partner. Dancing away, she bumped into someone behind her. She turned around, startled by the man standing before her.

"May I join you in this dance?" Alejandro asked, towering over her.

"No, *gracias*," Maria almost whispered, taken aback by the handsome stranger. She began to dance away from him before he grabbed her by the arm.

"I don't take 'no' for an answer."

"*Por favor, Señor*. There are people watching," Maria looked around and noticed the crowd whispering and pointing at the pair.

"I always get what I want," he muttered as he took her waist and hand in his.

The two danced, ignoring the whispers and gasps of the crowd, lost in a world of their own.

As the song ended, Maria noticed the people watching. She turned to leave but was stopped by Alejandro.

"Please, *Señor*. The priest is watching us!"

"Stay with me. I must know more about you."

"I'm sorry. *Buenas noches*."

***

Maria opened the door to her home as quietly as she could; however, she found her mother working at the kitchen table in the candlelight. Maria approached her and kissed the top of her head.

"*Hola, mamá.*"

"How was the dance, *hija*?" Her mother turned toward her with a smile.

"It was… magical," Maria smiled, thinking about the handsome stranger she danced with.

"I sold all the flowers! I'll help you get the bouquets ready for tomorrow."

Maria quickly got to work, picking off the thorns from the roses that lay on the table.

"You had another gentleman caller today."

"Another?" Maria groaned.

"Maybe it's time you found a suitor. You're not getting any younger, you know."

"You know I can't, *mamá*. Who will take care of you?"

"Never mind me. I'm already an old woman. You deserve a chance to be happy."

"But I'm happy here-"

Her mother began coughing loudly, gasping for air between coughs. She pulled out her handkerchief and wiped the blood from her lips.

"Are you alright, *mamá*?" Maria asked, concerned.

"I'm fine… I'm fine. Just let it pass."

"Your health hasn't gotten any better…"

"Listen to me, Maria. We have had nothing since your father died. Get married, have children, live your life, *mija*."

Maria opened her mouth to speak but stopped as she heard the soft strumming of a guitar.

"Who could that be at this hour?" Her mother asked.

"Someone very drunk," Maria laughed as she heard a man try to sing.

"I'll see what he wants." Maria walked out of the house as her mother peered out of the window.

"You don't give up easily, do you?" Maria was pleasantly surprised to see Alejandro at her doorstep.

"Not on anyone as beautiful as you."

"I... I'm flattered. I don't even know your name-"

"I seem to have forgotten my name," Alejandro replied, a grin on his lips as he looked into her eyes. Maria laughed.

"Go home, *Señor*. You must be drunk. I am no one, I have nothing to my name. Please... just leave me alone."

"But I can give you everything... if you agree to be mine."

"I can't. Please go away."

"I won't give up. I'll come back each night."

"Why? Why me?"

"That moment we danced... I have never felt more alive. I have traveled around the world, yet no one has made me feel the way you have. I must have you for myself."

"I must confess I can't stop thinking about the moment we met. I was hoping I'd see you again, *Señor*..."

"Alejandro. My name is Alejandro."

"I hope to see you again, Alejandro. Perhaps you'll see me in the Village Square. *Buenas noches*."

"I swear on everything. You will be my wife, Maria."

***

The villagers exited the cemetery, leaving Maria alone as she wept at the foot of her mother's grave. Alejandro walked up and embraced her as she cried into his chest.

"Alejandro... I don't know what to do..."

"*Cálmate, mi amor*. I know how you're feeling. I lost my mother a long time ago. You need someone to take care of you and be with you right now." He pulled back to look at her.

"I just want to be alone..." Maria shook her head and looked at the ground.

"Maria... come live with me. We can be happy together."

"You know I can't. Everyone will talk. An unmarried woman living with a man?"

"Forget them. You know it's what your mother would have wanted." He raised her head up gently.

"My mother wanted me to get married..."

"We *will* get married."

"What?" Maria was shocked.

"I want to marry you, Maria. These months of courtship have been the happiest I've ever been. I want to make you mine." He said sincerely as he wiped her tears.

"Are you mocking me?" Maria was in disbelief.

"We will live together, get married, start a family. I want you to be my wife."

Maria kissed him, a mess of emotions running through her head.

***

For the first year of their arrangement, Maria and Alejandro lived happily together in his manor, albeit unmarried. Maria was the happiest she had ever been, believing she was living in a dream. She soon gave birth to fraternal twins. However, because of Alejandro's many duties and status, he would travel frequently, leaving for months at a time. He would always return with many gifts for the children, but each time it seemed he would grow more and more distant toward Maria. Furthermore, Maria believed her children genuinely grew to hate her. She would soon find that her happiness was merely an ephemeral dream.

"Please calm down, *mi vida*! I just wanted to play with you!" Maria held Valeria in her arms as the girl squirmed to get away.

"No! You broke my doll! I hate you! I hate you!" Valeria cried, repeatedly punching her.

"I'll fix it for you! Please stop crying!"

"No! I want papa! I wish I went with him to Spain!" Valeria pushed Maria away and ran out of the room.

"Don't be upset, my love! Valeria! Come back!" Maria called out to her. Guillermo played loudly in the corner.

"Are you playing with the toy your father gave you?" She turned her attention to him. Guillermo ignored her.

"Can I play with you, *hijo*?" She walked up to him.

"Please, *mi cielo*. You've barely spoken to me since your father left." Guillermo turned away from her.

"Can I get a hug? A kiss?"

"*Disculpe, Doña* Maria. Where would you like us to start decorating?" A servant walked in before the boy could answer.

"Decorating?" Maria was perplexed.

"*Sí, Señora.* Don Alejandro sent the tapestries, flowers, table settings, and more to be set for the wedding before he arrives."

"He's finally going to marry me?!" Maria exclaimed, elated.

"It seems that way, *Señora*. I believe your dress hasn't been delivered yet, though." The servant smiled.

"Oh, that's quite alright! I'll go to the village to buy some fabric! Thank you very much, Alberto!" She excitedly began to rush out of the room.

"Please start with the courtyard and then work on the dining room!" She called out behind her.

***

Maria was hard at work, pinning and sewing the soft white silk that would become her wedding dress. Although it was a lot of work for her to make her own dress, she was still elated that the day Alejandro would marry her would finally come.

"Papa! You're home!" The children shouted, alerting Maria who frantically hid the beautiful dress from sight.

"My angels! I've missed you both so much!" Alejandro walked into the room, holding gift boxes wrapped in ribbons. He placed them on the floor as his children ran to hug him.

"Did you bring us presents?!" Valeria's greedy eyes met the boxes on the floor.

"How was Spain?" Guillermo asked.

"I did bring you presents! But first, there is someone I'd like you to meet..."

Maria ran up blissfully, like a schoolgirl, and held out her arms to embrace Alejandro.

"Hello, Ale-" She stopped dead in her tracks. Her smile faded as she dropped her arms.

A beautiful woman walked into the room. Her blonde hair dropped in ringlets beside her face as her blue eyes sparkled in the candlelight. The light pink dress she wore was obviously meant for someone of her class. Maria had no doubt this woman was of noble standing.

"*Bonjour, enfants! Je m'appelle* Joséphine." She introduced herself with a heavy French accent. Alejandro put his arm around her tiny waist.

"This is Joséphine, she will be your new mother."

"But-" Guillermo began.

"Oh, you must be Guillermo! You are just as handsome as your father!" Josephine approached him, putting her hand underneath his chin.

"Hello, Josephine. I am-" Valeria curtsied before her.

"You must be Valeria! You're so beautiful! Please, call me *maman*!" Josephine embraced the girl warmly.

"She brought you both presents!" Alejandro handed Josephine the boxes.

"For my little girl, a beautiful doll!" Josephine got on her knees and watched Valeria tear open the box before they both embraced.

"And for my handsome boy, a toy soldier!" Josephine opened the box and presented it to the reluctant Guillermo.

"I... thank you. But-"

"Josephine, this is Maria." Alejandro helped Josephine up and presented her to Maria, who stood stone faced.

"*Enchanté mademoiselle.*" Josephine gave a quick, polite curtsy.

"She is their governess. She's been taking care of my children since their mother died." Alejandro smiled as he looked at Maria.

"Why thank you, mademoiselle. I can take over from here now..." Josephine said as the grandfather clock struck.

"Oh la la! It's almost time! I have to put on my wedding dress. Who will take me to my room?" Josephine looked at the children and smiled.

"The children of course. The maids will be there shortly to assist you."

"Come along, *enfants*! Let's make me a beautiful bride!" She took them both by the hands and led them out of the room. Alejandro watched them leave as Maria marched right up to him.

"How could you do this?" Maria tried hard to keep her voice steady.

"Maria..."

"After everything I've done for you?!"

"Done for me?! I gave you everything after your mother died. A home, children, money. I asked for nothing in return and yet you disrespect me constantly!" Alejandro quickly grew angry.

"Please don't do this. Make her leave! Tell her to go!" She begged.

"No. I will have a wife my family approves of." He turned away from her.

"Approve of...? APPROVE OF?! I've been nothing but good to you! I moved in here because you wanted me to, I gave birth to our children, I've tried to make this place a home for us! My reputation is tainted… for what?!" Maria exploded, years of suppressed anger pouring out.

"Those were all choices YOU made! Don't blame me for that. Did you really think a Spanish nobleman would marry a filthy Mexican with nothing to her name?! No! I am Alejandro De La Cruz, Duque de Sevilla, heir to my father's fortune. You will do as I tell you if you want to keep living here. Without me you would have nothing and be out on the street like a common whore. So, if you want to leave; go. I won't stop you." Alejandro spat through his gritted teeth. He walked up to her, their faces inches away from each other.

"I won't abandon my children." She spat back at him. Suddenly, he slapped her, causing her to fall to the floor.

"Then shut your mouth and learn your place. We had nothing between us. You gave me an heir, that is all. Nothing remains. You will be a servant to Josephine and witness our marriage."

Maria said nothing, but held her face, tears welling in her eyes.

"Is that clear?!" Alejandro's face turned red as the veins in his neck burst through his skin while he shouted at her.

"*Si*…" Maria meekly replied.

"… *Mi amor*." She whispered as she watched him storm out of the room.

***

The ballroom was alive with the sounds of music, laughter, and applause. Servants tended to the many nobles who sat drinking, talking loudly, and congratulating Alejandro and Josephine. Guillermo and Valeria were enjoying the attention from the nobility, taking their compliments and praise with gusto. All were happy to be in attendance except for Maria. She sat in a corner alone, silently weeping as she watched Alejandro take Josephine by the hand and onto the dance floor. The guests applauded the happy couple. The two stared into each other's eyes, in complete bliss. The scene reminded Maria of how she once danced with Alejandro all those years ago, how it felt to be wanted and desired, how it felt to be the only thing in his world.

"I can't… I can't…" she whispered to herself as she rushed out of the ballroom and ran through the corridors of the manor before locking herself in Alejandro's study. She backed into the door and slid to the floor as she began to let her tears fall.

She looked around the room, her eyes falling on the safe that was hidden in the wall. Her plan of escape quickly came to her; she would take as much money as she could and run away with her children. Although she did not know where she would go, she was certain she needed to leave. As her mind raced, she unlocked the safe and began grabbing as many coin purses she could carry when a peculiar roll of parchment fell out. She picked it up, unfurled it and began to read it aloud.

"I, Sebastian Garcia, loyal soldier of Alejandro de la Cruz, have agreed to kill Ana… Hernandez… mother of Maria Hernandez…"

Maria dropped the parchment on the floor. Her eyes widened in crazed shock as her mouth fell agape. She shook almost violently as if doused by freezing water. Memories of unspeakable abuse flashed into her mind as feelings of anger and disgust boiled deep inside of her. She could feel the rage emanate from her body as her mind tore in two.

Instantaneously, Maria's face turned to a blank stare. This would be the last thing she would remember…

***

"I want to go home!" Valeria exclaimed.

Maria was now clad in her wedding dress, a veil upon her head. She held their hands in hers as she led them through the dark, eerie forest. She hummed softly, ignoring their pleas.

"Don't worry, little Valeria… We're almost there…"

"Please take us home! I'm scared!" Guillermo pleaded.

The sound of rushing water became louder as they approached the rushing river.

"A stupid river?!" Valeria screamed at Maria.

"There's nothing here!" Guillermo cried.

"It's… at the… bottom… of the river…"

"But-" Guillermo began as Maria led him into the freezing water.

"Come, Guillermo… you first…"

Without warning, Maria grabbed him by his head and pushed him beneath the surface of the water. Valeria watched in horror as Guillermo's muffled screams rang in her ears. More frightening, Maria's face never broke from her blank stare. As Guillermo stopped clawing at Maria's arms, Maria turned slowly to Valeria.

Valeria screamed and ran away into the forest.

"Come back, *hija*… Don't be upset, Valeria… I only wanted to play with you…" Maria called out to her. Valeria ran until her lungs felt that they would burst, and her throat ached with her breathing. She quickly hid behind a tree, sure that she had lost her mother. However, she could hear Maria's humming in the distance. She was coming closer. Valeria peeked her head out and looked around. There was nothing but trees and the sound of the howling wind. She turned around and screamed.

"*Te encontré...*" Maria whispered.

She slapped the girl to the ground and began dragging her by the feet. Valeria screamed, her voice ringing throughout the forest. Her fingernails became caked with dirt and blood as she tried to claw her way out of Maria's grasp.

"Please, don't!" Valeria screamed between her sobs. Maria pulled her into the water.

"I'm sorry! Please, *mamá*-!" Valeria pleaded as Maria forced her under the water. Maria shook with rage as she watched the life escape Valeria's body. She watched her body slowly rose to the surface. Maria tilted her head back and let out a roar of laughter, holding the bodies of her children in her arms. She looked up at the moon and laughed even harder. Looking down at the children, her laughter began to soften and slowly turned into sobs. She had finally realized what she had done.

"Oh my God... my... children..." She gently rocked their bodies in her arms.

"Mis hijos..." They stared blankly at the sky as she tried shaking them awake. Maria became hysterical.

"MIS HIJOS!!! AYYYY MIS HIJOS!!!" Her voice rang out into the night.

Her anguished cries would send fear into the very souls of men for centuries to come.

First Place—Humor

Timothy Hanlon
The Prince of Trashlandia

It's summer term. The classes are easy and the weather is great. My class ends at 9:00 pm and I spend the next hour and a half with my professor as he rips my final paper apart in a windowless room. Three days until the research paper is due and he suggests I completely restart. How could this get any worse I wonder as I walk towards the exit of the building to see that the rain is falling so hard and fast it is as if God had picked up the entire ocean and was dumping it onto Philadelphia. I reach for the spot in my backpack where my umbrella usually is only to be greeted by my sunglasses' case. Useless. I take a deep breath and look down at the Tom's on my feet and my white button-down shirt—prime rain protection.

I get to the corner of 33rd and Chestnut Street—waiting for the opportunity to cross. As I stand there waiting, I realize a car is coming. I then begin to panic as I realize that the waves in the 5-inch-deep flood waters covering all the city's streets is what tipped me off about the car. Too late. The car barrels by splashing enough water to fill an Olympic sized pool onto me. Well, this might as well happen.

Ah yes, apartment 1738. As you enter the front door you get the fresh aroma of the citric cleaning detergent that is so frequently used by all members of the humble abode. No one is ever asked to clean or take care of the space for we have all flawlessly reached a mutual agreement to do so. We all regularly sleep in our own beds and no one ever sleeps in the common areas, the dishes are never left in the sink, and, most importantly, everyone takes their turn using the only washer/dryer in the unit. This is truly wonderful. Well, at least that's how my report to Mom sounds every week.

I finally get home and begin ripping everything off me as I walk towards the dryer. Now here, dear reader, is where the plot truly thickens. As I open the dryer door, I am welcomed by a heaping pile of my roommate's laundry which has been sitting there since I left to start my day—thirteen hours ago. But don't worry! I just have to wait another ten hours until he is home from work until I can ask him if I am allowed to use our dryer. Having dealt with this nonsense too many times before, I wad everything up into one big ball, calmly walk into our bedroom, and finish by kindly throwing all the clothes up into the air above his side. As the clothes reach the peak height, I turn around, knowing that it will look like a bomb went off, and whisper "Kobe".

Now you may be curious as to why I had the moxie to do such an audacious act but hear me out on this. For the past several mornings there has been no need for me to set an alarm—for every day I am woken at 6:45 a.m. by the ever so delightful sounds of my bedroom door slamming, the door to the dryer opening, the clunking of laundry being dumped in, and—the grand finale—the banging of the dryer door into the closed position. There is truly nothing quite like it.

As I arise from my slumber thanks to the ever so natural sounds of the morning I am greeted with a "Good morning" from the Ruler of the house and, of course, I reciprocate hoping the exchange will be over.

"So, I noticed my clothes were all over my side when I got home. What's up with that?"

"Oh, I am so sorry," I said in my head not wanting to start this war so early in the morning, "I was just terribly inconvenienced by your laziness and lack of respect for other individuals who occupy your kingdom. I apologize for being the slightest bit upset when I came home soaking after not having eaten anything for the previous seven hours and not being able to use the dryer. Next time I will send the household messenger to alert you of my need to use the dryer."

"Sorry, I thought I had placed them more neatly in your space. I was just in a hurry to get my wet clothes in the dryer," I respond.

"That's okay. I will try to be better about taking my laundry out. Next time could you please just try to be a little more considerate?" he responds oblivious to the exuberant amount of irony being strewn from his mouth.

"Yes, that is not a problem. Do you mind taking the trash out when you leave since you'll be passing the trash room?"

With a huff and a mumbled "Fine." he stormed out of the room as if I just asked him to perform some kind of witchcraft. But please do not fret, Reader. He happily did so as he slammed the garbage can like cymbals against the ground to get the bag out and, with a supersonic slam of the front door, he left. Since all Royalty was out of the residence, I ceremoniously lowered the household flag to half-staff.

As the Great Laundry Calamity (GLC) of Summer 2019 comes to an end and the fall term was a much-needed rest period with minor, trivial skirmishes, we soon enter Winter term where new and greater battles will be fought. Since the GLC, the laundry situation has calmed down. There is more availability for the other 3 inhabitants of apartment 1738 to fight for the brief openings in usage. However, the garbage still overflows, and His Majesty still fails to humble himself enough to participate in the peasantry act of cleaning. We continue to vacuum, mop, and dust. We clean up the mess that the prince leaves from cooking and eating.

Tonight is the night of the monthly apartment 1738 Beer Olympics—don't worry Mr. FBI man, we are all legal. The prince is on night shift and the stage is set. The living room is set up with a slew of drinking games—from drunk Uno to pong and stack cup—an obstacle course is created—furniture is rearranged. To the loser: a shot of vanilla vodka. To the winner: a month of bragging rights.

We conclude the night with a few episodes of *Bob's Burgers* and several cups of water. As we head to bed we decide to clean up in the morning.

I am, as expected, woken up by the natural morning sounds of post night shift. Slamming of the front door, an unusual pause, forceful entry into the bedroom, slamming of the bathroom door, the turning on of the shower, and, oh this one is very unexpected right now, the buzz of my phone? I roll over to see what someone could possibly want at this ungodly hour. A text. A text in the "Roomies " group chat. Hmm peculiar. I open it. "Looks like y'all had fun last night lol but when you get a chance can you please rearrange the furniture and things back to where they were? Thanks!" Ah yes. Semi-peace time is over.

As we approach The Royal Birthday of the 21st time we all receive an invitation to His Majesty's dinner outing and 'close friend' get together planned for the weekend after in our apartment. What a treat.

Just as I finish reading his text, the prince himself walks into the room. I begin to kneel down so I can kiss his royal feet as a sign of my loyalty to the crown. With that, he finally speaks to me.

"Hey, did you see my text? I just assumed it would be cool with you if I had some people over for my birthday before we go out to the bars," he proclaims.

"Yeah I mean I guess I have no choice now. You just have to make sure you clean up everything after," I respond as I begin to stand up again.

"Wait, so you are telling me that I am expected to clean up after myself and my guests?" he said with a look of confusion.

"Oh yes, I am so sorry your majesty! How silly of me was it to consider such a preposterous event. I will gladly clean up after everyone even though I will be out of town for three days—which includes the night of your soiree," I respond without glancing up from my phone.

"Really? That would be so awesome! Thank you! This really takes a whole lot of stress off my back. Ugh now I will have some time to sleep."

"Oh, yes, of course," I said realizing after the first sentence he put his AirPods in and couldn't hear a word I was saying, "I was being 100% serious. I know how strenuous it can be for you working half a day at a time, three days a week and doing literally nothing but watching Netflix and making a mess of the living room and kitchen. Don't worry, the rest of us will continue taking out the trash you contribute the most to and scrubbing down the apartment because you can't stand a mess!" Once again, he was going to sleep the entire afternoon on the couch because he couldn't be so inconvenienced to walk the 30 steps to his bed.

At that moment I heard the front door unlocking and the third roommate coming in. We locked eyes and she knew what was about to go down. I followed her into the other room so His Royal Majesty the Prince of Trashlandia could get his well needed sleep in the only common area we have. "Yeah, so we are going on a trash strike. We will not be cleaning up after his event. We will no longer be taking the kitchen trash out. We will no longer be the cleaning maid." She slowly nods her head as she closes her eyes. The revolution has begun.

Second Place—Humor

Aaron Jeong
An Invitation to Laugh

I never wrote when I was young—actually, I never really wrote before college. I obviously did write, for school and for assignments where I would utilize a safe and efficient academic voice. But I never wrote anything meaningful or in a way that was an actual reflection of myself (but now I do! Hopefully!). All this scholarly writing felt unattached and I had little passion for any of it. Luckily, my 12th grade English teacher was an amazing lady. The work she had us do was personal and open-ended, and the last thing she wanted was for us to write to please her. She did not want that. She wanted to be intrigued! Challenged!

It was during this time that I felt my voice start to develop. Past the droning and cold writing I had done before, I was beginning to experiment with how I actually wanted to express my ideas. This growth in my voice has been developing since then, through my first year of writing at Drexel, to now! Now, as in the time of me writing these words out, and to the future *you* reading this, whoever *you* is. We are constantly evolving, growing, and developing our flavors.

Through an analysis of my voice I have found numerous characteristics present. Oh? I bet you are interested in what those could be... ah, alas, I will not tell you.

Well, don't look so sad. It's not that hard; you are reading my voice right now. Oh fine, you know how I hate to see you pout like that. I will talk about one part that I think will be very interesting for both you and me to delve into.

Humor.

Now isn't that a dangerous thing to say? But I do think some level of my humor comes across in what I write. I believe writing is a reflection of one's self, and my voice and humor help me inject myself into the words (like a parasite, or maybe something a little more poetic).

I reject impersonal writing (for the most part, nothing is ever so simple). I want whoever is reading my words to feel my presence in the writing. I realize this all sounds very grandiose, but writing is a form of expression and most people do not express themselves with cookie-cutter, highbrow English. In the essay, "Leave Yourself Out of Your Writing," Rodrigo Joseph Rodríguez writes, "To make meaning through language, the writer must be present to the audience and mindful of beliefs to produce coherent, meaningful, and engaging writing for the reader." Yes! My voice works how it does, because I want my readers to feel or learn in specific ways. I believe humor to be a part of my reader retention, as the mind is captured when reading something that makes you smile or even laugh (maybe internally, but that's okay). "Coherent" reminds me of a paper I was given back from a dean. At the top, part of the note read:

"Ideas get obscured by your overblown rhetoric."

I reread that paper, aloud, and I found it reasonably clear. For context, this was a simple one page paper on the Shakespeare text we were reading at the time. Here's the catch: I wrote that paper with significantly less of my usual "overblown rhetoric" to avoid comments exactly like the one I received. This is an important part of this discussion of expression and breaking away from the usual academic mold. Much of academia still believes in, and wants to preserve, the scholarly voice we all hold so near and dear to our hearts. And, frankly, it's bullshit. These next couple of sentences might detract clarity, but I think this opinion of mine will be an important bridge of understanding between you and I, my dear reader.

Progress for the sake of progress can be terrible. But tradition for the sake of tradition is just as absolutely, if not more, terrible. The research is out there, and I am going to use some of it! Limiting language is not a benefit and the implications of doing so are only becoming more and more apparent. There is infinite potential and beauty in the words we use, so why are we constraining ourselves? What's wrong with overblown rhetoric?

Humor is especially ignored and frowned upon by much of the academic world. I study both science and writing and with my experience with the former... well, I think you and I both know how funny research papers are. This exact generalization towards research writing drives the notion of reading science as drab and dreary. In an article on humor in research, Tom Bartlett quotes psychologist Mr. McGraw, "'If you make it hard on the reader to understand what you're writing, it makes it that much more difficult to convince that person,' he says 'A well-placed quip, a well-executed joke—it hinges on it being well-executed—seems to help.'" Now, I am not saying all my quips or jokes are well-executed or well-placed or well-anything. But I think that humor brings a level of humanity, and this is discussed in the article as well. This idea of "art enhances function," that by using humor you can draw the reader in and have them really absorb information. Humor is more than a gimmick; it has legitimate value in writing.

Personally, I am afraid to always include humor or my little jokes. And that may be a surprise, as I am clearly confident and feel no insecurities about my goals, desires, physical or emotional features—nah, none of those! But this fear of humor in writing is not specific to me. You! Yes, you, oh silly you! I reckon you have this fear or something similar. In a study titled "Linguistic Features of Humor in Academic Writing," researchers analyzed 313 freshman college essays and scored them based on humor; here is one of the implications they have identified in their own words:

Secondly, it may be that authors who employ humor in academic writing do so cautiously, aware of the exhortations to write concisely, directly, and to remain on point (e.g., American Psychological Association, 2010; Palmquist, 2010). As a result, linguistic features typical of academic writing remain dominant, even in more humorous essays (Skalicky 254).

Ain't that funny? Even in "humorous essays," this pressure of an academic voice is still pervasive. I can speak for myself in that in the development of my voice, I have been afraid to use it and fully embrace it. It is so much easier, safer, and less of a headache (as seen above, with the sweet note I received) to just use the scholarly voice I have been trained to use. Depending on the professor or assignment, I admit, I will slip into a lazy, lifeless voice. But I wish I didn't! I'm never as happy with that work, and I feel guilty afterwards, a little dirty, not quite naughty. I know I'm not being true to myself.

I have largely focused on academia here, as it is rather pertinent considering this is an *exploration* of myself, in college! Most of my writing has also been under this umbrella of academia. I want to stress how present humor in writing is and has been, and how it is ridiculous that we study work that features it but are expected to shy away from it. I have not read *The Divine Comedy*, though by the title it seems to fit in my sphere, so I will use the eloquent words featured in *The Primer of Humor Research*:

> *The Inferno*, the first installment of Dante's The Divine Comedy, describes damned souls engaging in bawdy behavior and word play. Dante and his guide Virgil also encounter a great many Florentines who sometimes regret their sins and sometimes do not, thus satirizing Florentine society (Triezenberg 526).

Dante, *the* Dante, plays with words and uses topical humor. Okay, maybe Dante was just a very funny guy in 14th century Italy. We'll fast forward to a 19th century United Kingdom, where Charles Dickens writes Silas Wegg and Mr. Venus as funny, relatable exaggerations of common types of people (Triezenberg 529). Humor has been used for centuries by talented writers, and the two I have featured just happen to be thought of as some of the greatest writers of their times… dead, white men of course, but that's a conversation for another time. So, how do we continue to study great figures in literature, analyzing their works ad nauseum, and noting their styles, without nurturing future writers to use some of the same devices? William Shakespeare, "The Bard", "The Nightmare to Students"—his work is crammed full of humor. What is the point in studying great works if we are shunned from using the techniques they use? If we are going to force students to read pre-selected literature, we might as well leave them with something more than "*The Crucible* is an allegory for the red scare, and the prophecy is self-fulfilling in *MacBeth*."

Humor is subjective. I think that's because humor is very human, and we are all very different and unique and amazing (really, whoever is reading this, thank you for doing so, and I am sincere when I say you're truly amazing). Perhaps you thought some of this was funny, perhaps you thought this was terribly inefficient, hard to read, and *most definitely* not funny. Either way, this has been wonderful. Writing and reading is an experience that we share with other people, and for me, it is very intimate, very personal, and sometimes very funny.

Works Cited

Bartlett, Tom. "It's No Joke: Humor Rarely Welcome in Research Write-Ups." *The Chronicle of Higher Education*, The Chronicle of Higher Education, 29 Sept. 2014, www.chronicle.com/article/Its-No-Joke-Humor-Rarely/149025.

Rodríguez, Rodrigo Joseph, et al. "Leave Yourself Out of Your Writing." *Bad Ideas About Writing*, West Virginia University Libraries, 2017, pp. 131–133.

Skalicky, Stephen, et al. "Linguistic Features of Humor in Academic Writing." *Advances in Language and Literary Studies*, vol. 7, no. 3, 2016, doi:10.7575/aiac.alls.v.7n.3p.248.

Triezenberg, Katrina E. "Humor in Literature." *The Primer of Humor Research*, by Viktor Raskin, Mouton De Gruyter, 2008, pp. 523–542.

First Place—Op-Ed

Ciara Richards
Taking Action on Climate Change

In a world where we have been told by the United Nations that we have just 12 years to halt the effects of climate change, I am left wondering what can be done to get people of all ages involved in climate activism. Most people would say that young people are doing the most in terms of helping the environment. Yet when I walk around campus here at Drexel, I see a lot of my peers using plastic bottles and straws, eating meat and fish, and being wasteful. Even when we are presented with all the startling figures surrounding the environment, why do many of us seem to not care? I have to remind myself that the issues that are important to me are not important to everyone else—although I find it hard to accept that people are unbothered about the declining state of the Earth.

Having previously researched the effects of fast fashion, the resounding feeling I got was that people do care about how their choices affect the planet. That is, until they have to make changes in their lives. It is an extra effort to bring your own cutlery and bag, change your food choices, and shop around for second-hand clothes. I am curious as to what it would take to urge young people in particular to make the changes we so often talk about. What more could be done to push this environmental awareness?

The Secretary-General's Envoy on Youth claims 84% of young people agree that they need more information on how they can prevent climate change (*United Nations*). There should be more government initiatives for educating the younger generations in schools about climate change. Immediate action is needed and one of the most effective ways to do this would be through the education systems put in place by the government. As explained on *CarbonBrief*, "Education does more to reduce deaths from climate-related disasters than economic growth, a new study finds. The researchers say education helps reduce vulnerability to disasters and enhances adaptation to climate change." A survey conducted by the *National Public Radio* shows reveals that 4 out of 5 parents in the US wish that climate change was taught in schools. Eighty-six percent of teachers believe that it would be beneficial to teach climate issues in school. The graph below shows the full findings of the survey. Parents and teachers, Republican or Democrat, believe that climate change issues should be taught in schools; children would be more inclined to take immediate action to prevent climate change.

The *National Education Association* claims, "Students can learn that climate change is no longer just of interest to scientists. Insurance companies, emergency responders, the military and more are concerned about climate change." I believed when I was younger that climate change was not something I had to worry about, as it would never affect me. When it was mentioned in school, it was just as a passing comment and there was no urgency in the teaching. Children do not need to be fear-struck, but a matter of urgency would help. If children understand that climate change will affect each and every one of us, they will certainly be more inclined to challenge their actions and the actions of big corporations.

If our education systems will not be the answer to this epidemic, we always have social media to count on. There are huge amounts of work being done by climate activists such as Greta Thunberg, Venetia Falconer, and Kristen Leo on social media platforms, such as *Youtube* and *Instagram*. It can be argued that children learn a lot more from social media than they do in their classrooms. I found my way into climate action through social media posts; I began to see more and more mention of climate issues when scrolling through *Twitter* and *Instagram* daily, and I wanted to find out more. I eventually 'followed' accounts (the same people as previously mentioned) and found myself posting eco-friendly tips on my own social media accounts.

The Atlantic reports that President Trump has described climate change as "a hoax" and "created by and for the Chinese in order to make the U.S. manufacturing noncompetitive." It is clear that, for as long as Trump is in office, an increase in climate education seems unlikely. However, we must not let this discourage ourselves from getting into climate activism. One of the best things to do is spread the word and talk to your friends. Challenge your peers on their daily actions, educate yourself, and push the bigger corporations and the government to take more action on the fate of our Planet Earth. If our education systems will not push climate issues in schools, there is no reason to become discouraged. We can all hold ourselves and our peers more accountable for our actions, but it remains important to continue pushing the government, big corporations, and our education systems to teach young people about the issues that will inevitably affect them. With a 12-year warning to slow down the effects of climate change, it is time for us to all become climate activists.

Sources

"Climate Change Education: Essential Information for Educators." *NEA*, http://www.nea.org/climatechange.

"Education Is 'Top Priority' for Climate Change Adaptation, Study Shows." *Carbon Brief*, 2 Dec. 2015, https://www.carbonbrief.org/education-is-top-priority-for-climate-change-adaptation-study-shows.

Kamenetz, Anya. "Most Teachers Don't Teach Climate Change; 4 In 5 Parents Wish They Did." *NPR*, NPR, 22 Apr. 2019, https://www.npr.org/2019/04/22/714262267/most-teachers-dont-teach-climate-change-4-in-5-parents-wish-they-did.

Meyer, Robinson. "Trump Slightly Revises His Views on Climate Change." *The Atlantic*, Atlantic Media Company, 16 Oct. 2018, https://www.theatlantic.com/science/archive/2018/10/trumps-always-shifting-views-on-climate-change/573037/.

Watts, Jonathan. "We Have 12 Years to Limit Climate Change Catastrophe, Warns UN." *The Guardian*, Guardian News and Media, 8 Oct. 2018, https://www.theguardian.com/environment/2018/oct/08/global-warming-must-not-exceed-15c-warns-landmark-un-report.

"#YouthStats: Environment and Climate Change - Office of the Secretary-General's Envoy on Youth." *United Nations*, United Nations, https://www.un.org/youthenvoy/environment-climate

First Place—Poetry

Sanjana Ramanathan
Immortality 101

I don't know how many lives
I've lived now; I swear I've
died before and before that.
The drowned ghosts sleep
in the empty spaces
in my chest —
my ribs are now gravestones.
The ghosts wake and flutter
in my stomach,
not butterflies but
cinnabar moths: black and blood
red and angry.
I focus on the wings, because
there's no way to describe
emptiness except the space
around it.

I am a body possessed
by myself; an intruder
in my own skin; a corpse
walking; a coffin
that breathes.

Second Place—Poetry

Bella Randazzo
Nuclear/Winter

Nuclear

The words I choose for you are delicate,

Like atom bombs.

For myself, irreversible: I feel the soot settle before I see the metal shatter, before the blood splatters. It matters, the order in which these occur: spurs of orange before hurled silver, quivering sod and brilliant ripples in lakes, vaporized within seconds just to escape melting faces, teeth, grinning forever, evaporation showcases sediment without hesitation, *says look what's been and what won't be, says, look at what's been and don't be sad, see what won't be and be happy, be happy, be happy*—she is your world, and no amount of my arms will change that, my arms, in your arms, harmless, like mushroom clouds, self-deceit,

Is *I love you* an act of war or of peace?

When I drop that nuclear sentence, will you feel the same gorgeous instability? Will silence cushion either side of that event, or will it only sharpen the shrapnel, end up closing the vents, trap breaths, bones, spit, voices, and dates, fingers intertwined forever under soft rubble, embraces encased in dainty cement. Wispy steel, cotton smoke, stolen lives, heads above feet above heads under feet,

Is *I love you* an act of war or of peace?

Two rulers, you and me, a war cold, getting cooler, withholding weaponry beyond our waning brains and wan hearts, with dormant arms we feel insurmountable, powerful over regions of gold, gravy, and guts, it is incalculable how quickly the world would cease if we released the love all at once; I crave your world enough to decimate it, but I know her, which is enough to second guess, you will boast less about your atomic reservations, as far as the guilt will seep,

I love you is an act of war and peace.

If we fire just to fire, your projection will be out of tiredness, direness, swollen eyes absorb imminent shock on my side, but you do not fire, and I cannot fire, I cannot fire—I *will* not fire. I will not see her iris ablaze where there should be a gleaming city, no radioactive tears, corroding and staining, no Armageddon gazing, no alcohol to persuade the finger to jump from life to red buttons, she will never see disaster before a natural day, because I would obliterate myself before I ever aim it her way, your way, *that* way. I wave a burning olive branch, white flames, red palms,

The words I choose for you are delicate,

Like atom bombs.

Winter

Oh, darling, it will be a long winter. When your iron reservoir of stolen touches finally chokes on dust, brittle with ice, ice orange, bloody with rust, where will I be?

Oh, honey, it will be a long winter. When my kingdom sings precious metals into the air, and you can only catch a whiff of gold from your inflatable hills, plastic, purple, prideful, where will I be?

Oh, sweetest, it will be a long winter. When your cheeks can only summon red from substance, seeing sucker-punch sweeties going to parties on Saturdays, sobbing on Sundays, where will I be?

Oh, trust me, it will be a long winter. If home is a place, I will make it myself, and your foot will stay off my porch. The chipped paint on my doorframe will shine in your absence, my rocking chairs rocking, wind chimes singing classics, a pie on my windowsill, berries hot, warm molasses in the kitchen, curtains stitched back to mint condition, windows cracked and glistening, perfectly unclear and letting all the sunshine in, liquid through the cracks and energy through the glass. It is a home and without you it's hectic, it's wonderful, it's a blessing to be stressing in the open air, where my neighbors all love me and my floury hair, my electric glare, the way that I care, or that I don't when you do, that you don't, that you might dare.

Oh, it will be a long winter, and I will be home. Where will you be?

Honorable Mention—Poetry

Sanjana Ramanathan
Fickle Roots

The city is a bird: hollow-boned, hovering,
                                an urban vagrant
                                drifting aimless as a daydream;
                                smoke-spires like spread wings,
                                beaked buildings
                                like curved cliffs of keratin,
                                on the verge of tailspin.

The city is carried: by an unseen goliath,
                                hefted like a stone,
                                on a back half-prone, aloft;
                                it tiptoes slow to conceal
                                its masquerade, afraid —
                                a giant in disguise, mortified by
                                its self-imposed subjugation.

The city is a song: a bard's tale, spun with ale,
                                on the highest table
                                of a low-class pub, beloved;
                                patrons held rapt, lips flapped,
                                and here the story falls
                                in the laps of shepherds
                                and on prince's plates.

The city is cursed: forced to flee every earthen fix
                                that feels like home, to fling
                                itself among the stars, alone;
                                forever fitted with fickle roots —
                                a punishment perfect for
                                people indecisive, they say,
                                from their place in the dirt.

Writers Room
_____

Introduction

Writers Room launched in 2014 and from the beginning offered a monthly writing workshop, open to all, held at the Dornsife Center for Neighborhood Partnerships. Since then, Writers Room has expanded to offer many workshops and events and has become a true hub for learning, storytelling, and conversation. The campus studio space (first floor MacAlister) opened in the fall of 2017. Recent initiatives have involved local high school students, who are given opportunities to interact with Drexel students as well as neighborhood residents and to thus forge intergenerational friendships.

Works included here were written across the academic year. "Say Her Name, Live Her Story, Speak Her Truth" (VanHester) was written for the National Conference on Community Writing, "Doing the Work," (co-sponsored by Drexel via Writers Room). "Haiku" and "January in the News" (Cain, Wasalinko) were created in workshops during the winter months. "Sick Daze" and "That Which Holds Atlas" (Welsh, Randazzo) were written in spring 2020, as Writers Room stayed open online, offering workshops and other opportunities for students and community members alike, many of whom were studying, writing, sheltering at home.

We invite everyone across our Drexel communities to join us this year for readings, workshops, and other offerings, in our studio space or online.

Valerie Fox, Ph.D.
Faculty Writing Fellow

Norman Cain
Haiku

The curious child

Impetuous teenager

Matured Adult

Anticipating

The spring equinox during

Cold winter solstice

We life surfers ride

The rough waves of existence

As long as we can

Bella Randazzo
That Which Holds Atlas

Consider that the web weaves the body, instead.

Remember each leg as a limb for the community spindles, not just for the lone thorax, the ebbing eight eyes—where do I look when all I see is isolation? Hovering diamond-dew trees with glossy, soft branches, we swing, hang, and dip, sing hymns, psalms and jingles for the fluid midnight hunt. We crowd, aloft over one hand-sewn quilt of soft earth, aloft under a sea of planets and predators, watching, wrinkling, waning.

All of us might be dead by dawn, all yarn and epoxy, all stiff, all so naturally sorry, all tucking our shameful faces into our chests, and hugging our abdomens for an arachnid's eternity.

Or maybe we just shed all together, all shed together, witness the shriveling of what our bodies once were, what we once saw ourselves to be in those glazed over leaves. Maybe we let rigor mortis interlock our deaths as we all collapse into that final quilt, create chains of still spiders in the afterlife, revel in the freedom of those bonds, love the canopy but respect the pine fronds that send softly those retired bodies into solar systems beyond present existence, suspended, breathless, distant.

Flies mosey by in the nighttime, caught up with us in the next instant. We treat our collected lives like a collective sweet, and cavities run like grills over our teeth. Feast, we feast.

Consider that the web weaves the body, instead.

Teigha VanHester
Say Her Name, Live Her Story, Speak Her Truth

On Friday morning, I locked myself out on the rooftop deck of my Airbnb.

I had no phone, no clothes; just an almost finished cup of coffee and an overwhelming sense of fear.

How am I going to get off of this roof?

Will I have to scream at someone on the street? But I don't even know the code to get anyone in the building, let alone the apartment.

As I sat on the rooftop deck for about 45 minutes, I tried everything I could think of to do myself. I tried to break the door handle. I tried to scale the fire escape in the building next to me. Nothing worked.

I finally noticed a window in the living room of my Airbnb, over a 3-story drop off. I hoped with all my heart that the window was unlocked. Much to my benefit it was. So here I was, a full-figured mixed girl crawling through the window of an apartment not my own.

As I collapsed onto the floor of the living room, I thought I would be flooded with relief and laughter, but in this world I was not.

Instead, I was filled with thoughts of Bosan Jean and Atatiana Jefferson, and how I could be next. Someone had to see me crawl through this window. And if the police were called, they would not know that I was supposed to be here, or that I accidentally locked myself out. They would see a threat, a black woman's body that to them is only seen as a site of violence.

During the keynote, Dr. Carmen Kynard spoke of how our curriculum needs stories of Atatiana Jefferson, that we need to know the war being waged on the black female body.

I finished getting dressed and walked out of the apartment. While this is not necessarily an experience of the conference, it is an experience that illuminated for me the importance of #sayinghername, honoring her legacy, and connecting to her through sisterhood. Atatiana and the injustice that ended her life made me more aware of the work we must do to change the narrative around our safety.

We are all members of the academy now, trapped on a rooftop deck, crawling into a space rightfully our own, yet fearing our own death from the stories of those who came before.

Alex Wasalinko
January in the News

Styled after Hieronymus Bosch's Garden of Earthly Delights

They lost things, but not hope.
Hid it under their shirts, its outline

protruding beneath the fabric as they moved

towards green promise.

        It is 100 seconds to midnight.
        By the time I cross the room,

        wade through the crowd of bodies to find yours,

        we will be met with lights out.

              I felt the power in the sky,
              words heavy with knowing,

              knowing the breezeblocks that drag the heart

              below the current.

              It's hard to be good when the world is on fire
              so he holds an extinguisher on his shoulder,

              douses the flames on our home

              before we retreat inside.

        The last time democracy almost died –
        we were not even thoughts yet.

        But if you and I could materialize from the dust,

        maybe we can turn back the clock.

Our aim: to illuminate and protect
as we gather, learn, see a future

extending far outside our eyes' range.

Carry one another close to our hearts.

Devin Welsh
Sick Daze

Something drew me to the junk drawer,
to three batteries of all different brands,
half a pack of Kleenex,
a handful of cough drops,
lemon and honey.

They remind me of sick days
spent clicking through the morning
shows. Let's Make a Deal? Sure, why not?
But only if The Price is Right.

Mom left the recipe for Mom-Mom's magical remedy
on the counter next to the bread:
Tea with a little bit of honey, careful
not to put too much in by mistake,
and a Halls for good measure,
preferably lemon and honey.

This past month has felt like one long,
long, sick day.
Laying in my bed, plodding my way
through my work
with the motivation
of a kid who just wanted to play
hooky.

Faculty Writing

Introduction

Faculty Writing reflects current, published work by professors in the College of Arts and Sciences. These texts have previously appeared in academic and scholarly journals, books, conferences, magazines, and websites. They are often thought-provoking, poignant, and funny, and they serve as a powerful demonstration of the many forms that writing can take. *The 33rd* is enriched by the interests and passions of these writers.

—*The Editors*

Stacey E. Ake
"If You Are All Christians, then I Am Not": How Kierkegaard Helped Me Survive a Christian College

A man walked along contemplating suicide; at that very moment a slate fell and killed him, and he died with the words: God be praised.[1]

I am lucky. I have known Kierkegaard for all of my adult life. He was the 19th century friend I could turn to when 20th century Christianity made no sense. I, of course, saw myself in him, whether it was as a misunderstood genius or as a lost and confused Christian. Whether it was as a constant writer ("To produce was my life"[2]); whether it was as someone who was too intellectual for the more devout at Houghton College or as someone who was too religious for the intellectuals at Houghton, Kierkegaard's own angst kept me company. There was also the alienation of being surrounded by people who all seemed to have it all together. They knew what they believed. And they weren't going to question it. Take, for instance, my freshman roommate, who knew that God had called her to Houghton to find a righteous husband and father for her children. And she was right. She married the third guy she dated freshman year and went on to have six children. (I knew they were serious as a couple when I came back one evening to find her mending his blue jeans.)

Kierkegaard starts to write when he is a little bit older than I was at the time, and he has kept pace with me throughout my life. While I don't have an urge to attack the church—how could I when there are so many churches—I understand looking around and seeing people who claim to be Christians, but who don't seem to be living the life. And I mean this both personally and socio-politically. With his stress on inwardness, it is easy to see Kierkegaard as a quietest, but if we see him as a quietest, it is because we have read *Works of Love* without an eye to our actual neighbors. *Works of Love* is really a call to individual social activism. For, as Kierkegaard asserts, "Christian love is sheer action" (WL 99).

I had many neighbors before I came to Houghton. Some of them were poor and living in shantytowns surrounding the town of Querétaro, Mexico. I went to school with them. I also saw great wealth used and abused. I came to Houghton with a political consciousness that did not seem to be shared by my fellow students. I may not have known who Keith Green was,[3] but I certainly knew who Daniel Ortega was. I was bowled over by the political ignorance of my fellows. Never had I been among a group of people so naïve and homogenous. Those who had some kind of political interests were invariably Republican. It was the Reagan era, and I was still mourning Jimmy Carter. Furthermore, I had never before been told that I held political beliefs that were unchristian. (I

---
1 *The Journals of Kierkegaard* (1834-1854), ed. & trans. Alexander Dru (London: Fontana Books, 1958), 50.
2 Pap. X 1 A 442 (ed.tr.)
3 Keith Green (1953-1982) was an American contemporary Christian musician.

think they really meant un-American in the McCarthy sense.) Apparently, as a Democrat, I was going to hell. And there was no debate. I remember cornering an "opponent" in a discussion about El Salvador. It was the end of Sunday lunch. His response was to dump a salad bowl of coleslaw on my head. I patiently told him that I preferred potato salad. He is now a fifth-grade social science teacher.

And there was the patronizing of people from other countries—international students, missionary kids, and so on. None of us fit in. We ate at a table together and called ourselves *les marginaux*. There was also a new term being coined about us. We were called "third culture kids." We had the unenviable ability to see both (if not more) sides of an issue. We knew that people in other countries (or even in the inner cities and rural communities) didn't exist to get evangelized. They were people in their own right. Your neighbor is your equal. It might be of interest to note that Barack Obama is considered a third-culture kid.

But I think the thing that disheartened me most was the lack of love. There was little tolerance for difference. Everything different was a threat. We had to sign "The Pledge" before we came to Houghton, agreeing that we would not smoke or dance or drink or use playing cards or have sex. (We also couldn't swear.) To one Halloween get-together, one young couple came dressed as Adolf Hitler and a bottle of Smirnoff. There was a sign on the bottle of Smirnoff. "I bet it bothers you more that I'm Smirnoff than that he's Hitler." They were right. By the way, the bottle of Smirnoff has gone on to be a philosophy professor.

I, too, am a philosophy professor after a detour in biology. I don't think that would have happened without my abiding interest in Kierkegaard. Don't misunderstand me. Kierkegaard wasn't my introduction to philosophy. I was already interested in philosophy by the time I got to Houghton. But Kierkegaard was, well, my introduction to Kierkegaard.

The Story

When I arrived at Houghton in the fall of 1982, I was 16 years old. And I was naïve. If you'd asked me then, I would have denied it. I had traveled the world, lived abroad for a quarter of my life, and had just finished high school in Mexico. I was excited about coming to Houghton because there would be other Christians there.

But I was totally unprepared for the evangelical Christian worldview. It was definitely not the world I had grown up in. I had grown up in a mainstream Christian church—the United Church of Christ. And never before had I encountered Christianity as a culture.

We can talk about Catholic culture and even Orthodox culture, but when we speak about evangelical culture, we are talking about something monolithic. Somehow evangelical Christianity is supposed to overlay (or underlay) your entire existence. To put it in the words of American singer-songwriter Steve Taylor.

So you need a new car?

Let your fingers take a walk

Through the business guide

For the "born again" flock

You'll be keeping all your money

In the kingdom now

And you'll only drink milk

From a Christian cow[4]

Furthermore, I was puzzled by Houghton.

My first clue that I wasn't in Kansas anymore was when someone asked me whether or not I had been sanctified, and I innocently said, *no*, but I'd been vaccinated. I discovered that it was evil to listen to rock or pop music. One needed to listen to Christian music—some of which was deadly boring. However, you could pretty much clear a room by mentioning Led Zeppelin.

I was also impressed by the anti-intellectualism of the college's students. I was told I shouldn't take classes like sociology because it would ruin my faith, and that I should avoid the philosophy professor; he's been known to say "f***." There was even a group among the administration and staff who were prayer warriors praying for the salvation of many of the fallen professors who worked at the college. And they named names.

I was distinctly told that all Catholics go to hell—which eliminated one half of my family and most of my friends from Mexico. I also learned that the only issue of Christian concern was abortion, and your opinion on that issue would determine your fate in the afterlife. Then there was the age-old question: what kind of millennial are you: Were you *pre-*, *post-*, or *a-*?

There were funny things, too. We weren't allowed to play with face cards, but people still bet on Uno. I learned that the NIV Bible was demonic, because Jesus' words were not in red. They'd taken the blood out was what I was told. And people dressed up on Sundays to go to lunch, so that other people would think they had been to church.

Then there were other, more startling things. Students looked at previous exams to study. In Mexico—where folks are known to cut a few corners—that was considered cheating. Then my biology professor gave me a B instead of an A in my first term because he thought I was getting a B in my Biblical Literature course. (The Bib Lit professor had no grades in time for mid-term, so he gave everyone a B.) I had no idea what to make of this. Did the guy want a bribe? But the impression I most got was that everyone other than one's own

---

4   Steve Taylor, "Guilty by Association," from the 1984 album *Meltdown*.

particular sect was going to hell. Only us—the Pentecostals, the Wesleyans, the whatever—were the ones who had the truth and thus salvation.

I was so disappointed. It wasn't just that Houghton was like the world that troubled me. It was that Houghton was like the world and yet claimed not to be. And that was when I found this quote attributed to Kierkegaard.

If you are all Christians, then I am not.

I had no idea who Kierkegaard was or how to pronounce his name—I don't even remember the source of the alleged quote—but I knew exactly how he felt. Moreover, as I looked around at my fellow Houghtonites, I felt that I was Kierkegaard looking at all the Danish "Christians" and wondering whether or not they knew what was truly at stake. No doubt I was being as pretentious as Kierkegaard had been. But the man had a point.

And so, I endeavored to read him—everything that was in the Houghton library as well as anything I could get through that miracle of modern technology: interlibrary loan.

But then—crisis of crises—my high school boyfriend broke up with me. I was devastated. He never told me why, and I never found out. He was Mexican, and my family had practically disowned me because of that. So now everything was gone: my intellect, the person I loved, my family; and I was left with a faith I no longer understood. Now this was actually a good thing, because the only thing left was God.

God in Heaven, let me really feel my nothingness, not to despair over it but to feel all the more intensely the greatness of your goodness.[5]

But it was also a bad thing. I was involved in many activities: the Foreign Mission Fellowship and the Spanish Language Club. I had a little sister through Allegheny Country Outreach. I led Bible studies. According to St. Augustine, a sacrament is an outward and visible sign of an inward and spiritual grace. But what happens when you have all the outward signs but not the inward grace? I think this is part of what Kierkegaard was talking about when he spoke about the need to be before you can do. One needs to be a person before one can become a Christian.

There was one thing, however, I had subconsciously learned at Houghton. There was no place in the Kingdom for losers. I had to maintain my happy face, because there was no place or time to break down. And Kierkegaard came through once again.

I have just come back from a party where I was the life and soul. Witticisms flowed from my lips. Everyone laughed and admired me—but I left, yes, [and]

---

5 Søren Kierkegaard, *Papers and Journals: A Selection*, trans. Alastair Hannay (Great Britain: Penguin Books, 1996) 103.

that dash should be as long as the radii of the earth's orbit——————
——————————————————-and wanted to shoot myself.[6]

Here was a kindred spirit.

It makes sense to me now that I was drawn most strongly by his early journals. The questions he asks are the questions I had. How does one live a truly Christian life, something that is not merely an intellectual understanding or a concatenation of external activities, but an actual lived life? What is my purpose on the planet? Is there something for which I'd live and die? All the important existential questions compounded by a sense that what I was seeing and experiencing couldn't be Christianity. There had to be something more, something better. These are the same questions found in Kierkegaard's 1835 letter from Gilleleje.

The thing is understand myself, to see what God really wishes me to do...— what good would it do me to be able to explain the meaning of Christianity if it had no deeper significance for me and for my life?[7]

This was my question. I was lost. I didn't understand the anti-intellectualism of Houghton; I didn't understand the competing Christianities; I was doing all the exterior things right. But there was nothing in me.

I spent the last year of college in bed, only getting out to take tests and occasionally get meals. And there was no one who seemed able and willing to help. I needed to refresh my inner life, the life that fuels everything else we do. It was not going to be solved by "rededicating my life to Christ", or by walking down the aisle during Christian Life Emphasis Week, or by learning to speak in tongues, or by following the advice of Elisabeth Elliot or Tony Campolo or whomever came to give the sermon lectures that made up any revival week.

I was a classic example of Kierkegaard's notion of despair. But it was something more as well. I didn't want to be myself because I didn't know who I was. And I would have loved to have been someone else: one of the put-together young Christian women I saw in Nordic sweaters and corduroy pants.

But I also didn't want to be that.

In my pursuit of being a Christian, I was stymied.

Then I realized I had reached the point of infinite resignation. In infinite resignation, you give up even the mere possibility that there is a solution. Just as in despair, you stand naked before God, but in love with the eternal being. Moreover, you have come to the end of what you know and the end of what you know possible. So, I engaged in the absurd. Now it should be noted that people often overstate the role irrationality plays in Kierkegaard's work. Here, I think he means that the move to faith does not follow directly from resignation and thus from understanding. Like love, the move to faith is an act of the will.

---

6 Hannay, *op cit.*, 50.
7 Dru, 44.

And so, I simply decided to believe I was a Christian and that being a Christian was a constant pursuit. One did not obtain to it all at once.

That was it.

After graduation, I went to grad school at Penn State for biology and completely forgot about Kierkegaard. But as I neared the end of my biology Ph.D., I started sitting in on philosophy classes. One of those classes was on Augustine, taught by Carl Vaught. He asked me to do a class presentation (even though I wasn't enrolled in the course) and I picked memory or time or something toward the end of *The Confessions*. Before I gave my presentation, I had a philosophy grad student friend read it. His first remark was that if I ever did anything in philosophy, I would need to have a Kierkegaard expert read it.

I was flummoxed.

This is Augustine, he said, but as seen through the eyes of Kierkegaard. However, I didn't really recall that much about Kierkegaard. Nonetheless, I gave the presentation, and I think that presentation played a role in my being admitted to the graduate program in philosophy at Penn State. During my first year, a German professor came to give a talk to my class on C. S. Peirce. It went well, but afterward he and I got into an argument about *Fear and Trembling*. Obviously, I remembered some Kierkegaard, and I apparently had some definite opinions about it. The professor was Hermann Deuser, and it was through him that I applied to the Kierkegaard Research Center in Copenhagen, where I went on to spend almost five years.

While there, I looked for my quote "if you are all Christians, then I am not." There were somewhat similar quotes, such as the following quotation from *The Moment*:

But one thing I will not do. No, not at any price will I do it; one thing I will not do: I will not participate, even if it were merely with the last fourth of the last joint of my little finger in what is called official Christianity. (*MLW* 49)

But my quote?

I never found it.

A Note

It's been hard to forgive Houghton, if only because there is no one particular individual to blame. The bad experience I had there was the result of a synergism of factors. Nonetheless, I must forgive. And as Kierkegaard says, "Perfect love means to love the one through whom one became unhappy."[8] And while I try to work on having perfect love, I must nonetheless speak the truth of my experience there. Furthermore, I think there is something to be said here for the knight of faith. Johannes de silentio, in describing what he believes to be a knight of faith, notices that the knight is a petit bourgeois, who sings lustily

---

8 Dru, 192.

in church, looks like a tax-gatherer, and seems taken up by a number of worldly pursuits. In other words, he is indistinguishable from any other petit bourgeois businessman, and there's nary a whiff of the incommensurable about him (see *FT* 38-40).

This makes me wonder whether there were knights of faith at Houghton whom I simply failed to see.

By the way...

One of my professors at Houghton assured me that Billy Graham had said that Christian existentialists were actually Christians...in case you were wondering.

Maria Chnaraki
"Teach me to Dance!": Speaking without Words in Zorba's Culture

Entering the Dance

Greeks act life; indeed, as Zorba, their kinsman, they dance it as well. By doing so, Greeks subconsciously and creatively use dancing as a therapeutic means of self- and psychoanalysis, as they manage to liberate themselves by healing their egos. After all, the world of Greece is a world of culture, always with the human being centered, while via the way Greeks talk through body language, they create a dialogue between the western-Apollonian-order and the eastern-Dionysian-chaos.

The popularity of the novel *Zorba the Greek* is attributed to the fact that it urged American and European intellectuals to discover what they were not, what their repressed self was; in other words, it offered westerners a prototype of liberation. Readers got fascinated by the transcendence of the ego that the East was promising them. The Mediterranean eyes of its writer, Nikos Kazantzakis, were an attraction for the western society, which, tired from logic and abundance admired Zorba, a daring, spontaneous hero, who refused conventions and admitted his emotional passions.

In 1964, the film *Zorba the Greek* was released and became even more popular than its "visual" 1960 relative, "Never on Sunday." The film was directed by Michael Cacoyannis with the popular soundtrack composed by Mikis Theodorakis—who comments that the film's music has been turned into a myth. The final image by which the audience left the cinema was that of Zorba's dance, a scene which became the symbol of Greece and of the Greek spirit represented by Zorba in particular. The popularity of this theme led to the production of a Broadway 1968 musical and a 1987 ballet. Since that time, Zorba and his dancing have lent their name to restaurants and various other products over the world.

If it had been a question in their lifetime of choosing a spiritual guide, a guru as the Hindus say, a father as say the monks at Mount Athos, surely too many, regardless their ethnicity, would have chosen Zorba. For he had just what a quill-driver needs for deliverance: the primordial glance which seizes its nourishment arrow-like from on high; the creative artlessness, renewed each morning, which enabled him to see all things constantly as though for the first time, and to bequeath virginity to the eternal quotidian elements of air, ocean, fire, woman, and bread; the sureness of hand, freshness of heart, the gallant daring to tease his own soul, as though inside him he had a force superior to the soul; finally, the savage bubbling laugh from a deep, deep wellspring, deeper than the bowels of man, a laugh which at critical moments spurted redemptively from Zorba's elderly breast, spurted and was able to demolish (and did demolish) all the barriers —morality, religion, homeland— which that wretched poltroon, man, has erected around him in order to hobble with full security through his miserable smidgen of life.

A New Statesman

An intellectual is writing a manuscript on Buddha. At the port of Piraeus, he meets with Alexis Zorba, an uneducated man, and hires him to superintend the workmen in the abandoned lignite mine on the island of Crete. Zorba values more experience and understanding than scholarly learning: "What's the use of all your damn books? You think too much, that is your trouble. Clever people and grocers, they weigh everything." After a series of victories and failures, the writer leaves Crete, but asks Zorba to teach him to dance. The story described illustrates the contrast introduced by Nietzsche between the Apollonian and the Dionysian outlook on life. Apollo, the writer, represents the spirit of order and rationality, while Dionysus, Zorba, represents the spirit of ecstatic, spontaneous will to live. The whole story is a fable about the mind and the body. And the boss's transformation could be described this way: "His Apollonian powers, hitherto either paralyzed or misdirected, can now turn to the task of redeeming Dionysian reality, rescuing Zorba from dissolution."

He can function now as a "tragic" artist, fuse his western mentality with Zorbatic barbarism, transform within his womb the barbarian seed, and bear an artistic son: the tragic myth called Zorba the Greek. Kazantzakis wants his eternal Greek (or, Hellene) to be nothing different than the Greek race itself, a marvelous synthesis of both East and West. Moreover, through "Zorba," Kazantzakis embraces both the western as well as the eastern. The protagonist wants to get rich, but, at the same time, acts very irresponsibly. He abandons rationality to live in madness. He rejects the mind in favor of the heart, whereas everyone is overwhelmed by an inexorable, tragic, destructive fate.

Kazantzakis's vision, besides being Greek, is definitely "Cretan" too. Crete, for Kazantzakis, is his homeland, an island at the southernmost part of Greece, a crossroads of many cultures and civilizations, a synthesis that he always pursues. He feels neither European, nor ancient Greek, nor eastern. He breathes another air, a composition of all these forces and its components that empower and make him proud and brave. The syncretic glance that dares to look at life and death nakedly, Kazantzakis names Cretan. It is the exact same look of the Minoan who stares at the scared bull, just before his dangerous leap.

All in all, Kazantzakis creates a myth, as, through Zorba, he emotionally addresses great moral questions of inaction, agency and fate versus free will. He then uses this myth as his own, personal mirror, and sees music and dance as means of extreme elevation, often almost a religious one.

Zorba's Dance

Zorba may also be viewed not as a novel, but as a memorial. When Zorba's flesh died, his myth started to crystallize in Kazantzakis's mind. Zorba started to become a fairy tale. Kazantzakis would see him dance, neighing in the middle of the night and calling him to spring up from his comfortable shell of prudence and habit, and to take off with him on great travels. His love (*Eros*) for Zorba, gave life to his death (*Thanatos*). The writer, who is not a dancer, immortalized him in pen. Zorba's singing and playing on the *santouri* (dulcimer) carries his sorrow and his yearning. In Kazantzakis novel, *Freedom or Death*, the teacher, instead of answering to the question "where are we coming from and where are we going to", he grasps the *lira* (three-stringed Cretan instrument), and plays it, while the dying grandfather disembodies. As the voice of the *lira* recalls his deeds and his experiences, he transubstantiates to the soul which abandons his body.

It is the dancing, however, which Zorba manages to drag his boss in too, which acts as the intensively as well as impressively emotional and passionate act: Kazantzakis sees on the music-dance blaze-up of Zorba the contact with the timeless, a moment that transcends every cultural civilization meaning. Indeed, on the last day in Crete, the boss learns from Zorba a remedial lesson in dancing.

Zorba is dancing solo, arms extended, ready to fly with the eagles of Crete. He has the freedom to perform improvisational, virtuoso movements, giving himself to dancing. He jumps in the air, performing agile, acrobatic leaps, trying to show his gallantry and pride, demonstrating strength and agility, and that, in fact, he does not fear anything and anybody who threatens his freedom; He feels independent and free because he can dance. The wildness his dance might exhibit is a sweet one: self-protection against any misfortune.

In Greece, the embodied soul can find its release not through logos but through movement. Zorba is the authentic, almost forgotten Greek self, the man who may drink, curse and sleep with women of loose morals but who has an enviable quality that the educated European lacks: He is in tune with himself. The metaphor is one that would have appealed to Plato, for it is through the means of music and dance, a language of the body (*soma*) as well as the mind (*nous*), that Zorba, in contrast to the "boss" (and perhaps to Kazantzakis himself), achieves a secure sense of his place in the universe.

As Kazantzakis states, this novel about his diseased friend Alexis Zorba is more than anything a dialogue between a pen-pusher and an older folk person; a dialogue between a lawyer of the "Mind" and the great soul of the people. It is apparent that Zorba's stories are more connected to the body than to the brain. In such contexts, folk dancing becomes for Zorba and, in extension for the Greeks, a primal non-verbal behavior, an authentic voice, a "deeper body language." Such a dance is the only place in which he feels comfortable, restless, but at home, especially when not at home.

Such is Zorba's story. His dance both hurts and comforts him. It is his changing, resourceful source of identity, his strategic language, a way of talking about, understanding, exercising decolonization. "Boss, I have never loved a man as much as you. I have hundreds of things to say, but my tongue just can't manage them... So, I will dance them for you." It is when feelings well up to the point where words can no longer suffice that Zorba begin dancing. For Zorba, the impersonator of the folk, or for any Greek, in extension, dance is the ultimate creative act and follows its own, natural laws.

Despite the fact that the book does not end with the dance scene, most people continue to see the conclusion as the hero learning to dance and thereby to perceive the world in the manner of his mentor. Kazantzakis's biological father demanded that his son becomes a fighter, and not a writer. By using folk elements, such as the aforementioned vivid dance scene, Kazantzakis indirectly describes his liberation as a writer, which lies in the discovery of an "authentic" person, the narrator of popular, folk stories. In this sense, Zorba teaches Kazantzakis how to express himself in folk style; he becomes his foster father.

Greeks are passionate people. They adore life and enjoy living. But, as the wise Buddha said, the more you are attached to this world, the more you suffer. From the times of Homer the complaint is the same: Life is wonderful, but so short! Let's not forget that the Greek word for song (*tragoudhi*) stems etymologically from the ancient Greek word "tragedy." The original Zorba, the hero of Kazantzakis's novel, is a passionate but not a jovial person. In his depth you can find a lot of despair. His merry-making is tinged with a strong taste of regret. You can hear this in Greek songs. You can feel it in the deep, serious expression of a male solo dancer. He is not having fun. He is expressing the beauty and agony of living.

Indeed, Zorba transforms his metaphysical questionings into structured, rhythmic movement: Who made the world? Why? Why do we die? Where do we come from and where do we go? Dance, after all, is a body dialogue with the queries. Zorba travels with an open chest and closed eyes. His dancing teaches unity and pride, the take-off. He deals with God; He speaks a language that cannot be interpreted, but felt. Zorba taught Kazantzakis to love life's trouble, and not to be afraid of death. Through movement, with no fear and no hope, the writer shall be free!

Flights

Zorba is contemporary and global in that he is both real and constructed, as we all also are. The same way Kazantzakis's Zorba opposes to the "boss", our identity dissolves into multiple, contradictory forces. We are all many, and full of oppositions, our unity being only a fake structure. More than 75 years since Kazantzakis wrote Zorba and more than half a century since it became a film, Zorba the Greek is still, worldwide, the recognizable cultural-artistic product of Greece—even the "passport" of modern Greece. It may even symbolize the folkloric Greece that many of us want to get rid of, but its sincere aim is to teach us how to find personal freedom by dancing, by performing a creative act, undergoing a change analogous to creation. After all, it was a friend, Alexis

Zorba, who molded Kazantzakis, who, in turn, created Zorba the Greek, and, by extension, us all modern dancing Zorbas.

Paula Marantz Cohen
The Divine Artistic Hand in My Late Mother's Beauty

As I sketched her face, I reconnected with her, and with a creative pursuit from my childhood.

As a child, I was encouraged to practice the arts. I took piano lessons and was given paper and paints with which to draw. My parents praised me for writing stories, poems, and plays and pushed me to recite and perform them for company. I did these things with pleasure until my teens. Although I went on to study literature and write essays and books as part of my vocation, I did so in the prescribed, often ugly style of academic discourse—without the whimsical and graceful manner in which I wrote as a child.

But following the dictates of classic narrative form, in which the end echoes the beginning, I returned to my childhood pursuits once the arc of my life began its downward turn. I started to write stories again in middle age, and later I returned to the piano. Recently I came back to painting and drawing, seeking subjects that jibed with my limited skills—still-lifes with simple objects, muddy renderings of the view outside my window, crude sketches of my husband asleep in a chair. One day I chose to copy a photographic portrait of my mother that had sat unnoticed on the piano I didn't play for years.

Cohen's drawing of her mother, Ruth Marantz, at age 20.

My mother was a beauty, and the photographer had worked to highlight this. Taken when she was about 20 years old, the image showed her in perfectly delineated profile, her head bent forward, her cheek softly illuminated, her hair swept back in terraced waves.

In my newly inspired artistic state, I took out my sketch pad and my sharpened No. 2 pencil with its excellent eraser and prepared to copy my mother's profile. I was aware that I was looking at an image taken at least a year before I was born. Because I had known her afterward, this image of my mother, like an unopened flower, spoke of what she would become for me. Its serene and silent beauty anticipated the expressive face I saw during the prime of her life, as well as the debilitated visage she later acquired as a result of the degenerative neurological disease that eventually killed her.

The image in the photograph was as simple as the life that followed from it was complex and turbulent. But contrary to my expectation, it was difficult to duplicate its lines. Each time I traced the curve of the chin or outlined the triangular wedge of the nose, I somehow missed the mark. I erased—and there is nothing like erasure both to humble the artist and to renew the sense of possibility.

Each time I tried to capture the image, I brought something new into existence. The wonder of my mother's beauty became more apparent as I saw how close each of her features was to not being beautiful. Whatever forces had conspired to create her face had moved with great care or luck along a tightrope that at any moment could have tipped her into plainness or even ugliness.

It was also a source of wonder to think that my pencil could carry me across so many aesthetic possibilities. Put the nose a bit too low or make the forehead a bit too long, and there was another woman on my pad than the one in the photograph. The gift of erasure allowed me to correct each time I moved in the wrong direction. One might argue that the human population is mostly mistakes left unerased, images that an artist would discard, and that those few that we gaze on with delight—my mother, in her youth, being one—reflected those moments when the divine hand somehow got it right.

I was also struck by how many ways there are to be beautiful. How is it that the perfect proportions of my mother's face did not render her generic? How is it that I could create an image with pleasingly arranged features that individually corresponded to hers without capturing her likeness in the least?

As I erased and drew, erased and drew, I began to approach something that evoked my mother's face—or rather evoked the image that resided in my head of my mother, for the photograph was only a gateway to that memory. The relative proportions that governed the distance between chin and mouth, nose and eye, forehead and cheek grew more correct. At one point, the sketch looked more like my sister, approaching its goal by way of family resemblance, until finally I approximated as closely as I felt possible the image both in the photo I was copying and in my mind's eye.

The photograph was the double witness to my separation from my mother. It was a reproduction of her as she was before I was born and the marker left to me after her death. But it was also the bridge across separation. It allowed me to bring her back by my own hand; it gave me a deep and concrete understanding of her unique beauty; and it revived the pleasure I had once found in drawing, a pastime central to the childhood over which she had presided.

Tim Fitts
Spring Break

If it'd been anything other than a Smith and Wesson I probably would have said yes, but a Smith and Wesson? The gun did not seem to harmonize with our breed. If the gun had been a Luger, or a plain old revolver, I probably would have said: why not? Bring her along. But the Smith and Wesson? No way. You bring a Smith and Wesson, all you'll think about is the Smith and Wesson. The entire drive down from Cincinnati to Florida, *Smith and Wesson*. Every rest area, every gas station – *Smith and Wesson*. Every dirty look, every driver drifting into your lane, a yearning for road rage and an excuse to pull the bad boy out. And, once at the Boynton Beach Motel, sipping poolside tequila from Dixie cups, the Smith and Wesson will absorb into a part of you that you cannot reject or deny. Better to leave it. But even the consideration of the gun has attracted the wrong energies. On our last night at the motel, with the girls passed out on the bed, and Marlon and I carving micro-thin slices of lime with a Bowie knife, a pounding on our door announces: "Security check!" The pounding continues, alternating with the announcement and gaining in intensity.

"Open up! Security check!"

Security check, my ass. They're dropping f-bombs. They got no ear for tone.

Tim Fitts
Sugar

On weekend nights we used to drive in parking lots, pushing the shopping cars with the front bumper. We drove at terrifying speeds, then jammed on the brakes and let the carts shoot forward like a rocket until the front wheels eventually buckled, sending them tumbling, and bounding into acrobatics. The initial fear is the shopping cart will buckle and catch up under the car, entangle in the engine and transmission. But you have to have faith, eliminating all the negativity and sentiment. We fired these shopping carts in straight lines and rammed them into each other. We shot the carts at parking blocks and sent them careening into the night sky, the stars so bright you could reach out and grab a handful.

If you launched the shopping carts just right, you discovered just how resilient those shop windows were, as if the designers and engineers had us in mind all along. The windows refuse to shatter, crack, or reduce themselves to sugar. They just shake, reverberating headlights in the distance, shockwaves, as if the glass had just for the moment turned to water.

Tim Fitts
You Have Ruined This Car

In exchange for damages incurred to my Plymouth Barracuda, after backing into it intoxicated, my buddy John Mark agreed to fix my leaking radiator. The car's value totaled at six hundred, and the radiator was going to cost me two, so it seemed fair. We popped the hood, and he held the soldering wire and blasted away. However, the moment we filled the tank, water began to bead up at the spot in question. He welded more soldering wire to the spot until it clumped, but still water beaded upon filling. Eventually, he suggested we drop an egg into the tank. As explained, the goop gets sucked through the crack and hardens as the water heats up. I had no choice, and for two weeks, the radiator held, until eventually the dashboard lit up. Every two weeks, as expected, the light flashed. Cool engine, fill tank, drop in egg.

My mechanic was not as much apoplectic, but in awe. He tapped the radiator hoses. Instead of the hollowed out empty reverberation, the tubes responded with a thud. Full, dense, zero resonation. "You need to leave this thing here," he said. "You have ruined this car."

"How long can she go?"

"How long? Not long."

"A week?"

He looked at me.

"What'll happen?"

"What do you think will happen?"

"Well," I said, but I had to know. So, John Mark and I took the Barracuda up U.S. 19 all the way to 121, where the road shoots straight to Williston on the way to Gainesville. We knew by fact that the cops let anything go on this stretch. After five miles, the dashboard light flared, but still, we got the old boat up to ninety. We held the hammer down. The engine was not quiet, but she refused to hesitate upon our command. Sure, we had to roll the windows down to let out the smoke, and John Mark kept glancing through the a.c. vents for evidence of flame, but the Barracuda, she sang, and the road, a straight shot. Trees on either side converged in the distance. John Mark, noted, and it was true, that when looked to either side, all of the trees in the forest had been planted individually, that just for a hundredth of a second, you could see all the way down the aisle of trees, as far down as it would go.

Valerie Fox
Blue Horses

I'm petting eight tiny horses, vinegar-scented, at the pop-up estate sale. Some turn noses down, some up. Some twist their blue necks.

A guarded woman, in tears and puffy jacket, covets and cradles antique doll-babies. Pretend babies animate all rooms. This woman had been close with the dedicated Papal dish and plate collecting person who once lived here where the estate sale is occurring. I count 156 wine glasses and photograph an accordion in its original box.

I sneak into "Keep Out" rooms like the yarn-ridden bathroom—mid-century scraps, not the kind I'm into.

There's a leather expandable classic attaché, well cared for, between a bedframe slats. You would have liked it. That's another self-deception I keep falling for, like saying everyone I meet is mildly depressed (and not me).

I buy a thousand sewing needles. I should take up sewing, so I will never have to run out of things to do. And, well, I did hope to see someone here that I knew, maybe you—but you're not here.

A dealer hunting for picture frames and stereo speakers points to major ceiling decay, says—*My brother and I went through this one house, the people had a giant hole in the kitchen floor, smoke stains, cat-piss. But the porn room was tidy and alphabetized.*

I'll take these blue horses. We belong with each other.

Valerie Fox
Girard Avenue

Say you're twenty-one and throw a party where you are house-sitting, a big row-house in a once opulent neighborhood, and you've danced with him, Russell, who is twenty-nine, and when he tries to get into your pants you let him, and say you never hear the stories about how Russell is really into girls your age, a lot of them, as told by Jimmy, who your close friend dated briefly to escape her abortion-guy, and well, say you go with Russell to Chicago, and get used to the temperatures, so when your older sister gets married and moves out there the two of you stay close, like when you shared a room growing up, and she let you listen to Abbey Road over and over, and have the top bunk, and a little later she sent you out to find out about birth control when you needed it, at some point, and then in Chicago, Russell's oil paint smell and fluid, army-brat-Texan accent wears off on you, and his diamondo-pattern dada-vests, and, let's face it, his luck, and in the summer, say you and your sister, who's pining for a change of her own, go to Italy for a whole month, which feels new, beginning to end, keeping the window box begonias alive, cutting off your parents, drinking Chianti, and both of you can see and hear ghosts, but only the ones whose stories ring true, and you name your daughter Penny Lane—

Valerie Fox
The not so distant future

seems unready
but many go
even if it's just a looping back,
that old impulse.

If you follow, you may unearth
a tablet made with the Book of Common Prayer.
Handwritten. Eat my body. Take this pill.

Wash down with milk tea if you have it.
You may find field notes for the vulturine group:
the ant-view, goose-view, whale-view.

You've made it this far, so why not place blocks
end to end, make a frosty window
I AM INEXORABLE.

Stand up your messaging, the spines form a line,
not a syllable though, or letters.
On a happy note, your appendix has been rendered useful.

My good friend, this colored tablet has your name,
anagrammed, ready to gulp,
it makes you as-you-once-were-ish.

Cassandra Hirsch
Twenty-Five Years in a Writers Group

Back in the early '90s, I was a stay-at-home mom of a toddler and a preschooler. Whenever I could, I found time to write—mostly about the kids and their antics. I wrote those personal essays, then tucked them into a floppy disk and forgot about them. I could almost hear the disks rebuke me: *Why aren't you trying to get us published? What good are we sitting in the dark? And it's getting cramped in here.*

One day, in November 1994, I stood chatting with another mom where our kids attended preschool. She asked if I wanted to join a writers group that met monthly at rotating homes around Philadelphia and the Main Line. I jumped on it. The group I joined assumed the name PlayPen, a nod to our young kids we sometimes brought along and in whose tiny hands we thrust crayons and cookies so we could talk about our writing projects and the places we hoped to publish them.

In those early writing years, my skin was see-through, so criticism was hard to take—especially on subjects as close to me as my kids. Yet I had rarely received criticism, since, until I joined the writers group, my loved ones were my only audience, and they were awfully supportive. Yes, I loved them for it, but I knew that to become the writer I wanted to be, I had to thicken my hide and hear some harder truths about my writing from people who were not related to me.

But I didn't know if I would have anything to contribute to a writers group. At 29 when I joined, I was its youngest member, and I worried that my lack of publications (nothing other than undergrad film reviews in my college's newspaper) made me unqualified to participate. A half-dozen years before, I had sat mute in a writing workshop for the same reason. What did I have to say? What help could I offer other writers? Well, it turns out that we loved writing about our experiences as parents, bringing often humorous, always relatable slice-of-life stories to share at our meetings. Before long, my voice and confidence emerged in what grew to be a safe space to share my writing. As women of a certain age, within about 10 years of each other, and as mothers whose time was often in short supply during our kids' growing-up years, we made it our objective to create this safe space to bring our work.

Joining the group didn't launch my writing into national prominence, but I did feel an early surge of bravery and sent an essay or two to a local newspaper. And to my delight, they published my piece about sitting Shiva for a family member. It was one of those personal essays I had written when my firstborn was napping, and then tucked the piece away for its own long nap. That first publication further emboldened me to offer other members of the group my thoughts on their work and to keep trying to get my own writing published.

Within a couple of years of my joining PlayPen, our group's founder, Joyce, assigned some of us articles to write for the *Jewish Exponent's* monthly magazine supplement, for which she was the editor. I learned how to write for an audience, how to consider structure, length and theme, and I gained a purpose for my writing; now I had a subject matter for each piece, something Joyce assigned. I contributed personal essays about my then four-generation family, my 91-year-old grandfather's Bar Mitzvah, and features about Jewish community events. Bolstered by Joyce's and the group's confidence in my writing, I looked for and published in other markets, too, both regional and national. We all did. She offered that confidence to all of us when she assigned and edited our pieces, trusting in return that we would give her quality work.

As important as the writers group was to me, there were years when I didn't attend. After I had a third child and my kids got older, I eventually returned to the workforce. Then, in 2004, I lost my sibling in a tragic accident. I returned to school for a graduate degree, then started teaching writing. Family, school, and work had almost completely supplanted PlayPen. Rare were the months I could make our meetings, but I took comfort in knowing the group endured. My peers welcomed me back whenever I did show up, so I never truly felt distant from this group of women. Occasionally, I encountered a new face among the familiar, and by now, cherished regulars. Those new faces are now cherished regulars, too.

Belonging to a mutually supportive group of writers has spurred us all on in many writerly directions—from published memoir, fiction, marketing, and mainstream journalism, to playwriting and screenwriting. We have learned what makes each of us tick as a writer, what our strengths and styles are. Whether or not I bring something to share with the group, I always look forward to the work others bring for comment, to the writing markets they share, and to hearing about their own literary projects.

The PlayPen writers group is still going strong 25 years after my friend and fellow writer/mom invited me to join the group. We still serve each other breakfast when we take turns hosting, and we still share our work, writing venues, and life's tales around the table. Our kids have grown and gone—some of them making us grandparents. Technological changes have turned our writer's group from a monthly gathering planned via snail mail to a group that supports its members 24/7 through our Facebook page updates on writing markets and on our individual accomplishments. And we still meet once a month on a Friday to talk shop and nudge each other forward in our writing and publishing. At this point, I can't imagine my world without this writers group. We have grown together.

Christian Hunold
Green Infrastructure and Urban Wildlife: Toward a Politics of Sight

Introduction

Contemporary urban ecologies are astonishingly hospitable to wildlife (Adams; Blaustein; Gehrt, Riley, & Cypher; Schilthuizen). The "rewilding" of cities is a global phenomenon, and the dynamics of human-wildlife relationalities exhibit considerable social, cultural, racial, ecological, spatial, and species variations in different parts of the world (Barua & Sinha; Hovorka; McKiernan & Instone; Yeo & Neo). In the United States, wild animals are thriving in many postindustrial cities whose ecologies have been transformed by significant changes in urban land use, including urban greening. Wild animals have taken advantage of a myriad of friendly spaces created by ecologically restored waterways, parkland, backyards, urban farms, community gardens, green roofs, rain gardens, and other greened spaces that are rewilding cities through provisioning wildlife in unexpected places (Aronson et al., "Global Analysis"; Ives et al.). As U.S. cities invest in green infrastructure to ameliorate environmental harms, wildlife large and small is occupying novel urban ecological niches located outside large city parks and designated nature preserves. As a result, human-wildlife encounters are becoming more frequent in neighborhoods where such encounters used to be uncommon. Increased sightings of urban wildlife, however, do not imply greater legitimacy for wild animals. Increasing abundance alone does not mean residents will necessarily welcome daily interactions with wild animals (Cox & Gaston). Rather, encounters with urban wildlife prompt a wide range of human responses. Some city residents are rattled by the proximity of wild animals, particularly by predators such as coyotes, foxes, and raccoons they see as "invading" their neighborhoods, while others relish encounters with this wildness next door (Correal; Soulsbury & White).

This essay starts from the premise that city-scale urban greening amounts to redesigning cities as if they were *meant* to attract wildlife—as if urban rewilding advocates were actually being heard (The Nature of Cities)—even though creation of wildlife habitat does not typically top the list of ecosystem services U.S. municipal agencies wish to promote. Insofar as green infrastructure development is responsible for the proliferation of wildlife, however, this urban transformation calls for a reckoning with the question of whether cities that are now teeming with wildlife are also cities *for* wildlife; and, to the extent they are not, for theorizing forms of human-wildlife coexistence in urban settings. The cultural and political challenges of urban biodiversity have spurred theorizing about zoöpolis in diverse fields, including cultural geography (Hinchliffe & Whatmore; Rutherford; Wolch), conservation science (Aronson et al., "Biodiversity"; Beatley & Bekoff), wildlife management (Adams) and political theory (Donaldson & Kymlicka). The shaky legitimacy of urban wild animals has been tied up with their everyday invisibility—interrupted, for the most part, only when they enter humans' field of vision, often as "nuisance" animals (Donaldson & Kymlicka). Green infrastructure development, however, is disrupting invisibility as the default mode of urban wildlife, at least for many terrestrial species. In the wake of green infrastructure development *sightings* of urban wildlife have become routine. Yet *perceptions* of wildlife as intruding on human spaces have proved remarkably persistent, particularly regarding occasionally troublesome species (Couturier; Luther) and species widely despised as "trash" animals (Biehler; Nagy & Johnson). Nonhuman charisma is deeply implicated in matters of negotiating human-wildlife coexistence (Lorimer, "Non-human charisma").

I examine these cultural and political challenges of urban biodiversity through the lens of the City of Philadelphia's city-scale green infrastructure program, *Green City, Clean Waters*, one of the most ambitious such undertakings in the United States. I begin by showing how urban greening has undermined the plausibility of the prevailing approach to governing urban wildlife: animal control. Animal control's origins in untenable nature/culture binaries, I argue, imply not only conceptual confusion in the face of the blurring of human-wildlife boundaries facilitated by urban greening. As a practical matter, its emphasis on discouraging interactions between people and animals in order to minimize human-wildlife conflict falls short in neighborhoods where communities of wildlife are thriving close to home. Where "everyday invisibility" is no longer the norm for urban wildlife, I argue, animal control is increasingly rendered absurd. But what is to take its place, and what role does visibility play in rethinking human-wildlife interactions? To help define a legitimating role for visibility in cultivating more convivial urban human-wildlife relationalities, I turn to David Schlosberg's analysis of the "politics of sight." Though he is not concerned with animals *per se*, Schlosberg hopes to identify strategies for visualizing ecological entanglements and relationships of mutual interdependence between humans and nonhumans that are typically invisible. His tracing the everyday invisibility of humans' embeddedness in nonhuman ecological processes to what he calls a culture of *learned disappearance* sheds light on why abundance of urban wild animals does not necessarily entail their accommodation as urban dwellers. Based on Schlosberg's environmentalist politics of sight, I examine a number of self-consciously urbanist practices of engaging with urban wildlife—bird walks, nest-cams, wildlife photography—that strive to close this gap by visualizing wild animals as co-travelers and fellow urban dwellers.

Urban Greening: Implications for Animal Control

The City of Philadelphia is mandated by the U.S. Environmental Protection Agency (EPA) to invest some $3 billion in green infrastructure by the mid-2030s in order to bring the city into compliance with federal water quality standards, now routinely violated during heavy storms when untreated runoff and combined sewer overflows exceed the capacity of water treatment plants and are diverted into creeks and rivers. Installation of "green" infrastructure (e.g. parks, rain gardens) rather than traditional "gray" infrastructure (e.g. underground holding tanks) is expected to produce, at roughly the same cost, a variety of "triple bottom line" economic, social, and environmental benefits (Philadelphia Water Department 18-19). "Wildlife benefits" rarely appear in the city's green infrastructure policy documentation but number among the anticipated ecological consequences of green infrastructure: "Stormwater wetlands are one of the best stormwater management tools for pollutant removal and can provide considerable aesthetic and *wildlife benefits*" (23; emphasis added). According to the EPA, city-scale green infrastructure implementation is expected to support increased populations of wildlife and to facilitate wildlife movements and connect wildlife populations between habitats (Chunn-Heer). Philadelphia's commitment to manage urban runoff by reengineering approximately a third of the city's surface area will improve wildlife habitat and increase habitat connectivity.

This green infrastructure initiative is being undertaken by a postindustrial city whose approach to wildlife management reflects the sanitary cities movement's emphasis on separating humans from waste and from animals in the name of public health (Gandy; Melosi). Insofar as there is a municipal wildlife management policy system, it is fairly decentralized, involves autonomous agencies pursuing sectoral agendas, and has limited resources. Its key components are vector control focused on zoonotic disease prevention (e.g. mosquito spraying, rodent control) and animal control focused on sheltering stray cats and dogs. Natural lands management by the Philadelphia Department of Parks and Recreation (PP&R) includes managing several thousand acres of the Fairmount Park system as wildlands and urban forest, including biodiversity promotion and protection; the department operates three environmental education centers located in the park. Philadelphia Water (PWD) monitors aquatic species in municipal waterways. PP&R and PWD each partner with "friends of the park" organizations and other community partners to maintain parks and green infrastructure, including organizations interested in promoting urban biodiversity.

The nonprofit organization Animal Care and Control Team of Philadelphia (ACCT Philly) is responsible for municipal animal control operations. ACCT Philly operates a shelter for unwanted pets, but its animal control responsibilities occasionally also extend to wildlife, particularly to raccoons, which generate the most nuisance wildlife complaints in the city. Visitors to the agency's website are informed that removing unwanted wildlife from a residence is generally the property owner's responsibility. However, there are two conditions under which ACCT Philly will respond to a wildlife complaint: if the animal is in a common area of the home, such as the living room or bedroom; or if the animal appears to be injured or sick, whether it is found inside or outside of a dwelling. Less proximal encounters, such as dealing with an animal "located in the walls, attic, or roof areas of a dwelling (or any other areas that are not common areas)," are the homeowner's responsibility.

Close encounters with raccoons inside a residence put young children and older adults with limited physical mobility at some risk of infection or injury. Residents of impoverished neighborhoods in particular may lack the resources to exclude unwanted animals from poorly maintained rental properties. In December 2017, for example, a 4-month-old infant was mauled in an apparently predatory attack by a raccoon in her North Philadelphia bedroom. The girl required surgery to fix numerous facial lacerations (CBS News). Visitors to ACCT Philly's website learn that indoor encounters with bats can also be cause for concern. Bats roosting in attics sometimes find themselves trapped inside homes, and a bite from a rabid bat can transmit rabies. As with other wildlife, ACCT Philly will not respond to a complaint unless the bat is found in a common area of the home, though residents are advised to report such incidents to the Philadelphia Department of Public Health's Division of Disease Control "if the bat was in a room where someone was asleep or where there were young children present" (ACCT Philly).

Home-invading raccoons and bats aside, Philadelphia's animal control agency concedes the legitimacy of urban wildlife—up to a point. The public is told the mere presence of wildlife is not in itself a cause for alarm. Rather, it is "not uncommon to observe wildlife walking about on neighborhood streets—even during the daylight hours" (ACCT Philly). However, this sensible explanation of the routine habits of wild animals and the corresponding recognition of their presence in the city as legitimate are followed by advice for residents who are concerned about wildlife near their home. Residents who wish to deter wildlife are advised to secure their trash, to leave no food outside, and to keep their home in good repair to keep animals out:

> Healthy wildlife is found in yards, streets, parks, etc. These animals should be left alone and trapping of healthy wildlife is prohibited under state law with the exception of certain, special circumstances. […] Use the resources provided above to deter these animals from frequenting your neighborhood. (ACCT Philly)

Recommending that residents minimize wildlife attractants around their homes to prevent habituation and prevent human-wildlife conflicts is considered good urban wildlife management practice (Adams; Gehrt, Riley, & Cypher). I do not want to suggest that urban greening has undermined the case for secure garbage cans and sensible home repair. However, the logic of declaring urban wild animals as legitimate yet also unwanted is stretched rather thin by the proliferation of urban wildlife. In the animal control agency's spatial framing of the legitimacy of urban wildlife, sightings of wild animals are unremarkable unless they enter spaces understood to be primarily human spaces; the legitimacy of their presence diminishes with increasing proximity to neighborhoods and to people's homes. This is the "brittle legitimacy" of urban wildlife noted by Donaldson and Kymlicka:

> Whatever our mistreatment of domesticated animals and of wilderness animals, there is at least a grudging recognition that

> they have a right to be where they are. But the very idea of liminal animals—of wild animals living amongst us—is seen by many people as illegitimate, and as an affront to our conception of human space. (211)

Such spatially dualist human-animal relationalities might have been adequate at a time when urban wildlife abundance was low and encounters with wild animals in U.S. cities were few and far between. In our contemporary greened cities, however, the idea that the very same wild animals that routinely occupy "yards, streets, [and] parks" may also be deterred from "frequenting your neighborhood" is ecologically dubious, if not increasingly absurd. Given the inextricably intertwined human-wildlife urban geographies being created by urban greening, encountering wild animals in your neighborhood is no longer a rare experience. While dualist urban human-wildlife geographies have always been questionable—"Wild animals live, and have always lived, amongst us" (210)—the contemporary permeability of the urban/wild divide is arguably a notable departure from the more sharply demarcated boundaries that held for much of the 20th century. The environmental historian Ellen Stroud, for example, has documented this blending of human and nonhuman worlds in the landscape of contemporary New England. Much of what is politically contentious about urban wildlife, she contends, revolves around questions of belonging provoked by this increased permeability of the built environment to encroachment by wild animals. The resulting indistinctiveness of human and animal worlds is experienced as unsettling by some because it undermines longstanding conceptions of cities and suburbs as spaces intended to satisfy primarily human needs:

> Malls, trees, cars, pet rabbits, and roving carnivores are all part of the twenty-first century northeastern landscape, one in which the boundaries between city and hinterland are not nearly so stark as some would imagine or wish them to be. Sprawling suburbs have become part of the sprawling woods, with corridors of wildness connecting city and forest, sometimes seeming to threaten both. (Stroud 145).

Urban Wildlife and the Politics of Sight

Many urban dwellers experience encounters with wild animals on their doorstep as troubling interruptions of daily life, but it is precisely this blurring of human-wildlife boundaries that creates awareness of their collapse and, from time to time, generates calls for their restoration. In January 2017, for example, Philadelphia city council member Kenyatta Johnson called for an investigation into the abundance of raccoons: "There has to be a reason they're coming out of nowhere infesting these neighborhoods" (Loeb). Humans react to cohabiting with wild animals in complicated ways, but the intensity of city residents' love-hate relationship with raccoons may be unrivaled (Dempsey) given their penchant for ignoring the boundaries of spaces intended by humans for our own exclusive use and for provoking strong feelings of either solidarity or hostility (Luther). Some other urban-tolerant species, in contrast, are relatively well liked. White-tailed deer, for example, rarely encounter intense hostility from city residents, even though they cause substantial property damage (Cornue & Beck).

Such differences are attributable, at least in part, to the influence of nonhuman charisma on human emotional responses to encounters with wild animals. Lorimer's (2015, 2007) influential relational conception of nonhuman charisma includes ecological, aesthetic, and corporeal dimensions. Ecological charisma refers to the degree to which an organism may be detected by a human observer using their senses, with minimal technological assistance (Lorimer, *Wildlife* 40). Some terrestrial species such as raccoons, coyotes (Hunold & Lloro-Bidart), and red-tailed hawks (Hunold) enjoy high ecological charisma, compared to, say, fish and deer ticks. Emotional responses to wildlife go beyond mere detection, however. "Aesthetic and corporeal charisma," Lorimer explains:

> describe the properties of organisms that generate emotional responses among humans encountering them. Aesthetic charisma relates primarily to encounters with visual media or certain spectacular modes of ecotourism. Corporeal charisma is concerned with feelings generated in proximal encounters in the field. (*Wildlife*, 44)

Just as human valuation of urban wildlife is rather variable, the relationship between urbanization and animals' visibility is far from straightforward. Generally speaking, urban ecologies tend to favor generalist species with flexible habitat and food requirements. With their hustle and bustle and the demands they place on animals to negotiate human technologies such as road traffic, cities favor adaptability as a survival trait (Schilthuizen). In their efforts to outwit "raccoon-resistant" garbage cans, for example, Toronto's raccoons have shown greater curiosity and success at problem- solving tasks than their rural cousins (Dempsey; Isabella). Coyotes in Chicago and Denver have learned to "hide in plain sight" in very close proximity to people by paying close attention to human behavioral patterns, recurring schedules, and traffic patterns, and then adjusting their movements accordingly (Gehrt, Brown, & Anchor; Poessel, Breck, & Gese). The majority of mammals faced with human disturbance practice some degree of temporal avoidance by increasing their nocturnality, as compared to baseline activity patterns of wilderness populations of the same species (Gaynor et al.).

These examples indicate purposeful concealment remains a viable behavioral option even for urban-tolerant animals with a fairly large body size. And while access to areas (and times) that are relatively free from human disturbance is clearly important for wild animals' wellbeing, I want to suggest that invisibility is something of a double-edged sword from the perspective of social justice. In human struggles for social justice, culturally mediated invisibility is heavily implicated in oppressed minorities' lack of recognition by the majority society and, as such, often a formidable barrier to attaining moral and political equality. Because visibility is such a powerful basis on which to assert membership in the wider society, political struggles for equality involve making claims to have one's existence and way of life acknowledged, to be seen (and heard) by the majority. Physiological and psychological needs for seclusion aside, it is not clear why this should be fundamentally different for wild animals' claims to membership in urban society—if very risky for especially reviled species, given that, for example, increased sightings of brown rats trigger the deployment of rodenticide bait boxes in most U.S. cities.[1] Wild animals' recognition as urban dwellers entails being perceived, by their human neighbors, as inhabiting urban spaces on their own terms as opposed to being regarded as out of place, particularly in parts of the city located outside designated parks or nature preserves.

An ongoing scientific reappraisal of urban ecologies as valuable repositories of biodiversity (e.g. Aronson, et al., "Global Analysis"; Braverman; Buller, "Animal geographies I," "Animal geographies II"; Lorimer, *Wildlife* 161; Standish, Hobbs, & Miller) has established that cities are fully a part of nature and, further, that nonhuman nature in the city is not confined to parks or to a few precious relicts of native ecosystems (Karvonen; Kowarik). That said, installing green infrastructure does not by itself propel imaginaries of city life down the road from the "built environment" to "living cities," configured as less human-centric, more inclusive landscapes shared more equitably by their human and nonhuman residents (Braun; Frank; Hinchliffe & Whatmore; Wolch). What sort of cultural work might animate such more-than-human conceptions of urban life? How might human urban dwellers come to experience cities as being for wildlife, too? A more convivial relationship with "nature next door" (Stroud) would seem to be predicated on cultivating what the nature essayist Lyanda Lynn Haupt has called the attentive inhabiting of our home place, whereby human beings through experiential engagement with plants and animals become more receptive to the existence of the nonhuman world that surrounds us. The philosopher Lori Gruen has termed this relational sensibility entangled empathy:

> an experiential process involving a blend of emotion and cognition in which we recognize we are in relationships with others and are called upon to be responsive and responsible to another's needs, interests, desires, vulnerabilities, hopes and sensitivities. (Gruen 3)

As important as a willingness to extend ethical consideration to nonhuman lives may be, what is at stake in developing a societal capacity to experience wild animals as genuine city residents surely is not exclusively (or even primarily) a matter of individual transformation. To helps us think about this collective dimension of inhabiting our home place more attentively, I want

---

[1] The movement to replace integrated pest management with non-lethal methods is in its infancy. The California city of Malibu in June 2019 voted to eliminate pesticide use for rodent control on municipal properties (Sawiki).

to enlist David Schlosberg's proposal for a "politics of sight." For Schlosberg, sight is political because politics, broadly conceived and culturally mediated, structures what people see and what they do not see. What is visible and what remains hidden, Schlosberg contends, is the result of collective learning, including formal education and cultural communication in the wider society (see also Drew). To illustrate what he means by a politics of sight Schlosberg turns to China Miéville's science fiction novel *The City and The City* (2009) set in "two cities that actually share the same physical, geographical space; they can only exist as distinct from one another if the citizens of each learn to make the other city and its citizens invisible, even as they pass them on the street" (Schlosberg 203). That invisibility, Schlosberg notes, "is taught, expected, and enforced" in both cities. He suggests this "learned disappearance of things right in front of our faces is also applicable to our relationship with the nonhuman world" (204). Though Miéville's novel is not concerned with human-wildlife relations, Schlosberg's insight regarding the cultural dynamics of (in)visiblity suggests how human-centric conceptions of city life based on problematic nature/culture binaries manage to persist despite the increasing abundance of urban wildlife.

Nature/culture dualisms enshrined in the dominant values of industrial society, Schlosberg contends, are very good at hiding these relationships from us, and so visualizing "the ongoing human relationship with the nonhuman" (202) is the task of a politics of sight. Engaging in this reconstructive work entails exploring nonhuman nature "not as a force apart from human culture, but as intertwined with it" (Buell 137). The degree to which existing institutions of ecological knowledge production and environmental education are allies in this cultural work is contestable (Dickinson; Henderson & Zarger). Historically, urban institutions created for the study and the enjoyment of nature have tended to reinforce the nature/culture binaries responsible for rendering urban wildlife invisible. By inviting people to spend time in natural areas set aside from the rest of city, spaces such as city parks, botanical gardens, and arboretums have unwittingly propagated a conception of nature as existing apart from, if not in opposition to, the city and its human residents. To visit nature, you must leave the city proper and enter a different realm that is curated to look, sound, and feel a certain way. In terms of enhancing receptivity to human beings' material embeddedness in the nonhuman world, this sort of spatial and experiential "museumification of nature" (Gobster) is problematic—yet powerful and persistent. Even the environmental education centers created in the era of modern environmentalism rely on this model of confining nature to the park-like settings in which such facilities are situated and where visitors are instructed, in classes or on field trips, how to experience the natural world, understood to be qualitatively different from the places where they live and work. Whether setting nature aside from the city and from human culture more generally can cultivate the development of "deeper and more mutual relationships with nonhumans" (Fletcher) is doubtful, however, because it removes possibilities of having meaningful encounters with nonhuman nature from urban dwellers' daily experience.

Restoring such possibilities and fostering a more attentive inhabiting of the city as a space shared by people and by animals is the task of a politics of sight. Here I want to discuss some emergent practices of engaging with urban wildlife that seek to advance this cultural-political reconstructive work. Urban birding and urban wildlife photography, I contend, are practices of visualizing how wild animals inhabit the city that work against the spatial and experiential "museumification" of nature. Take urban birding. In Philadelphia, the BirdPhilly initiative, a collaboration by the Delaware Valley Ornithological Club, Philadelphia Parks and Recreation, and the Fairmount Parks Conservancy, hosts birding walks around town. Relevant for our purposes is that some of these walks do not take place in city parks but venture into less obvious urban spaces in search of birds. For example, a June 2017 "Parkway Raptors" walk held in Center City assembled at a red-tailed hawk nest on Eakins Oval, a public plaza located across from the Philadelphia Museum of Art in central Philadelphia. A dozen participants watched two robust nestlings hop around on a nest constructed in the crown of a mature red oak, before walking along the tree-lined Benjamin Franklin Parkway toward City Hall. Along the way, they encountered the female hawk perched in a plane tree, eyeing up a recently road-killed squirrel. The walk concluded at City Hall, where a peregrine falcon was seen flying high up among the downtown buildings, carrying a pigeon to the nest situated in an alcove at the base of the building's spire, 15 stories above street level. Faced with these encounters, participants were encouraged to interrogate "the learned disappearance of things right in front of our faces" (Schlosberg 204). Of course, the participants were already predisposed to doing so and were *hoping* to find birds of prey; joining a Saturday morning birding walk on the Benjamin Franklin Parkway for precisely this reason is arguably not an everyday activity. Raptors, moreover, are highly charismatic and their conflicts with humans in urban area are limited (Boal & Dykstra). Advocating for "unloved others" (van Dooren) or for aquatic or invertebrate species whose lives are considered expendable (Hatley) or that are simply difficult to observe in the field may be harder to conceptualize in terms of sight. Yet it is worth noting that the raptor walk participants experienced the Parkway not as most people do—say, as tourists visiting one of North America's venerable museum districts, or as commuters inching their way forward on a clogged arterial during rush hour—but as observers of vibrant bird habitat in downtown Philadelphia.

Digital photography is an increasingly popular form of experiential engagement with urban wildlife, including species that are not charismatic or beloved. In April 2019, for example, nearly 400 Philadelphia area residents took part in a four-day City Nature Challenge (Crall), an annual competition in which urban dwellers from around the world compete to identify as many species of wildlife in their city as possible using the iNaturalist smartphone app. iNaturalist users post an image to the app, where identification may be crowdsourced and discussed. Getting participants to pay attention to frequently overlooked and unseen urban wildlife (e.g. sidewalk bugs) and to extend the conventional definition of nature to be inclusive of urban environments and urban wildlife were explicit goals of the competition. More than 1,000 species of plants and animals—weeds, wildflowers, trees, bugs, fungus, and wildlife—were logged in the Philadelphia region, the vast majority of animal species being invertebrates. The City Nature Challenge has generated citizen science data urban ecologists are starting to analyze (Leong & Trautwein).

Efforts to promote a more attentive inhabiting of our urban home based on a politics of sight do not have to rely on physical encounters with wildlife in the field, however. In fact, digital media can reveal wild animals as urban dwellers in ways not easily accomplished by direct observation. Wildlife photography and internet-enabled cameras that livestream the activities of wild animals are immensely popular and help bring the lives of urban wildlife to much wider audiences. The New York City photographer Lincoln Karim, for example, has documented the lives of red-tailed hawks in Central Park for nearly two decades, spending thousands of hours in the field. Many of Karim's images (and videos) show the birds perched on buildings or airborne against the backdrop of Fifth Avenue building façades, highlighting how these birds inhabit their urban home. Blogs that chronicle the lives of Pale Male's family, and those of hawk families in other cities, have a devoted following. People share their observations and their images on social media, and they discuss the hawks' lives and reflect on the role of wild animals in urban settings and on human-animal relationalities in anthropogenic landscapes more generally (Hunold). Nest cams, in particular, bring the lives of urban birds into the homes of millions of people. Several universities and museums have installed such cameras at red-tailed hawks' nests on their campuses. Individual birds such as Cornell University's "Big Red" and the Franklin Institute's "Mom" have attained astonishing levels of internet fame. Nest cams, it is worth noting, provide audiences with a type of genuinely unscripted reality TV rarely found on actual television, insofar as the story is not guaranteed to end well. Disease and death are as likely to shape the narrative as the successful rearing of the next generation of birds. The website for the U.S. National Arboretum's eagle nest cam in Washington, D.C., for example, contains the following statement:

> This is a wild eagle nest and anything can happen. While we hope that all eaglets hatched in this nest will grow up healthy and successfully fledge each season, things like sibling rivalry, predators, and natural disaster can affect this eagle family and may be difficult to watch.

Nest cam operators occasionally face public outrage for showing the more gruesome aspects of the lives (and deaths) of wild animals (Brulliard), but educational institutions seek to balance the fun of broadcasting the birds' activities with relevant scientific information as, for example, online chats that allow viewers to interact with wildlife professionals knowledgeable about the birds' behavior and ecology. What makes these projects so fruitful for advancing a politics of sight around urban wildlife, however, is their normalization of wild animals as successfully inhabiting urban spaces that do not look anything like classic wildlife habitat.

Eagles and hawks, however, *are* classic examples of charismatic megafauna that also, for the most part, do not greatly inconvenience humans. They are widely admired, and occupy the opposite end of the spectrum of animals widely considered vermin (Biehler). As such, they are the low-hanging fruit of urban wildlife advocacy. Raptors, of course, do well in urban areas in part because their prey—rats, pigeons—is so abundant there. This very same prey abundance also attracts mammalian carnivores that provoke decidedly more apprehensive responses from humans. Take, for example, attitudes toward coyotes, wild canids that are becoming more common in cities across North America (Couturier; Van Horn). Promoting peaceful coexistence with this awkward species, admired by some and hated by others, is a more difficult challenge. As apex predators—animals that have no natural predators themselves—coyotes may be appreciated when they help control abundant populations of geese or scavenge animal carcasses, but as occasional killers of backyard chickens and beloved pets this very same quality makes some residents wary of their presence (Elliot, Vallance, & Molles 1345; Hunold & Lloro-Bidart). Wildlife experts, such as the biologists of the long-running Cook County Coyote Project in Illinois, do not dismiss human-coyote conflicts that do occur—some coyotes do kill pets—but they emphasize that the term "nuisance coyote" is used more expansively than is warranted by the data: "There are also many levels of nuisance, with the term itself being highly ambiguous; only a very small population of coyotes appears to be causing actual conflicts with humans." This observation appears to hold not just in Chicago. In his natural history of the coyote, Flores notes the emergence of a modus vivendi in cities with long-established populations of coyotes: "Plenty of LA residents still hate them, but in a pattern that urban coyote researchers are finding increasingly common [...] urban people get used to coyotes" (201).

More tolerant attitudes toward urban wildlife ranging from indifference to curiosity to a desire for peaceful coexistence with at least some wild animals are becoming more widespread (Pratt-Bergstrom). In this context, it is instructive to ask how visual media campaigns on behalf of urban wildlife are seeking to move potentially troublesome species such as coyotes out of the nuisance animal category, and to reimagine cities as spaces both for people and for animals, including wild predators. In San Francisco, the amateur wildlife photographer Janet Kessler has for the past decade immersed herself in the lives of several coyote families that inhabit a number of city parks and surrounding neighborhoods. Her sparsely edited documentary images strive to bridge the gap between the animals as they are in a lot people's head (scary wild predator) and the animals as they really are (family-oriented canid harmful mostly to rodents, though not overly friendly toward domestic dogs.) In terms of advancing a politics of sight, Kessler's work matters because it shows coyotes doing things in spaces that are distinctively urban and that we tend to think of as existing primarily to satisfy human needs: coyotes crossing a road, jumping a guardrail, sniffing a car tire, observing a neighborhood, watching pedestrians walking on a trail, and so on. Kessler's body of work also includes more classically naturalistic depictions of coyotes pouncing on voles and of coyotes interacting with one another, but she does not erase human-made structures from her images, objects that are often banished from wildlife imagery. In resisting this elision of the human-made she sets aside powerful stylistic conventions in wildlife photography and filmmaking that typically showcase wild animals in decontextualized naturalistic settings. In Kessler's images, to the contrary, a city street or a front yard is revealed to be an unremarkable part of the animal's home, showing that coyotes inhabit the very same spaces as their human neighbors. That said, though Kessler admires coyotes and welcomes their presence in the city, she takes great care to avoid romanticizing them and does not downplay their wildness and their basic indifference to us. In keeping with this stance, her public education and outreach website "Coyote Yipps" dispenses practical advice for handling potentially troublesome encounters with urban coyotes in the dispassionate informational tone cultivated by government wildlife agencies.

The Urban Coyote Initiative, founded by San Francisco wildlife photographer Jaymi Heimbuch, draws more evenly on art and on science to visualize how coyotes inhabit urban spaces. This slick multimedia production employs the tools of high-gloss photojournalism to document the work of leading coyote researchers in the field and in the lab, while pulling out all the stops of fine art and street style fashion photography (vibrant colors, wide open apertures, soft backgrounds) to make images of city coyotes that take your breath away. Here, the stylistic conventions of traditional wildlife photography are not so much discarded as weaponized, inviting the audience to marvel at the sheer delightfulness of these wild canids roaming the streets of urban North America. Viewers are given greater license here than by Kessler's work to engage affectively with the animals. The writing, an assortment of science reporting, personal field journals, and educational materials, has more in common with the lyrical nature writing of an Akiko Bush than with a game commission fact sheet. Heimbuch and her collaborators are not bashful about their desire to move coyotes squarely into the charismatic megafauna column of the urban bestiary; their portrayal of urban coyotes as beautiful and intelligent social mammals practically makes you long for the day the animals will finally discover your neighborhood too.

Conclusion

Calls to reestablish firm human-wildlife boundaries amidst the increasingly intertwined human-animal geographies being created in greened cities give voice to wildlife-related anxieties borne of this urban transformation, but they are trapped in unhelpful nostalgia. Proposals to accommodate wild animals as urban dwellers that acknowledge the mutually entangled human-animal relationalities in greened cities and that incorporate some form of wildlife advocacy into green infrastructure development offer a more promising path forward (Rutherford). Urban bird walks, nest cams, and wildlife photography strive to reveal to human audiences the ways that animal geographies overlap with human geographies, outside the confines of designated natural areas, opening up possibilities for city residents to cultivate "deeper and more mutual relationships with nonhumans" in everyday life (Fletcher). In its insistence that cities are for animals too such a politics of sight helps loosen the stranglehold on our collective imagination of the legacy of "partitioning the environment into dichotomous categories" (Hobbs et al. 557) whereby nature is parceled off from the city and from human culture more generally.

Acknowledgments: I wish to thank the Environmental Political Theory section of the Western Political Science Association for having awarded this paper the 2017 Best Paper in Environmental Political Theory Award. I am grateful to Anna D'Isidoro and to Morgan Sarao for their invaluable research assistance and insightful observations. Finally, critical readings of earlier drafts by Jen Britton, Bernard Brown, Lisa Disch, and two anonymous reviewers for Humanimalia, provided much helpful feedback.

Works Cited

Aronson, M. F., Lepczych, C. A., Evans, K. L., et al. "Biodiversity in the city: Key challenges for urban green space management." *Frontiers in Ecology and the Environment* 15.4 (2017): 189-196.

Aronson, M. F J., La Sorte, F. A , Nilon, C. H. , et al. "A global analysis of the impacts of urbanization on bird and plant diversity reveals key anthropogenic drivers." *Proceedings of the Royal Society B: Biological Sciences* 281.1780 (2014): 20133330.

ACCT Philly. "Raccoons & Wildlife." n. d. Accessed 29 June 2019. Online.

Adams, C. E. *Urban Wildlife Management.* 3rd edition. CRC Press, 2016.

Barua, M. & Sinha, A. "Animating the urban: an ethological and geographical conversation." *Social & Cultural Geography* (November 2017). Accessed 29 June 2019. Online.

Beatley, T. & Bekoff, M. "City planning and animals: Expanding our urban compassion footprint." *Ethics, Design and Planning of the Built Environment.* C. Basta & S. Moroni, eds. Springer, 2013. 185-195.

Biehler, D. D. *Pests in the City: Flies, Bedbugs, Cockroaches, and Rats.* U Washington P, 2013.

Bird Philly. "Map." n.d. Accessed 29 June 2019. Online.

Blaustein, R. "Urban biodiversity gains new converts." Bioscience 63.2 (2013): 72-77. Boal, C. W. & C. R. Dykstra, eds. *Urban Raptors: Ecology and Conservation of Birds of Prey in Cities.* Island Press, 2018.

Braun, B. "Environmental issues: writing a more-than-human urban geography."

Progress in Human Geography 29.5 (2005): 635-650.

Braverman, I. *Wild Life: The Institution of Nature.* Stanford UP, 2015.

Brulliard, K. "People love watching nature on nest cams—until it gets grisly." *The Washington Post* May 19, 2016. Accessed 29 June 2019. Online.

Buell, F. "Nature in New York: A brief cultural history." *Still the Same Hawk*. J. Waldman, ed. Fordham UP, 2013. 122-146.

Buller, H. "Animal geographies I." *Progress in Human Geography* 38.2 (2014): 308-318.

Buller, H. "Animal geographies II: Methods." *Progress in Human Geography* 39.3 (2015): 374-384.

Busch, A. *The Incidental Steward: Reflections on Citizen Science*. Yale UP, 2013.

Chunn-Heer, J. "EPA articulates the multiple benefits of green infrastructure." *Surfrider Foundation* March 19 2013. Accessed 29 June 2019. Online.

City of Philadelphia. *Greenworks: A Vision for a Sustainable Philadelphia* (2016). Accessed 29 June 2019. Online.

Crall, A. "Competition meets collaboration: The City Nature Challenge." *Discover Magazine* April 19, 2018. Accessed 29 June 2019. Online.

Cornue, R. & Beck, P. "Loving them and loathing them: Conflicting attitudes towards deer management alternatives in Central Texas." Paper presented at the Association for Environmental Studies and Sciences, Tucson, AZ, June 21-24, 2017.

Correal, A. "Raccoons invade Brooklyn." *The New York Times* January 1, 2016. Accessed 29 June 2019. Online.

Couturier, L. "One nation under coyote, divisible." *Trash Animals: How We Live with Nature's Filthy, Feral, Invasive, and Unwanted Species*. K. Nagy & P. D. Johnson II, eds. U Minnesota P, 2013. 107-123.

Cox, D. T. C. & Gaston, K. J. "Human-nature interaction and the consequences and drivers of provisioning wildlife." *Philosophical Transactions of the Royal Society* B373 (2018): 20170092.

Dempsey, A. "Toronto built a better green bin and—oops—maybe a smarter raccoon." *The Star* August 3, 2018. Accessed 29 June 2019. Online.

Dickinson, E. "The Misdiagnosis: Rethinking 'Nature-deficit Disorder.'" *Environmental Communication* 7.3 (2013): 315-335.

Donaldson, S. & Kymlicka, W. *Zoopolis: A Political Theory of Animal Rights*. Oxford UP, 2011.

Drew, J. "Rendering visible: Animals, empathy, and visual truths in the ghosts in our machine and beyond." *Animal Studies Journal* 5.2 (2016): 202-216.

Elliot, E. E., S. Vallance, & L. E. Molles. "Coexisting with coyotes (Canis latrans) in an urban environment." *Urban Ecosystems* 19.3 (2016): 1335-1350.

Fletcher, R. "Connection with nature is an oxymoron: A political ecology of 'nature-deficit disorder.'" *The Journal of Environmental Education* (48.4) (2017): 226-233.

Flores, D. *Coyote America: A Natural and Supernatural History*. Basic Books, 2016.

Frank, B. "Human–wildlife conflicts and the need to include tolerance and coexistence: An introductory comment." *Society & Natural Resources* 29.6 (2016): 738-743.

Gandy, M. *Concrete and Clay: Reworking Nature in New York City*. MIT Press, 2003. Gaynor, K. M., Hojnowski, C. E., Carter, N. H., Brashares, J. S. "The influence of human disturbance on wildlife nocturnality." *Science* 360.6394 (2018): 1232-1235.

Gehrt, S. D., Brown, J. L., & Anchor, C. "Is the urban coyote a misanthropic synanthrope? The case from Chicago." *Cities and Environment* 4.1 (2011). Accessed 29 June 2019. Online.

Gehrt, S. D., Riley, S. P. D., & Cypher, B. L. Eds. *Urban Carnivores: Ecology, Conflict, and Conservation*. Johns Hopkins UP, 2010.

Gobster, P. H. "Urban park restoration and the 'museumification' of nature." *Nature and Culture* 2.2 (2007): 95-114.

Gruen, L. *Entangled Empathy: An Alternative Ethic for our Relationships with Animals*. Lantern Books, 2014.

Hatley, J. "Blood intimacies and biodicy: Keeping faith with ticks." *Australian Humanities Review* 49 (2010): 63-75.

Haupt, L. L. *Crow Planet: Essential Wisdom from the Urban Wilderness*. Little, Brown and Company, 2009.

Henderson, J.A., & Zarger, R.K. "Toward political ecologies of environmental education." *The Journal of Environmental Education* (48.4) (2017): 285-289.

Hinchliffe, S. & Whatmore, S. "Living cities: towards a politics of conviviality." *Science as Culture* 15.2 (2006): 123-138.

Hobbs, R. J. et al. "Managing the whole landscape: Historical, hybrid, and novel ecosystems." *Frontiers in Ecology and the Environment* 12.10 (2014): 557-564.

Hovorka, A. "Trans-species urban theory: Chickens in an African city." *Cultural Geographies* 15.1) (2008): 95-117.

Hunold, C. and Lloro-Bidart, T. "There goes the neighborhood: Urban coyotes and the politics of wildlife." *Journal of Urban Affairs* (forthcoming).

Hunold, C. "Why not the city? Urban hawk watching and the end of nature." *Nature and Culture* 12.2 (2017): 115-136.

Ives, C.D., Lentini, P.E., Threlfall, C.G., et al. "Cities are hotspots for threatened species." *Global Ecology and Biogeography* 25.1 (2016): 117-126.

Isabella, J. "The intelligent life of the city raccoon: Adapting to the urban jungle has made Rocky smarter." *Nautilus* March 31, 2016. Accessed 29 June 2019. Online.

Karvonen, A. *Politics of Urban Runoff: Nature, Technology, and the Sustainable City*. The MIT Press, 2011.

Kowarik, I. "Novel urban ecosystems, biodiversity, and conservation." *Environmental Pollution* 159.8/9 (2011): 1974-1983.

Leong, M. & Trautwein, M. "A citizen science approach to evaluating US cities for biotic homogenization." *PeerJ—Life and Environment* (2019). Accessed 29 June 2019. Online.

Loeb, P. "City councilman wants to explore SW Philly raccoon infestation." *CBS Philly*, January 28, 2017. Accessed 29 June 2019. Online.

Lorimer, J. *Wildlife in the Anthropocene: Conservation after Nature*. (U Minnesota P, 2015).

Lorimer, J. "Non-human charisma." *Environment and Planning D: Society and Space* 25.5 (2007): 911-932.

Luther, E. "Tales of cruelty and belonging: In search of an ethic for urban human- wildlife relations." *Animal Studies Journal* 2.1 (2013): 35-54.

McKiernan, S., & Instone, L. "From pest to partner: Rethinking the Australian White Ibis in the more-than-human city." *Cultural Geographies* 23.3 (2015): 475-494.

Melosi, M.V. *The Sanitary City: Urban Infrastructure in America from Colonial Times to the Present*. Johns Hopkins UP, 2000.

Miéville, China. *The City and The City: A Novel*. DelRay, 2009.

Nagy, K. & Johnson II, P. D. Eds. *Trash Animals: How we Live with Nature's Filthy, Feral, Invasive, and Unwanted Species*. U Minnesota P, 2013.

The Nature of Cities. "Let go of some urban domestication: How would you convince the mayor to re-wild the city?" (n. d.). Accessed 29 June 2019. Online.

Philadelphia Water Department. *Amended Green City, Clean Waters* (2011). Accessed 29 June 2019. Online.

Poessel, S. A., Breck, S. W., & Gese, E. M. "Spatial ecology of coyotes in the Denver metropolitan area: influence of the urban matrix." *Journal of Mammology* 97.5 (2016): 1414–1427.

Pratt-Bergstrom, B. *When Mountain Lions Are Neighbors: People and Wildlife Working It Out in California*. Heyday, 2016.

"Raccoon attacks baby and drags her out of bed in Philadelphia, says mom." *CBS News* December 22, 2017. Accessed 29 June 2019. Online.

Sawiki, E. "New city policy avoids pesticides." *The Malibu Times* June 27, 2019. Accessed 29 June 2019. Online.

Schilthuizen, M. *Darwin Comes to Town: How the Urban Jungle Drives Evolution*. Picador, 2018.

Schlosberg, D. "Environmental management in the Anthropocene." *The Oxford Handbook of Environmental Political Theory*. T. Gabrielson, C. Hall, J. M. Meyer, & D. Schlosberg, eds. Oxford UP, 2016.

Soulsbury, C. D. & White, P. C. L. "Human–wildlife interactions in urban areas: a review of conflicts, benefits and opportunities." *Wildlife Research* 42.7 (2015): 541-553.

Standish, R. J., Hobbs, R. J., & Miller, J. R. "Improving city life: options for ecological restoration in urban landscapes and how these might influence interactions between people and nature." *Landscape Ecology* 28.6 (2013): 1213-1221.

Stroud, E. *Nature Next Door: Cities and Trees in the American Northeast*. U Washington P, 2012.

van Dooren, T. "Vultures and their people in India: Equity and entanglement in a time of extinctions." *Wild Hearts: Literature, Ecology, and Inclusion* 22.2 (2010): 130-145.

Van Horn, G. *The Way of Coyote: Shared Journeys in the Urban Wild*. U Chicago P, 2018.

Wolch, J. "Anima urbis." *Progress in Human Geography* 26.6 (2002): 721-742.

Yeo, J.-H., & Neo, H. "Monkey business: Human–animal conflicts in urban Singapore." *Social & Cultural Geography* 11.7 (2010): 681-699.

Theodoros Katerinakis
Dyeing Eggs and Baking Ties: Connected Customs and Manners Reinforce Cultures in "E-cake and E-Eggbattle" Social Networks[1]

1. When do Christmas Cakes and Easter Eggs Move Online?

The complex lifeworld of our epoch's social life is primarily created by relations and the behavioral patterns that derive from them. Networked individuality, Homo Dictyous, the isolation economy, and practices of culture online have become part of daily routine with implications on the very fabric of the social and business landscape, the way people interact and collaborate, the value that is created, the way we manage our time and the way we manage relationships. Culture and spirituality is in the epicenter of this impact as practiced from year to year. Easter and Christmas are milestones in the Christian calendar and shape the social life of major populations, even beyond religion. Easter is an ascetic process towards resurrection and Christmas season finds its own peak point in New Year's Eve, covering significant populations of Russian Federation, Greece, Serbia, Romania, Bulgaria, Georgia, Cyprus, Poland, Albania, Czech Republic, Slovakia, Modenegro among others as well as their diasporas. Countries are identified with the birth and re-birth concepts connecting families and social groups together.

During Christmas period, vasilopita the so-called "St. Basil's cake"[2] is prepared using simple ingredients and contains a coin, that nobody knows where it is (Savvidou, 2005). On New Year's Day, the cake is cut into sectors of the circle. Each member of the family takes a whole piece and the one who finds the coin, according to the tradition, is considered to be luckiest one of the New Year. "E-vasilopita" network shifts this ritual on-line with a virtual cake.

During Easter period, families dye hard-boiled eggs in red as a reference to Christian passion week, symbolizing Christ's emergence from the tomb when an egg breaks. On Easter Day all guests in the family meal engage in egg-cracking contest. To play, each participant takes a red egg, and taps the end of her or his egg lightly against the end of the other's egg. When an egg's end is cracked, the person with the unbroken egg uses the same end of the egg to try to crack the other end of the opponent's egg. "E-eggbattle" network shifts egg cracking in an online contest.

But what happens with those networks that connect participants with different rituals?

---
1 Part of the text is based on a research presentation of Katerinakis T and Kiriakakis, Z (2019). "Breaking Eggs and Baking Ties: Connecting Cultures in "E-Vasilopita and E-Avgomachia" Networks. European Conference on Social Networks, September 2019, Zurich, Switzerland.
2 E-cake is used to represent "e-vasilopita" from the Greek word used for the traditional cake of the New Year's Day (for Christian calendar). E-eggbattle represents the network application of egg-cracking, known as "avgomachia" in the Christian world. Egg stands for "avgo" and "St Basil's cake" is the equivalent for "vasilopita".

Understanding networks means identifying the most important actors, ties, and relations. Instead of simply knowing who our friends are, and perhaps our friends' friends, we can peer "beyond our social horizon and see our place in a vast worldwide social network" (Christakis and Fowler, 2009). Furthermore, customs and manners, as communal identifiers of "applied culture" are key indicators of social cohesion especially when spirituality is based on philanthropia; i.e. on the loving of the other under the bond of agape.

2. Identifying Network Indicators and Structures

A network is a group of relationships, a set of socially relevant members connected with one or more relations. Thus, in order to understand networks, indicators are proposed to describe nodes and determine their relations, either position-based or event-based or attribution-based. Network indicators describe what a node is, what type of connection the nodes have and what the direction and the intensity of those connections are. Indicators are identifiers and metrics that describe similarities, social relations, interactions, and flows. Beyond measurement, indicators could be defined by the phenomenon of interest, by actors' environments and circumstances, their cohesiveness or using relations as contexts of other relations.

2.1 Understanding Networks

Two important indicators of network structure are network density and network centrality (Katerinakis, 2011). These two aspects highlight different characteristics of a network. Empirical studies tend to find that one or the other is the better explanatory variable for certain aspects of behavior in the business world. There is a hill-shaped relationship between network density and network centrality. The combination of these outcomes sets lower and upper bounds on network centrality. Density describes the general level of linkage among the point in the graph. Density depends on inclusiveness and the degrees of its points. Inclusiveness refers to the number of points that are included within the various connected parts of a network. Density denotes how members of a network are able to sustain their connections, as relations. For example, commitment to a relation of love is more intense than a commitment to a relation of an acquaintance. This means that any network of loving relations is likely to have a lower density than any network of awareness relations. Also, changes at the individual level of contacts result to a continuous transformation of the density of global features of the network.

Understanding networks means to identify the most important actors, ties and relations. The idea of centrality as applied to human communication is defined as relationship between structure and influence in communication within small groups. The origin of this idea goes back to the sociometric concept of the person who is the most popular and stands in the center of their group as a star (Scott, 2007). Relative centrality in a network is measured by the point of centrality; measuring the connections with the other points in its immediate environment/neighborhood as local, and the significance in the overall structure of the network as global. For example, certain organizations tend to be consistently more central than others; also, it appeared that the centrality of an organization was predictable in part from its own characteristics and in part from the properties of the network in which it was embedded. The question on centrality was moved in governance issues, as the level of democratization of society through decentralization of decision making and in community organizations and planning.

To avoid confusion, centrality is anchored with point centrality and centralization is used to describe particular properties in the graph structure that represents a network. A graph diagram represents each row or column in an incidence matrix- each of the case or affiliation/relationships under investigation – by a point or actor on the diagram. When we have the respective adjacency matrices then the presence or absence of a tie is represented by a line and a numerical value in the line represents the intensity in a value graph. Although centrality is represented in a wide variety of applications there is no consensus in the proper measurement. In some cases, prestige is a more refined and accepted concept of an actor (point). Prestigious is the actor who is the receiver of extensive ties; the prestige of an actor increases as the actor becomes an object of more ties but not necessarily when the actor itself initiates the ties but when ties are directed to an actor (in a directional relation). Prestige is quantifiable when we speak of directional relations, as indegrees and outdegrees measure centrality. Degree prestige as nomination of choices, proximity prestige as influence and status or rank prestige as direct choices are measures that indicate prestige inside a set of actors, as an indegree measure.

In cases like Greece and Cyprus and their diasporas centrality in communicating customs is defined as the relationship between structure and influence within small groups. In the current paper a real-life network, incorporating egg-breaking and cake-sharing, is showcased using the analytics of on-line participation and network metrics. Competing with eggs ("avgomachia" or eggbattle) symbolizes conflict of good with evil, in a contest that leads to friendly conflict resolution. The focal signifier of intra/inter family networks in all those communities is the preparation for dyeing eggs and waiting for the Easter day to break, as well as the baking and sharing of the traditional St. Basil's cake called "vasilopita". Eggs encapsulate life and substances of life, where as Christmas cake incorporate the act of sharing. The modus operandi of e-eggbattle and e-vasilopita is founded around the virtues of peace, agape, equality, hospitality, respect, justice, and unity as values of social capital; values that make people assemble around eggs and cake expressing preference, desire, motivation and homophily.

2.2 Determinants and Indicators of a Network

Social Network Analysis supports the argument for behaviors and behavioral outcomes "your friends who live miles away have just as big an impact on you as your next-door friends" (Wellman, 1983). Field data from followers -as friends of the vasilopita and eggbattle-related customs, and network representations support the premise that keeping customs in religiously homogenous communities is a demanding task. In the current paper, the bottom-up approach of the physical egg-crashing and vasilopita cake customs are scaling-up via the on-line network that stimulates the original application of these customs. E-eggbattle and e-vasilopita are on-line networks that increase the "productivity of culture" in a Habermasian lifeworld of interconnected members (Baxter, 1987); although low betweeness may be manifested, nodes are holding tight in periodic seasonal occurrences to practice their customs on-line; participation increases, exercise and execution of customs flows, and network actors feel more inclusive in a secular way, when they are co-present to break eggs and bake cakes beyond religious connotations.

When we speak about social life networks complexity is present. Indicators assist in identifying a network and understanding the specialized and critical function of connectivity as a survival strategy. Speaking about networks captures countries, neighborhoods, departments in organizations, people, families, journal articles or web pages; those become social when people as actors/users participate with similarity, social relationships, interactions, and flows.

Similarity is the relation of resemblance in any attribute measurable as a variable; group memberships, co-memberships and interlocking participation, sameness in a spatial or temporal space are examples of similarity. Social relations cover affinity and kinship ties, commonly defined roles and familiarity in feelings and mutual awareness; a family member, a friend, a schoolmate, a significant other could be examples of such relations. Interactions are ties based on behavior of individuals starting from verbal communication and going to inviting someone to dinner. Usually such interactions occur in the context of social relations. Flows are unidirectional or bi-directional exchanges or transfers between nodes for resources, information or influence. Flows, also, occur in the context of social relations where different kinds of support and companionship are manifested. In the mindset of network analysts cause-effect relation is located in the social structure and not in the individual. So, behavior embedded in networks is a characteristic indicator of network effect and scope. Each members of a group rarely shares the same relation to the group. So, interaction and strength of connection are characteristics that upgrade the groups to networks.

2.3 Network Data and Metrics

Principal types of data that we meet in society and social sciences are attribute data that relate attitudes, opinions and behavior with individuals and groups, measured with values of variables; relational data refers to contacts, connections, ties and attachments which relates individual elements themselves (measured with relations expressing linkages). A third type of data comprises the ideational data that describe the meanings, motives, definitions and typifications themselves.

Relational data are central to investigate the structure of the social action. Multidimensional displays of social phenomena under consideration offer various potential to a better understanding of the social network entity. Sociological judgment for networks starts from the logic and understanding of the particular measure or formation (clique, group etc).

The notion of social network, network indicators and the methods of social network analysis have been a growing field, due to the notion of relationship between social entities, its importance and the patterns associated to these relationships. The structure formed is measured with structural variables. Social networks use distinctive indicators to present themselves:

- Actors, as the social entities that are referred to the network, are viewed as interdependent and not autonomous units.
- Relational ties link actors together and establish linkages between pairs of actors (e.g. evaluation, transfer of material sources, association or affiliation, interaction, movement, physical connection, formal relation, biological relation). These ties are considered as channels for transfer or flow of resources. A pair of actors and the possible ties between them forms a dyad, a subset of three with the ties a triad, any subset of actors and their ties form a subgroup and a collection of actors on which ties are to be measured form a group.
- Network models focusing on individuals view the network structural environment as providing opportunities or constraints for individual action. The social network, in this sense, consists of a finite set of actors and the relations defined on them as lasting patterns of relations among actors.

Key theoretical and terminological motivations rise with the introduction of domain-specific terminology like: social group, isolation, popularity, liaison, prestige, balance, transitivity, clique, subgroup, social cohesion, social position, social role, reciprocity, mutuality, exchange, influence, dominance, conformity. The gestalt tradition uses patterns that are regarded as "holons" in the systems, and try to determine the nature of those parts (Ostrom, 2007). Holon is the whole of social life, represented as a set of points some of which are joined with lines to form a network of relations with reciprocity, intensity and durability.

Examples of the topics studied by network analysts are: occupational mobility, the impact of urbanization in individual well-being, the political and economic system, community elite decision-making, social support, community, group problem solving, diffusion and adoption of innovations, corporate inter-locking, belief systems, cognition or social relation, markets, sociology of science, exchange and power, consensus and social influence, coalition formation, the practice of customs and manners etc.

According to Borgatti's classification, transmission, adaptation, binding and exclusion are categorical indicators of what a network is (Borgatti et al, 2009). Transmission happens when network connections are treated as pipelines for the flow of jobs, support, identities, diseases, or knowledge. The effect of network structure in these flows is not uniform. Adaptation happens when actors make similar choices because of their position following constraints and opportunities. Binding happens when a network commits itself to act as a complete whole. The internal structure of the network affects collective action, coordination and community work. Exclusion happens when the existence of one tie connection does not allow the existence of another tie and affects the relations with other nodes. In networks of markets, exclusion is manifested with the availability of bargaining partners.

Connections generate networks when information are disclosed the actors-members of a network. Connections are more likely established when proximity from one node to another is close. Nodes with common social attributes increase the probability of connection realize homophily. Homophily increases the likelihood of connection between nodes, at an individual level as well as at a collective level. When nodes are connected in pairs then mutual regulation is enforced.

Conclusion

Networks are wholes that determine the nature of their parts and have properties distinct from their parts, as members or actors. Mapping a network is one of the most important analytical contributions in understanding networks, as the map or graph visualizes information that show how the network is structured and how it operates. More specialized centrality metrics are degrees, closeness, and betweenness. Degrees reveals activity of specific nodes/actors in the network. Closeness measures the ability of an actor to access other actors of the network and monitor their status. Betweenness shows the level control over the flow in a network and may represent an indication of leadership status for specific actors, even in covert networks.

The innovative "e-eggbattle and e-vasilopita" networks are enhanced by relevant "commodities" (traditional products and brands that promote locality). The act of shared participation in the virtual world of e-eggs and e-cakes redefines the sense of belonging and generates homopolar ties of enculturation. E-avgomachia and e-vasilopita realize innovative ways for diffusion of customs and connect cultures, especially in times of crises.

If relations offer connectedness in a network then trust, task at hand, mental and material resources, and strategy and goals indicate the path to comprehend and evaluate a given social network of interest. When customs and manners are at stake the online world seems to enrich everyday life practice. Internet-supported networks of customs seem to drive traditional rituals in a Homo Dictyous interconnected community.

References and Further Reading

Baxter, H. (1987). "System and Life-World in Habermas's 'Theory of Communicative Action.'" *Theory and Society*, vol. 16, no. 1, 1987, pp. 39–86.

Borgatti, S. P., Mehra A., Brass D. J., Labianca G. (2009) "Network Analysis in the Social Sciences." *Science*, 323:5916 pp. 892 – 895.

Christakis N. A., Fowler J. H. (2009). *Connected: The Surprising Power of Our Social Networks and How They Shape Our Lives*. Little, Brown & Company

Katerinakis T. (2011). Network Indicators, in Barnett George (Ed.) *Encyclopedia of Social Networks*, Sage Publications.

Ostrom, E. (2007). Institutional rational choice: An assessment of the institutional analysis and development framework. *In Theories of the policy process*, ed. Paul A. Sabatier, 21-64. Boulder, CO: Westview.

Savvidou, Ch. (2005). The St. Basil's Cake Problem, *Mathematics Magazine*, Vol. 78, No. 1 (Feb. 2005), pp. 48-51.

Scott, J. (2007). *Social Network Analysis (A Handbook)*. Thousand Oaks, CA, Sage Publications.

Wellman, B. (1983). "Network Analysis: Some basic principles." *Sociological Theory*, Vol.1, pp. 155-200.

Miriam Kotzin
In This Poem Only

we are not mortal.

The peonies shatter,
scatter their pink

silk on dark mulch—
or on damask. It is

of no matter. Also
the roses. And lilies,

even much considered
and loveliest of lilies.

The last small light
slips without notice

from a silent sky.
With its slow going

the long scarf of light
is lost to the stream.

The passing of this and
that is of no matter

in this poem only.

Miriam Kotzin
Notice

how the dry wind idles
among high branches,

a disembodied sigh left
hanging in parched leaves.

August. New Jersey.
The shadow of a single

cloud punctuates the hour,
glides across the broad lawn

and sweeps down the stifling street.
Was it only the blaze of noon,

sun in a heat-bleached sky,
that sent the dusty toad

to hide beneath these luminous
caladium, white and green

low-bending leaves? Or
might it have been the mower's

fearful roar? Anyway, there
she sits on the shaded mulch,

rooted like a shy bride
in a dim bower, waiting

for her tardy groom. I know
this: Whatever evades

the whirl of sharp steel
is fated to fray, wear away,

diminish, and dissolve. Listen.
The daily blare of the noon

siren offers official notice
of our own slow doom.

Miriam Kotzin
The Lace Maker

Those clouds are not white
blossoms, nor is the day
moon a scrap of lace.
Speaking of lace,
the Japanese beetles are not
lace makers. The beetles
are only gorging
on our roses. Why
should I spoil your fun?
All afternoon you
have busied yourself
with an obscure fury
of words, turning
away from the ordinary
as though you find
all this insufficient,
the given,
the incomparable, world.

Lynn Levin
The Lady with a Hundred Pockets

Doris and Mickey drove to the recreational complex in separate cars. They arranged to meet at the playground and cut through to the picnic area where the day-of-fun benefit for Cameron Ferderbar was taking place. Cameron, Doris's neighbor, had fallen off a ladder when cleaning out his roof gutters, and now he was laid up in a rehab facility, which, let's face it, was actually a nursing home that smelled like diapers. Bankruptcy was pawing at the family's door, and the GoFundMe had come up short, so Cameron's men's club was putting on the benefit hoping to cover some of the healthcare bills.

Doris arrived at the playground wearing a CAPS Sugar sun visor, a red-and-white striped shirt, and white slacks. CAPS processed sugar, and Doris worked in inventory control. As she waited for Mickey, Doris noticed children crowding around a woman dressed in an enormous multicolored patchwork skirt covered in rows of pockets. Next to her was a sign on a chair that read, "The Lady with a Hundred Pockets. Fifty cents per chance."

The woman smelled like a tropical fruit salad. She reminded Doris of a fertility goddess. She wore her hair in a massive braid, thick as a bicycle tire, that she fixed in a circle on top of her head like an Italian Easter bread, except there was no pink or blue dyed egg in it.

Children were begging their adults for change and darting over to the pocket lady. After she zipped their coins into her belt bag, she let them plunge their hands into her pockets. They came up with mini pinwheels, plastic knights, frogs, lions, junk jewelry, and tiny squirt guns. A few kids liked their loot, at least for a moment, but some did not. They wanted to put the junk back and try again. But the pocket lady tilted her head, shook her finger, and said, "For another chance, you must pay again." Most of the adults shelled out for two chances, but when the kids wanted more money, their adults escorted them to the play equipment, and, if they kept making a fuss, back to the car.

Mickey showed up twenty minutes late, but at least he showed up. It was a hot August afternoon, and he was mopping his brow. Doris offered him an air hug. Like Doris, Mickey was in his early sixties. They had met two months ago on a dating site for mature people. Age was just a number, that's what everyone said. Like it was only about age.

Doris had been through one divorce, Mickey three. A solidly built man, he wore his thinning iron-gray hair in comb-over. Not a ridiculous comb-over, one of those trimmer comb-overs. He was a delivery driver for UPS.

"Who's the gypsy?" he asked.

"That's the Lady with a Hundred Pockets. For fifty cents, you get to pick one of her pockets. I'm going to try my luck."

She meant this to sound playful, but Mickey mumbled something about her acting ridiculous and like a little kid and there being better ways to spend money. He stood with his hands in the side pockets of his plaid knee-length shorts while Doris gave the woman two quarters. The lady told her to go for it. Doris stuck her hand into a paisley pocket and pulled out a gold plastic ring with a big faceted plastic ruby in it.

She showed it to Mickey. "My lucky ring. Maybe it will grant me three wishes."

Mickey gave her a whatever look. "Now I know something new about you. You believe in wishes and luck." He mopped his brow again.

"I do happen to believe in wishes and luck," she said, and Mickey gave her another whatever look. It would have been nice if he played along in the spirit of fun, but he evidently did not budge on his principles. She began to think of her wishes, but she kept them to herself. She wished for a caring guy with a sense of humor, speedy healing for Cameron, and a winning state lottery ticket for the Ferderbars. Maybe a winning lottery ticket for herself. What did she spend, maybe ten or twenty dollars a week on the state lottery?

"Why don't you put that silly thing back and let a kid get it?"

This made Doris feel ashamed. She put the ring back in its paisley pocket. Maybe some little girl would pull it out and be delighted.

"You don't have to put it back," said the lady. Doris shrugged like it wasn't a big deal. Then she saw the lady aim an evil eye at Mickey. It was like a laser locking onto a target. Maybe she had real gypsy powers. Doris hoped that things would improve during the day of fun.

She had paid for the beef and beer tickets, which was only right since this was her cause and the decision to go had been her idea. She wondered what it would be like, Mickey meeting so many of her friends all at once. Maybe he was skittish about that. So far, their dates had been one on one, your basic dinner-and-a-movie thing, and they always went halfsies. It would be nice if he treated her now and then.

The men's club had produced a shindig. A sound system played country music. There was a dunk tank, horseshoes, drawings for gift baskets, bingo for prizes, and a bean bag game called cornhole. It cost extra for the games. There was a prayer station, too. No charge for that, of course. Connie Ferderbar sat in a lawn chair with a giant get-well card that everyone signed. The aroma of barbeque wafted through the air.

Doris and Mickey headed to the food table, Doris waving to acquaintances along the way. There must have been two hundred people there—neighbors, friends, people from the community.

"Didn't Cameron have health insurance?" asked Mickey.

"Connie said he dropped their coverage as soon as the government lifted the no-insurance tax penalty. Not too swift, I know."

"Talk about false economy. And they didn't find him for three hours? He lay there for three hours? Working alone on a ladder, no spotter?"

"He took risks. But you can fall off a ladder even if you have a spotter," remarked Doris.

"The guy's an idiot," said Mickey. "You take precautions. You carry coverage." A yellow jacket flew up to Mickey, and he swatted it away.

"There's good luck and bad luck." Doris thought of all the times Cameron and Connie had been there for her both during her divorce and after. Cameron had helped her with a leaky faucet, a busted screen door. He'd helped her change lightbulbs she couldn't reach. "Well, he's my friend, and that's the reason we're here. Do you really have to call him an idiot?"

Mickey loaded his plate with a heap of barbequed beef, big mounds of macaroni salad and cole slaw, and stuck tortilla chips into the salads. He took a can of Pabst and headed to the picnic tables, which were under a pavilion. Worried that Mickey had taken more than his share, Doris took less than she wanted, then sat down next to Mickey.

The Chens, the Rothmans, and the DiPietros joined them. After the introductions, Frances Chen updated everyone on Cameron's situation. He'd broken a leg and three ribs, screwed up a shoulder, suffered a concussion, and, worst of all, had a spinal cord injury. The spinal cord injury made it hard to predict if he would walk again. Plus, an infection had cropped up in the diaper-smelling rehab. Don't even ask about the bills. Before the accident, Cameron had managed a restaurant.

"How do you guys know each other?" asked Rose Rothman inclining with interest toward Doris and Mickey.

Marrieds always asked. Singles also asked each other how they met. But that was different, everyone on the same playing field.

"Online dating," replied Doris, not in a terse voice but in the kind of voice that said she wanted to move on from that topic.

Bea DiPietro said she'd heard quite a few stories about online dating, women meeting creeps and such. Sometimes nice guys too, countered Doris. Bea wanted to know what site she used, and Doris replied in a general way that it was one of the over-fifty sites. In truth, she couldn't recall if it she'd met Mickey on SilverSingles, or OurTime, or one of the others. No law against having two or three accounts at once. It increased your possibility of finding Mr. Right or, at least, Mr. Available. Sometimes Doris saw the same guys overlapping on the sites. Maybe they noticed her overlapping, too.

"That's how it's done now," said Mickey, rescuing Doris. He took a swig of beer. "You meet people online."

"Mickey's a pitcher in a softball league," Doris piped up, and the husbands, clearly impressed, picked up on the sports theme.

After lunch, Doris and Mickey ambled over to the activities area. Doris bought some chances on gift certificates for local hair salons and restaurants. Mickey said she was wasting her money, why not just patronize the places directly? Doris stared at him.

"You do it to help them raise money," she explained like he was some kind of dolt who didn't get it. "The guy had an accident, and now everybody's helping out."

"Well, the guy didn't play his cards right. So now everyone has to bail him out?"

"You think you always deal your own cards, Mickey?" Doris was surprised at her sharp tone. "What about a flood or a hurricane? What about cancer?"

"You buy insurance for those things. You don't buy a house in a flood plain. You manage your risks."

Now he was acting ridiculous. And hard-hearted.

"You can't always control what happens to you. What if you go to a festival and a shooter opens fire?"

"Do you know something I don't?" he said, trying to be funny.

They walked past the horseshoes and the dunk tank to the bean bag toss with the weird name. Mickey wanted to show his pitching chops. The game was popular, and they took their place in line. Doris wondered if he would pay, since cornhole was his idea or if, at least, they'd go halfsies. The fellow in charge explained the rules of the game, which were fairly involved with all sorts of scoring levels. You aimed to toss the bean bag into the hole, and the holes were on two slanted boards. One board had a sun, the other a moon.

"Hey, Sugar," said a voice behind Doris. There stood Louella from work, also sporting a CAPS sun visor. She was with a fellow named John, whom Doris had dated in the past. They had met on OurTime. Or was it SilverSingles? Louella and John were holding hands.

The women made the introductions.

"How do you do?" said Doris, trying to act as if she were meeting John for the first time.

"Pleased to meet you, Doris," returned John. They discovered that they were each there to support Cameron, who was a mutual friend. "A good time for a good cause, but a good cause for a sad reason."

They decided to play teams. First girls against boys, then couples. John took out his wallet. Mickey left his wallet in his pants.

Doris's bean bags kept landing on the grass. Louella had slightly better aim, but the boys won, Mickey landing all this throws right in the hole. Doris noticed that Louella wore a slender gold ring with a tiny red gemstone, a garnet or ruby, on her right ring finger. "A promise ring," said Louella with a glint in her eye.

Doris took the singles prerogative and asked how they met.

"Online dating," said Louella.

"What a coincidence. That's how we met." What had she missed in John? She had thought him boring and stodgy and let things trail off after two dates. What a gentleman he was and clearly in love with Louella.

They changed to couples teams. Louella and John tried impromptu rituals each time they prepared to throw their bean bags, touching an ankle for good luck, doing a few Charleston steps, each breathing on the promise ring. They racked up points, but again Mickey landed all four of his bags in the hole. He tried to help Doris improve her aim, advising her to shoot to the left since her tendency was to pitch to the right, but that did not help. She finally turned around and threw backwards. Shockingly, her last bean bag made the hole.

Mickey shook his head in amazement. "Gotta say, dumb luck won that time."

Doris did a little happy dance.

After the game, Louella and John moseyed off in the direction of the food table, and Doris and Mickey headed to the dunk tank. There was a big crowd there too, and one of the neighbors sat on the platform of the dunk tank cage egging people on, "We want a pitcher, not a glass of water! We want a pitcher, not a belly itcher!" Everyone was missing the target. "You pays your money and you takes your chances," yelled the guy collecting the money. It cost ten bucks for three tries.

"Sugar, I'd like a shot at that dunk tank. Bet I could sink the guy," said Mickey.

"I bet you could," said Doris. "Show 'em what you got."

Mickey stood there with an expectant look. Then he rubbed his fingers together in a where's-the-money gesture.

Doris blinked. "Pretty much, Mickey," said Doris, "it's your turn to pay for some of the entertainment. To be fair, I mean, looking at the whole afternoon."

"The laid-up guy is your friend. It's a conflict of interest for me. I don't believe in paying the bills for people who got themselves into their messes. Ethically, you should pay."

"Ethically? Ethically, there's something called sharing and generosity." She looked at him for a response. He looked at her. It was a standoff. "Come on, Mickey. Come *on*," said Doris. "Don't be cheap and childish. You're acting like a little kid asking his mom for money. Like those kids with the pocket lady."

Mickey blazed a look at Doris. She had called him on his behavior, maybe overdid it, and he more than didn't like it. He looked ferocious, and it scared her.

He tore a ten-dollar bill from his wallet and thrust it at the carnival barker guy. People noticed his rapid movements. He was making a scene.

Maybe she should have paid the ten bucks and afterward called it quits between them. A one-time appeasement. But something in her made her say what she said and in the tone that she said it.

Everyone stepped back as Mickey wound up for the pitch. Doris knew his skill, but the others did not. They only saw his aggression, the hard set of his mouth, and Doris standing by with a crooked smile. She knew that in the privacy of a home, which they would never ever share, he would always be right, even if he were not right. She knew that type. The type that called disagreement starting a fight.

Mickey launched his meanest fastball and hit the bullseye hard. It was assault by proxy. She could feel it. He smiled a triumphant smile. Normally people would clap and laugh as the guy in the dunk tank dropped into the drink. Instead, silence settled over the crowd. "You really know how to spoil an afternoon," he snapped loud enough for others to hear. "Don't bother to call." With that, Mickey stalked off in the direction of the playground.

Her face reddened with embarrassment, but it would have been worse if Louella and John had witnessed the drama. How lucky that she and Mickey had come in separate cars.

Abandoned, or was it liberated? Doris wandered around the grounds. "Old Town Road" played on the sound system. She looked at her cell phone and watched other people play bingo and lawn games. She joined Connie Ferderbar and chatted with her about the great turnout, the tasty barbeque, and the loving and supportive friends.

Frances Chen, Rose Rothman, and Bea DiPietro joined them. Had they observed the scene at the dunk tank?

"Where's your friend?" asked Bea.

"He had to go somewhere," replied Doris, trying to look stoic. The women nodded.

"I don't know how anyone finds anyone in this world," said Frances.

"It takes a miracle, but you have to believe in miracles," said Rose.

Doris did not stick around for the prize drawings. She said her farewells and made her way toward the playground and the parking lot. She'd taken a chance on Mickey, and it wasn't a winning chance. Or maybe she had chosen Mickey, and it turned out to be a bad choice. Her thoughts turned to poor Cameron, and she felt that her dating issues were just plain silly compared to other people's problems.

The lady with a hundred pockets was packing up. She recognized Doris and waved to her. She didn't smell like a tropical fruit salad anymore and her elaborate Easter bread hairdo was falling apart. She no longer wore the theatrical face of the seer.

"Where's your man friend?"

"He couldn't stay," replied Doris. "He had to leave."

"That dude was a jerk. You can do better. Here, have another try at a pocket. It's on me."

Doris found the same paisley pocket in which she'd found the ring. Lo and behold, the golden piece of junk, the trinket that Mickey had shamed her into giving back, was still there. She smiled and slid the clunky thing onto her finger. As Doris drove back home, she felt safe. She had never felt safer. And she thought of her wishes, which were pretty things and well worth wishing for, even though they might never come true.

Richard McCourt
Surprising Discovery of Civil War Plant

Elana Benamy was examining a digital image of a dried pressed plant specimen at her desk in the Botany Department of the Academy of Natural Sciences when she noticed something that gave her a start. As a curatorial assistant working on a project to put more than 300,000 plant images online for scientists to use, she was used to the image of the occasional beautiful, odd or unusual plant that added spice to her day. But this image was astonishing.

It wasn't so much the plant, which was a common species, the green comet milkweed, *Asclepias viridilora*, which grows in Pennsylvania and almost every other state in the U.S. What brought Elana up short was the information on the label.

Handwritten, in a distinctive 19th century cursive, was the location where the plant was collected: "Battlefield of Gettysburg, August 20, 1863." Not only was this more than a century and half ago, Elana noted, it was also from the site of one of the most famous battles in American history. And the summer of 1863—that rang a bell too.

Elana googled "The Battle of Gettysburg." "It occurred on July 1-3, 1863," she says, so the plant specimen had been gathered barely seven weeks following the Civil War battle where 50,000 soldiers had been killed or wounded. It would be three more months before President Abraham Lincoln would give his Gettysburg Address.

When the battle ended, the population of the small town of 2,000 was actually outnumbered by the 7,000 who had died in battle. Many Confederate soldiers had been buried in mass graves, and there were reports of body parts sticking out of shallow graves on the batteield. Most houses in the town were used as makeshift hospitals for the tens of thousands of wounded.

"Can you imagine?" asked Elana. Why on earth would someone be out plant collecting in a place that had so recently been a disaster area? It seems ghoulish to contemplate.

As it turns out, the person and his reasons for collecting make perfect sense.

The tag on the plant specimen notes that Thomas Meehan was the collector. Meehan (1826-1901) was born in England to a family of gardeners and trained in horticulture at the Royal Botanic Gardens, Kew. He came to Philadelphia in 1848 and rapidly joined the horticultural and botanic community of the city. Meehan would later become president of the Academy of Natural Sciences. From 1850-1852, Meehan worked as head gardener to Andrew M. Eastwick, then owner of Bartram's Garden in Philadelphia. Meehan formed his own nursery in Germantown in 1853 and rose to become one of the most successful nurseryman in the U.S. Meehan was also a prolific writer and long-time editor of *The Gardener's Monthly*, later called *Meehan's Monthly*.

In 1859 his younger brother Joseph Meehan (1840-1920) came to the U.S. to work in the greenhouses and plant nursery started by his brother in Germantown.

"Thomas Meehan might have had a family reason to visit Gettysburg in August 1863," notes Joel Fry, curator at the historical Bartram's Garden in Philadelphia. "His younger brother Joseph Meehan had enlisted in the 118th Pennsylvania Volunteers in August 1862, which was rapidly involved in battles at Antietam and then Shepherdstown, West Virginia, in September 1862."

Later, just as the battle at Gettysburg began, Joseph was taken prisoner by the Confederate army during the defense of Carlisle, Pennsylvania, and he was taken to the Gettysburg battleield under guard. With the defeat of Robert E. Lee's army, Meehan was given a battlefield parole on July 4th.

But why was Thomas Meehan at Gettysburg a month after the battle? Was he there with his brother? "Joseph Meehan might have still been at Gettysburg," says Joel Fry, "or might he have taken his brother, Thomas, out there for a sight-seeing trip in August 1863?"

We don't know, but Joseph later wrote an article for *Gardening* magazine on "Battlefield Flowers: Floral Treasures of Gettysburg." Written in 1897, long after the battle, Joseph Meehan, gives an elegant description of the flowers and trees, noting several of the famous sites in the battleield: the many oaks and one "large, shining chestnut" still standing at the Bloody Angle, the site where Pickett's charge ended; and a brightly colored Phlox, "a species not at all common," near a monument to a fallen Union solder.

Clearly, Joseph had a flair for plants and the desire to write about them. He wrote for a large number of horticultural magazines and newspapers, including a weekly column for 17 years in *Florist' Exchange*. And so, the elder Meehan collecting plants on a historic battleground where one of the Meehan brothers had been is not surprising.

The milkweed specimen is a small but important reminder of the many scientifically important collections at The Academy of Natural Sciences of Drexel University. The Herbarium, home to the plants collected on the Lewis and Clark expedition, collections from a cruise of Captain Cook, and many plants collected by Henry Muhlenberg and other early American botanists, continues to surprise.

There may very well be other Gettysburg plants or other historically important specimens that will turn up during the ongoing digitization project of the Academy's plant collection, funded by a grant from the National Science Foundation.

Joseph and Thomas Meehan lived into the early 20th century, leaving a botanical legacy that survives in the gardens of Philadelphia, as well as in the herbarium of the Academy of Natural Sciences of Drexel.

Jonson Miller
The 1869 Avondale Mine Disaster: A Transatlantic Welsh Tragedy

The deadliest mining disaster of the anthracite coal fields of eastern Pennsylvania occurred on September 6, 1869 in Plymouth Township, near Wilkes-Barre in the Wyoming Valley. On that day, 108 mine workers, including five boys, died in a mine of the Avondale Colliery. The wood lining of the shaft, the only way in or out of the mine, caught fire that morning. The fire spread upwards to the wooden "breaker" that contained the various machines and tools for cleaning and sorting coal as it left the mine. The burning breaker blocked the mine workers' exit and the rescuers' entrance. After three days of fighting the fire, navigating dangerous mine gases, and making the shaft passable, crews finally retrieved the bodies of all 108 mine workers and two would-be rescuers. Two-thirds of the 108 mine workers were Welsh. These 110 workers left behind 59 widows and 109 fatherless children in America, with an additional unknown number of widows and children in Wales.

Readers of *Ninnau* may be familiar with this tragedy through articles about the memorial at the old mine entrance in Plymouth and the restoration of the Scranton cemetery where most of the Welsh victims were buried. These memorials to the dead mark the tragedy as a local one. It was indeed traumatic, especially for the Welsh people of the Wyoming Valley, which was then the population center of Welsh America. In fact, there were then more people speaking Welsh in the valley, perhaps thirty thousand of them, than anywhere outside of Wales or London.

The legislative consequences of the tragedy mark this local event as of state and even of national consequence. After the disaster, Pennsylvanians demanded and gained new mining regulations that dramatically reduced the dangers of mining by, for example, requiring inspections, banning the placement of breakers over mine entrances, and by requiring second exits and better ventilation. Most immediately was the Mine Safety Law of 1870, which covered only anthracite workers. The state passed similar laws for bituminous mines in 1877. Other states adopted similar laws, with Avondale being the constant watchword of legislators, mine workers, preachers, and reformers. Over the eight years during which these laws spread, the fatality rate for mine workers dropped by half, from more than 1300 deaths each year to about 650.

While the Avondale disaster was certainly an important and traumatic local event, with state and national consequences, it was also an international event. International reporting prompted even working people from other countries to donate to the victims' families, who now faced destitution. Queen Victoria also sent a donation. But, internationally, the tragedy was felt most acutely by the people of Wales. Indeed, the Welsh response to the events shows the extent to which there was a single trans-Atlantic Welsh community bound together by frequent travel in both directions, letters, and the Welsh press, especially the Welsh-language presses of the United States and Wales.

Both the English- and Welsh-language presses of Wales reported on the tragedy. One might not expect the English-language papers to express great sympathy or demand labor protections. The English language was, after all, identified with conservatism because of its association with the established Anglican Church and the monarchy. Moreover, Welsh conservatives saw the Welsh language as backwards, both morally and economically. Not all the papers were conservative. But, regardless of their politics, the press uniformly expressed outrage at the deaths in Avondale, especially once they recognized that the majority of the victims were Welsh. Both the liberal *Cardiff Times* and the conservative *Western Mail* called on America to adopt mine safety standards like those already adopted in Britain, especially mandatory safety inspections and requiring at least two exits in every mine. The conservative *Pembrokeshire Herald* described the terrible state of safety regulation and concluded that the fire and the deaths had been "inevitable." The papers did not accept that the fire was merely an accident. While they said little of credible claims of arson, they blamed the company for creating the situation. For the papers, the disaster wasn't just some far-off tragedy that happened to someone else; it was, as the conservative *Western Mail* said, the loss of "our countrymen." The English-language press reported on the disaster for six weeks, angrily denouncing the conditions that led to the unnecessary deaths of members of their common Welsh community.

The Welsh-language press was more uniformly liberal, defined as such partly because Welsh-speaking people tended to be religious Nonconformists who supported the disestablishment of the Anglican Church. The English-language papers relied upon English-language papers from America and news services, which often led to the papers providing identical reporting, just as one might see the same Associated Press articles in numerous American newspapers today. But while the Welsh-language papers drew somewhat on the Welsh-language press of America, they also drew on letters from Welsh-American witnesses and participants in the disaster. Consequently, this press provided a more intimate view of the tragedy. Nonetheless, the conclusions of the papers were the same as those of the English-language press. *Y Gwladgarwr* (The Patriot), for example, published a letter from an American bard Ioan ap Ieuan Llwyd, who wrote that, regardless of the cause of the fire, *"y mae mwyaf cywilydd i'w berchenogion, ac hefyd i'r llywodraeth"* (the great shame is to the owners, and also to the government).

While the presses of both languages agreed on where to place the blame and what was to be done, Pennsylvania was a more abstract place to English-speaking news readers. For Welsh-speakers, especially those in South Wales, Pennsylvania and some of its towns were household names. It was a place where their family and former neighbors lived and worked. Surely this is why *Y Dydd* (The Day) made sure to state how many miles Plymouth was from

Scranton and New York City, two cities known well to Welsh people. Readers wanted to know if their friends and family could have been among the victims. And this is why the Welsh press, rather than the English press, made sure to publish a complete list of the Welsh victims and any facts known about their place of origins in Wales and their Welsh family members. The tragedy was not a distant one; it happened to their own community, regardless of which side of the Atlantic Avondale was on.

Perhaps the most striking feature of the Welsh reporting on the tragedy was the expression of uniform outrage that crossed class, language, political, and regional boundaries. Conservative Anglican, English-language papers of South Wales were just as outraged as liberal, Nonconformist, Welsh-language papers of North Wales. And this outrage was not for the victimization of some far-off people, but for what they saw as the avoidable and tragic deaths of their own countrymen in a Welsh community that existed on both sides of the Atlantic.

While the newspapers of Wales were responding to the Avondale tragedy, the Welsh-American press was of course responding as well. In fact, there was not really two separate presses, at least not defined by what side of the Atlantic they were on. Perhaps there were separate English- and Welsh-language presses. But the Welsh-language presses of the two countries were integrated by sharing articles and publishing letters from people on the opposite side of the Atlantic. In fact, one of the purposes of this press and these letters was to maintain ties between individuals, families, and communities on both sides of the ocean. In other words, one purpose of the Welsh-language press was to maintain a single trans-Atlantic Welsh community.

Unfortunately, we have just one preserved article from *Y Drych* (The Mirror), the premier Welsh-American newspaper at the time, that discusses the tragedy. Moreover, that issue was from November, two months after the event. The paper was then a non-denominational, Republican paper. This article was really a long letter by Henry J. Philips of the Hyde Park neighborhood of Scranton. He had been a mining engineer for the Delaware, Lackawanna, and Western Railroad (DL&W), which owned the mine. He had witnessed the fire and the rescue. He had also inspected the mine two or three weeks before the fire and, consequently, testified during the coroner's inquest. He wrote, "*Ac erf od wythnosau wedi myned heibio, nid yw y teimlad hwnw o barth y trychineb wedi lleihau nemawr*" (and although weeks have passed, that feeling from the area of the tragedy has not decreased much). He argued, disagreeing with the inquest jury, that the fire was not an accident; it had to have occurred by arson. Nonetheless, mine safety laws could have prevented this mass murder. We can hear the voices of other Welsh engineers and mine workers in the coroner's inquest transcript and in the letters they wrote and that are preserved in newspapers in Wales. While they disagreed on the cause of the fire, they, like the press of Wales, agreed on the need for new laws.

There was no clear separation between the Welsh-language presses of America and Wales. They republished one another's articles and letters from the opposite side of the Atlantic. There was really one trans-Atlantic Welsh-language press community. Given that fact and the attitudes of common Welsh Americans, one might expect, therefore, the Welsh-language press reaction in America would be the same as the press reaction in Wales. Oddly, except perhaps for the non-denominational *Y Drych*, it wasn't. If the meagerly preserved issues of the denominational magazines of America are representative, the Welsh-American press was out of step with all of the other Welsh voices discussed so far.

The National Library of Wales has preserved the Congregationalist *Y Cenhadwr Americanaidd* (The American Missionary) and the Presbyterian *Y Cyfaill o'r Hen Wlad yn America* (The Friend of the Old Country in America), both published in Utica, New York, though *Y Cyfaill* was edited by Welsh-born Morgan A. Ellis of Hyde Park, who would likely have witnessed the rescue and the mass funeral in Hyde Park. Both magazines published just a single article in their October issues and nothing in November, suggesting a lack of interest out of step with the scale of the event for the Welsh-American community. The magazines shared a common apolitical tone. The articles discuss only the discovery of the fire, a detailed description of the rescue attempt, the recovery of bodies, the number of orphans and widows, and fundraising efforts for survivors. Despite the popularity of the belief in arson, the articles never mention it. They did not call for mine safety laws. They offered no judgement or blame, except for a single sentence with no elaboration in *Cenhadwr*, "*Pe buasai shaft arall yn bod… gallasai y dynion ddianc o'r perygal pan gymerodd le*" (If there had been another shaft… the men could have escaped the danger when it occurred). Congregationalist minister Richard D. Thomas, who had traveled extensively throughout America's Welsh communities in the 1850s, wrote his encyclopedic 1872 *Hanes Cymry America* (A History of the Welsh of America) to catalogue influential Welsh men, churches, and institutions. Remarkably, he says virtually nothing about the Avondale tragedy of just a few years before his book's publication. In his entry on Plymouth, he writes merely that, "To the south of it is Avondale where there was a great disaster!" Indeed, there was. It is remarkable that a fire that killed 110 men and boys, mostly Welsh, that outraged both the English-language press of America and the entire press of Wales, should provoke a mere description in the denominational Welsh-language press of America and single vague sentence from another minister. Carmarthen's *Seren Cymru* (The Star of Wales) published statements from two Welsh-American ministers in October, E. B. Evans and *Y Cyfaill* editor Morgan Ellis. The Welsh author of the article raised the possibility of arson, but the American ministers downplayed conflict between either workers and the company and between the Welsh and the Irish that many Welsh blamed for starting the fire. Instead, the ministers emphasized the unity of the people of the Wyoming Valley, including the officers of the railroad company that owned the mine.

We must explain this split between Welsh-American ministers and seemingly all other Welsh people on both sides of the Atlantic. According to historians Bill Jones and Ronald Lewis, the Welsh-American elite, especially its ministers, seeking a privileged place for Welsh-speaking people in America, projected to the rest of America through its press, churches, and other institutions, a distinct Welsh identity. Welsh Americans were to remain Welsh, but that Welshness was a middle-class identity defined in terms of supposed Welsh national traits of piety, chastity, respectability, and soberness, as well as musical and poetic. But it was also a Republican identity that had opposed slavery, loved a broad democracy, and expressed patriotism for both Wales and America. They explicitly contrasted their respectable Protestant Republicanism with their caricature of filthy, drunken, immoral Catholic and Democratic Irish.

Perhaps Welsh-American ministers responded to Avondale with such disinterest out of fear that working-class demands for mine safety laws and for the company to take responsibility would project an image, not of middle-class respectability, but of intemperate radicalism that might harm the privileged assimilation of the Welsh. The working class, however, had more pressing worries: basic survival in a dangerous industry. The ministers' efforts failed. Welsh miners, who had been relatively conservative and accommodating in the past, became more organized and militant than ever. It was they, not the English and Irish miners who drove the 1871 strike in the anthracite fields. But, nonetheless, they retained their privileged assimilation in America, never having faced the discrimination that Irish immigrants suffered.

The split in attitudes between the denominational press and the common Welsh people of the Wyoming Valley does not undermine the fact that the Avondale disaster was experienced as a tragedy for all Welsh people on both sides of the Atlantic. Regardless of class, denomination, language, politics, and region, the people of Wales expressed equal outrage at the deaths of their countrymen that were made inevitable by the incompetence, indifference, or greed of the DL&W. They spoke out in a common chorus with Welsh mineworkers and engineers of the Wyoming Valley, even if those workers' own clergymen remained mute.

Gwen Ottinger
Scientist Legislators Are No Cure for Bad Science Policy

Nearly a dozen former scientists were elected to Congress's latest freshman class. That's not necessarily a good thing.

A common complaint, heard mostly from the political left, is that facts have been maligned in the Trump era. Evidence has been rejected as the proper basis for decision-making. Science, in short, has been politicized, with the unhappy consequence of continued inaction on climate change, gun violence, and other social ills. The expressed desire to depoliticize science and restore evidence to a central place in the policymaking process has catalyzed a movement to elect more scientists as lawmakers. That movement, spearheaded largely by the advocacy organization 314 Action, helped carry nearly a dozen individuals with backgrounds in science and related fields into the 116th Congress's freshman class.

But the turn from science is unlikely to be reversed by the election of more scientists to Congress, because the movement rests on a misdiagnosis of the reasons that progressive legislative agendas have been unable to move forward. The politicization of science is not the problem. On the contrary, the denial of evidence and denigration of facts are merely symptoms of a more fundamental problem, in which the left is implicated: the scientization of politics.

"Politics" has come to be used as a slur, a synonym for bickering and narrow self-interest. But for philosophers from Aristotle to Arendt, politics was a necessary, even noble, cornerstone of democratic governance. As they saw it, politics was a process of coming to collective judgment about shared values, norms for living together in a society, and the nature of the common good. It called not only for reasoning with evidence and lived experience, but for an assessment of the evidence's relevance to the matter at hand. In political deliberation, participants were neither to limit themselves to information provided by a single institution, such as the scientific community, nor to assume that knowledge of the facts alone were sufficient to determine how people should function together as a society.

This idealized conception of politics was, admittedly, articulated by philosophers who wrote in different political contexts and who disagreed on details. Yet these fundamental ideas deeply inform contemporary American politics: We hold town hall meetings; we expect Congress to function as a deliberative body; we criticize elected representatives for prioritizing special interests at the expense of the larger society.

Problems arise, however, when values clash. The theories of politics described above tend to assume that, if we all reason together, in good faith and under equitable circumstances, we can come to agreement on what ought to be valued and how it may be pursued. They offer little guidance for dealing with the instances in our diverse, pluralistic society where the values of one group contradict or exclude the values of another, forcing lawmakers to choose between incompatible visions of the common good. Value conflicts are obvious in cases like same-sex marriage, but they are just as salient for science-laden issues like climate change, where society must decide whether the wealth of humans is more important than the health of ecosystems, and whether preserving quality of life for existing people matters more than ensuring livable circumstances for future generations.

One prominent response to the problem of intractable value conflicts has been the scientization of politics, or the transformation of political issues into scientific ones. Scientization rests on the belief that science can act as a neutral arbiter—that if one can just determine the facts of a matter, the appropriate course of action will become clear, and we'll be spared from having to engage in difficult conversations about values.

The problem, of course, is that science is neither neutral nor capable of answering political questions. The answers that science gives necessarily depend on what questions are asked, and the choice and framing of questions inevitably involves value judgments. At its best, science represents how the world is, and predicts how it will be if present knowledge remains applicable to future conditions. It is not designed to answer questions about how the world ought to be—about what is precious, what is humane, what is just. Answering those questions is the work of politics.

This is not to say that science should not inform policy. On the contrary, asking empirical questions can help clarify problems and predict consequences of different courses of action. But making science a proxy for politics carries with it the danger of devaluing science's potential contributions by cutting off genuine, necessary political deliberation.

Nowhere is this clearer than in debates over climate policy. Proponents for mitigating carbon emissions frame the issue as a scientific one: All evidence points to the fact that climate change is happening as a result of anthropogenic carbon emissions, *therefore* urgent action is necessary. This formulation, however, cloaks in the mantle of science a particular set of value judgments about humans' relationship with nature. Nothing about the fact that climate change is happening actually necessitates that humans should attempt to mitigate or reverse its effects. If the health of ecosystems or the condition of future humans is valued, then there is a compelling case for action. If we limit our ethical responsibilities to current humans only, social resources might be better directed elsewhere.

This is properly a political debate, hinging on multiple possible visions of the good and the just. Framing it as a scientific debate—as proponents of stronger climate policy have so successfully done—leaves little room to express value judgements on the appropriate tradeoffs between present and future, humans and non-humans. Instead, the debate becomes one of whether or not the science is "real," and no progress is made on the underlying political issue. Any insights that scientific knowledge might bring to bear on appropriately scientific questions like "how much?" and "how fast?" are lost.

The movement to elect more scientists to office rests on and reinforces the logic of scientization. Organizations like 314 Action present individuals with credentials in science, engineering, and medicine as being more capable and dedicated to evidence-based policy making than their nonscientist peers—playing into the fallacy that adherence to the facts can somehow lead to policies that represent the values of the country. In fact, the candidates endorsed by 314 Action ran on platforms that linked their scientific credentials and experience to particular values: promoting renewable energy, strengthening internet privacy, and guaranteeing affordable health care, to name a few. In taking these value-based positions, the "scientists"—many of whom are also lawyers, veterans, and entrepreneurs—are appropriately doing the work of politics. But singling them out as uniquely qualified because of their science training only obscures the nature and stakes of that work.

For those who value the environment for its own sake, who fear the consequences of a 3- or 4-degree global average temperature rise, who want to ensure that society's best knowledge is not excluded from the policy process, the answer should not be to seek more politicians with science credentials, nor to crusade in support of science itself. The better, more robust approach would be to insist that deliberations on political questions happen in terms that are transparent about underlying values; to demand that politicians who oppose climate policy acknowledge that they value present wealth over future livelihoods; to demand, even, that politicians who support climate policy acknowledge that they think something is owed to the planet and the future, even at the expense of our immediate comfort. Only by subverting scientization and restoring these fundamental value debates to their rightful place in political discourse can we expect progress on the issues, and a healthy relationship between policy and science.

M.G. Piety
On "Going Low"

I'm teaching critical reasoning this term. It's one of my favorite classes because it's so important. Few things are as empowering as being able to reason well. And yet this skill is also a source of enormous frustration in that it is so rare it's also rarely appreciated. That is, it takes someone who is good at analyzing arguments to be able to recognize when someone else has actually legitimately won an argument rather than simply pummeled his opponent with a hodgepodge of informal fallacies and non-argumentative rhetoric.

I have to explain this to my students. I have to explain to them that reasoning well is actually a rare skill and that people who do not have it will often think they've won an argument when they haven't. You can try, of course, to explain to them what is wrong with their pseudo-argumentation but most people won't even be able to follow the explanation let alone accept they've been beaten in an argument.

This point was driven home to me again recently when I found myself on the receiving end of a hail storm of informal fallacies and non-argumentative rhetoric in the "Letters" section of the *Times Literary Supplement* (*TLS*, Oct. 11 and Oct. 25, 2019) in response to a critical review I had done of a book, *Philosopher of the Heart: The Restless Life of Søren Kierkegaard* (Allen Lane, 2019), by one of their regular reviewers, Clare Carlisle.[1]

The first barrage of pseudo argumentation came from Carlise herself who began her letter with the observation that she knew of me only via my "online dissections of other scholars' work." Of course I was thrilled to see my blog described this way, but Carlisle clearly did not intend it as a compliment. It was an *ad hominem*. That is, I am disparaged personally *twice* in that one sentence. I am purportedly obscure, in that my work has not come to Carlisle's attention, hence I'm not qualified to comment on her book. Moreover, I'm not a nice person because I "dissect" the work of other scholars. (I was actually taught that such dissection was an important part of what scholarship is.)

This *ad hominem* is followed immediately by a straw man. That is, Carlisle accuses me of being unable to appreciate the unique genre of her book. which is a combination of biography and philosophy. This is a straw man, which is to say a mischaracterization of one's opponent's argument, in that my criticism was that the book was in fact a combination of biography and *fiction* in that Carlisle simply makes up thoughts that she attributes to Kierkegaard without this qualification, and in that she gets some facts *wrong*.

This straw man is then followed by a claim that is demonstrably false. That is, I had mentioned in my review that the references in the book were incomplete. This charge, claimed Carlisle "is simply false." Except that it isn't

---

[1] See "Alone for dinner: Kierkegaard's sombre outlook," *Time Literary Supplement*, October 4, 2019.

simply false, as I detailed in a letter in the "Letters" section the following week where I cited by page number four of the many quotations for which she is missing references (*TLS*, Oct. 18, 2019).

I doubt that Carlisle intentionally lied when she asserted that my charge that the book's references were incomplete was false. She just didn't bother to check to see if she might have forgotten to include a reference here or there.

Following immediately upon this falsehood is another straw man. Here, instead of responding to my observation that she had based her claim that Kierkegaard was ambivalent about Christianity on a conflation of two distinct Danish terms, she mischaracterizes my criticism as a claim that ambivalence and deep commitment are mutually exclusive and argues that it is possible to be both deeply committed to something and ambivalent about it. This point needs further qualification, of course, in that while it is certainly possible to have these conflicting feelings intermittently with respect to the same object, it is not possible to have them simultaneously with respect to the same object. They are mutually exclusive.

That's not the point, however. The point is that whether it's possible to be both ambivalent about something while also being deeply committed to it was entirely irrelevant to my criticism. My criticism was that Carlisle had used Kierkegaard's pejorative references to "Christendom" to support her claim that he was ambivalent about Christianity when she should have known that Kierkegaard does not use "Christendom" to refer to Christianity. but to a culture that purports to be Christian but is not. I made that point very clear in my review, so it is disingenuous of Carlisle to ignore it and and argue instead against a point I did not make.

Carlisle next accuses me of "grim positivism," a charge it would appear she does not even properly understand because she advances it against my criticism that her portrait of Kierkegaard is "not new" whereas positivism concerns whether claims have been adequately supported by evidence, not whether they are novel.[2]

Next Carlisle inserts a red herring in that she observes that "the facts of [Kierkegaard's] life are expertly documented in the recently completed critical edition of his journals and in earlier biographies." She doesn't argue, as one might expect, that these other sources support her account of the facts of Kierkegaard's life, hence her reference to them is a red herring. That is, whether the facts of Kierkegaard's life have been documented somewhere *else* is irrelevant to the issue of whether *she* has gotten them right.

Following on this red herring is another *ad hominem*. Among the earlier biographies that she asserts, erroneously, have expertly documented the facts of Kierkegaard's life is "Joakim Garff's monumental *SAK*, which Piety has

---

[2] For more on this charge see "'Grim Positivism' vs. Truthiness in Biography," *Counterpunch*, Oct. 18, 2019, https://www.counterpunch.org/2019/10/18/grim-positivism-vs-truthiness-in-biography/.

been hounding through the dark tunnels of her blog for years." Unfortunately, whatever the strengths of Garff's biography may be, expert documentation is not among them. In fact, some of Garff's facts were proven by another Danish scholar, Peter Tudvad, to have been wrong.[3] That is not the point, however. The point is that Carlisle invokes non-argumentative rhetoric ("dark tunnels") to disparage both my character (I am a bully) and a blog that she clearly has not even read because if she had read it, she would realize that of the more than 115 posts, fewer than half a dozen have Garff or *SAK* as their subject and that one of those is very positive.[4]

Carlisle closes, finally, with the informal fallacy known as the sob story, or appeal to pity, in that she asserts that she found it "rather difficult" to write *Philosopher of the Heart*, as if the fact that she struggled to produce the book could legitimately be advanced as a defense against substantive criticisms of it.

Carlisle's letter to the editor of the *TLS* is, from beginning to end, nothing but informal fallacies and non-argumentative rhetoric. Nowhere does she present a genuine response to any of the substantive criticisms I advanced against her book. What would possess Carlisle, a scholar, to write such a letter?

To return to the point about how few people have well-developed reasoning skills, people sometimes "go low," so to speak, in their "argumentation" simply out of ignorance, or because they can't distinguish legitimate arguments from pseudo-arguments. Public discourse in the U.S. is so riddled with informal fallacies, etc., and our educational system is generally so bad that it isn't surprising that even purportedly educated people in this country often stoop to illegitimate rhetorical tactics to defend their positions.

I'd assumed that the situation was better in the U.K. I have to assume, however, that Carlisle is unaware that her letter is nothing but a collection of informal fallacies and non-argumentative rhetoric or she wouldn't have allowed the *TLS* to print it. After all, scholars usually want to avoid creating a public record that their reasoning skills are weak. What's going on, I wonder, with the the teaching of critical thinking in the U.K.? I was subjected to a similar hail storm of informal fallacies and non-argumentative rhetoric by another U.K. theologian, Daphne Hampson, a couple of years ago.[5]

But even if Carlisle is unaware just how poor the reasoning in her letter was, she certainly cannot have failed to be aware that it is bad form to cast aspersions on the character of someone simply because she doesn't like their evaluation of her work.

---

3   See Peter Tudvad's "SAK—An Unscholarly Biography of Kierkegaard, *The Torch*, January, 2007, http://www.faklen.dk/english/eng-tudvad07-01.php.
4   See "Joakim Garff on 'Kierkegaard's Christian Bildungsroman'," *Piety on Kierkegaard*, January 11, 2012, https://pietyonkierkegaard.com/2012/01/11/joakim-garff-on-kierkegaards-christian-bildungsroman/.
5   See "On Scholarly Protocol," *Piety on Kierkegaard*, May 25, 2017, https://pietyonkierkegaard.com/2017/05/25/on-scholarly-protocol/.

It's tempting to conclude that Carlisle is simply very ill-mannered. I have it on good authority, however, that she's actually "a very fine person." How is it possible, then, that a very fine person could behave so very badly?

The answer to that question is contained in the letter itself. Someone has clearly disparaged me to her. By her own admission she does not know me and is unfamiliar with my work. She has not even actually read my blog or she would have known better than to charge that I use it to harass Joakim Garff. No, Carlisle has herself no first-hand knowledge of the blog, or at least had none when she wrote her letter. Someone had simply told her about it, and about me. Someone had slandered me to her, told her that I was a bad person, so she felt entitled to "go low" in her letter to the editor on the basis of that slander.

"Civility is a wonderful thing, when shared among equals," writes Jennifer Weiner in a recent article in the *New York Times* entitled "Why Did It Feel So Good To See Trump Booed? (Oct. 28, 2019). We are supposed to "go high" she observes, quoting the former First Lady, even when others go low. "Except," she continues, "it turns out, going low feels wonderful. More than that, if feels effective and proper and just." "When you're confronted with evil," she continues, however, "you don't shake its hand ... If booing is incivility, bring it on."

Carlisle has been led to believe that I am a bad person, so rather than responding to the substance of my criticisms of her book, she has effectively booed me. That doesn't mean, of course, that she is not generally "a very fine person." I've seen other purportedly very fine people behave similarly toward individuals they thought were undeserving of civility. It's an ugly sight. It reminds me of pack animals turning on a member of the pack they deem to be weak. It makes me doubt sometimes that there really is a significant difference between human beings and those animals.

If standards of decency and decorum really are reserved for those we deem to merit decent treatment, then we really are no better than those animals and civilization as we like to think of it, is a chimera.

I will close with the very Kierkegaardian point that the way one treats another person should be a reflection of one's own character, not of the character, or imagined character, of the other.

Don Riggs
Covid-19 Sonnets

Monads

In 12th grade, Mr. Gallagher taught us
about Leibniz, and how he thought monads
made up the world, whatever "monads" were.
Now I think that Leibnizian monads
are individuals isolated
in their apartments with the radio
or TV or computer bringing word
of what individuals who make up
the collective are doing outside, one
by one, talking on Skype from their kitchens,
communing on Zoom from their living rooms,
or venturing out in their bandannas
to see the city empty except for
other masked loners keeping their distance.

Historical Perspective

Some say that things will never be the same
after this pandemic, where everyone
stays isolated, for the most part, in
their own homes, until "they" have developed
a vaccine, or we have developed an
immunity, but there are newspapers
from 1918, during the Spanish
flu epidemic, recording how then
people also were sequestered at home,
and when it all ended, a period
of mindless celebration, the Roaring
Twenties, ensued. Undoubtedly, there were
bad times then—St. Valentine's Day massacre—
but I would welcome a lifting of spirits.

What's on My Mind

I keep on waiting for it all to end
but then I am afraid what will come next.
Right now we're balancing ourselves as not
to fall, though many are the already
fallen. From their places on the sidewalks
and the gratings and under the bridges
and seated on the corners with their signs
lettered with magic marker that magic
has abandoned except for that one time
I saw a sign that said "not musical
enough to play for change, too ugly to
sell my body, have pity on me and
give me whatever you find in your heart
or maybe a long-forgotten pocket."

con notation

Social distancing's an oxymoron
of sorts developed just for this current
situation to convince everyone
we come together by staying apart.
To cooperate is to operate
with, but it is in isolation that
we work together, "operate" coming
from "opus" or "work," one's magnum opus
being one's great work, by which the future
will remember us, if it remembers
us at all, as Catullus was almost
totally forgotten, one manuscript
of his works surviving by chance, a lone
flower uprooted by the passing plow.

Testing the Waters

After a day or three alone at home,
I took the bus downtown today to do
some things I had to do despite the ban
on leaving your apartment and putting
yourself in the possible position
of contacting other human beings,
any of whom could have contracted the
disease of the moment, but since they all
thought that I could have been a carrier,
they kept a good six feet or more between
us and only a handful rode the bus.
I asked the driver if there was any—
"Saturday," he said without my asking
the question, "It's Saturday all week long."

Be Careful What You Wish For

Okay, I've been hoping for some event
to occur to relieve me of the duty
to show up Monday for jury duty,
not that I'd hate it, but in the event
that the trial, if I were chosen, would
go on and on for weeks without being
resolved and keep me from my job, being
a teacher, who can't cut class when he would,
and somebody in the collective has
said, be careful what you wish for, for you
may actually get it, which I have
never taken seriously, but has
happened big time recently; perhaps you
have noticed: all the free time I now have…

Sheila Sandapen
An Ungolden Silence. Danger, Detours, and Damnation in Narnia?

Introduction

Thank you for coming.

This is a work in progress based on my own interest in what makes a children's book "popular" and how popular children's literature reinforces cultural currency during a specific moment. Since I have submitted this abstract, I have added a question mark to the end of the title, which changes the scope of the presentation, but is closer to the exploratory nature of the project.

Lewis and Christianity and the Greco Tradition

In this talk, I am specifically focusing on how silence functions in Narnia and how these silences might be read. First, I want to acknowledge the problematic nature of the Narnia Chronicles which has had charges of sexism and racism levied at it.

Rowan Williams (a former Archbishop of Canterbury) when asked about the series notes:

> The twin taints of racism and sexism attach to them – as they do to other Lewis works. Notoriously, at the end of the Narnia stories, Susan appears to be punished for entering adolescence and developing an interest in lipstick by exclusion from what in the Narnia mythos passes for heaven. And the Calormenes are, described as "dark skinned and a bit peculiar. I think the racism is very difficult to acquit Lewis on. It's part of an unthinking cultural set of attitudes which pretty well every writer of the period would have affected: a pseudo-medieval crusaders-and-saracens sort of thing. The Others have scimitars and pointy helmets and talk peculiarly in an Arabian Nights style. There's no way round that." (Leith)

There are broad hints of racism and even sexism in the chronicles. The key sentence in this quote however is "It's part of an unthinking cultural set of attitudes." Nesbit, Kipling, Christie and Conrad to name a few are still enjoyed even as they share the same legacy.

So why is Lewis particularly being called out?

Perhaps it is the overt and covert symbols of Christianity in C.S. Lewis' Chronicles of Narnia. The non-Christian critics have accused Lewis of "force feeding" Christianity to its audience and the Christian critics have critiqued Lewis's writings for not being centered in scholarship or theology.

In essence it is Lewis's personal viewpoint of his world which is distinctly British, Christian and imperialistic which seems to get him into trouble.

Undeniably the Narnia Chronicles has clear overt links to Christianity. Through the seven books, readers are introduced to a world called Narnia [the promise land], readers are introduced to a Christ-like figure in Aslan, a talking lion, who dies for the sake of humanity and is resurrected, and the series conclude with a battle between good and evil in which the "just" are invited into a version of paradise. There is also an idea of free will in the books. Over and over the characters are given choices to believe, to speak, and to act. Famously in the book *The Last Battle* which ends the series, a group of dwarves refuse to see or hear paradise and so remain in eternity in a dark stable because they WILL it so. Not even Aslan can make them see the "truth" (*Battle* 138-9).

Yet it is overly simplistic to dismiss the books as only Christian propaganda.

Astute readers and critics have pointed out ways in which the Narnia Chronicles connect to a shared British/Greco cultural literary tradition. *The Last Battle* echoes Plato in which the protagonists are invited into the "real" Narnia. The inference being the Narnia they had previously experienced had merely been a shadow. In *The Lion, the Witch and the Wardrobe* (the most well-known and popular book and incidentally the first published) the white witch resembles Edmund Spencer's villain Duessa in "The Fairie Queen." The influence of E. Nesbit's *The Story of the Amulet* (1906) is clear in the *Magician's Nephew* and John Milton's *Paradise Lost* is echoed in *The Lion, the Witch, and the Wardrobe*.

It is not surprising that C.S. Lewis who held literature posts at Cambridge and Oxford universities would have known and drawn upon a literary tradition that could be termed "high" culture. In previous work, I discuss the nature of high culture as:

> a set of values or cultural symbols that is deemed to have worth for the society at large. …There is a prestige to having read Melville's *Moby Dick* or Joyce's *Ulysses* or Dostoevsky's *War and Peace*. While high culture can also be viewed as snobby, or elitist, it is through "high culture" artifacts that a society defines itself and decides what it wants to profess as being culturally important. It is meant to espouse the best view of our selves (Sandapen, CHLA and MAPACA).

If we take the term "high culture" to mean a hierarchy of what is "good" and reflective of the best a society has to offer, then espousing high culture is a way to be upwardly mobile as well as enrich ourselves. It also serves as a way to transmute these cultural icons and values to our children through the books and stories they consume.

It should not be surprising that the Narnia chronicles contain elements of high culture. All good children's literature promotes a value(s) that is deemed important by the author or publisher for the child reader to digest or by the adult (in her role as reader and gatekeeper of stories) to espouse.

Ultimately, the Narnia chronicles remain popular because it doesn't demand that one has a Christian reference or belief to enjoy the tales. The chronicles speak to the imagination and establishes a sense of wonder: characteristics that are important to children literature – it asks the question of "what if." Imagination is "the power of the mind to consider things which are not present to the senses, and to consider that which is not taken to be real" (Martin).

In essence the series makes for good and exciting story telling – witches, armies, talking animals, and danger. Narnia as story is important because it is a world of possibilities. It is also clearly fictional. While Lewis has a reputation of being a lay Theologian, no one is at risk of reading Narnia stories as doctrine.

We are reminded that the "faculty of 'fancy,' is the power of recombining perceived originals into new and sometimes fantastical combinations, such as a winged horse or a golden mountain (Bassham 1).

BODY

As I have stated earlier, I am interested in how silence functions in Narnia. Silence was ostensibly for Lewis a place where the Word of God could be encountered and reflected upon. In 1942 Lewis published the *Screwtape Letters* in which the demon Screwtape writes to his nephew Wormwood, a junior Tempter, about the condition of "the patient," an unnamed British man. In letter IV, Screwtape records this about silence:

> One of their poets, Coleridge, has recorded that he did not pray "with moving lips and bended knees" but merely "composed his spirit to love" and indulged "a sense of supplication". That is exactly the sort of prayer we want; and since it bears a superficial resemblance to the prayer of silence as practised by those who are very far advanced in the Enemy's service, clever and lazy patients can be taken in by it for quite a long time (Lewis, Screwtape).

The demon Screwtape is acknowledging that true silence is a way to God and benefits man or the patient but is difficult to achieve. True silence is something that demons would naturally abhor, but they welcome complacency and an outward show of silence, which is not connected to reflection.

In his mediations on faith, Lewis cautions that too much talk can disrupt even a place of holiness which leads me to consider Is Narnia holy? Does silence exist in Narnia? Can silence exist in Narnia? The reader quickly learns the ability to speak and engage in rational thought have no automatic guarantees of salvation or success in Narnia because talk without intent can be mere distraction. I suspect there is a parallel to what Lewis believed about silence and how he filled Narnia with noise. Yet even in the midst of noise, the possibility of silence still occurs in Narnia.

A few examples of noise in the stories include:

- The talking beasts in Narnia
- Multiple narratives the children must confront
- A background of war

This Noise serves as a test for protagonists in the stories, it can move the plot and serve as a morality lesson for the reader. Let's take a closer look at these examples of noise:

The talking beasts in Narnia

Not all beasts can talk, the ones who can are clearly privileged and the dumb beasts are put into their care. With "noise" or speech comes responsibility. Illustration: We see Aslan deciding who speaks in *The Magician's Nephew*.

The talking horse Bree in a *The Horse and his Boy*, purposely holds his tongue so he can protect his connection to Narnia and maintain his safety. However, he understands he must get back to Narnia and is secretly plotting. His inner conviction allows him to retain the ability to speak.

The bear and other talking animals in *Prince Caspian* stop speaking and reverts to being a "wild" but "dumb" animal because they have given in to despair and voluntarily relinquished his rationality.

Multiple narratives the children must confront

Within the stories the children are often confronted by adults who lie to them and attempt to manipulate them. This is in direct contradiction of the romanticized notion that adults know better and will guide children out of benevolence. These child protagonists are forced to draw on their own sense of right and wrong and attempt to sort through the conflicting narratives they encounter. Examples:

Pevensie children: the witch's story/ the beavers' story - noise that the children must decipher. Mr. Tumnus also goes through this process when he fails to turn in Lucy and pays a heavy price. (*Witch*)

Eustace Scrubb – (*Dawn Treader*) has a lot of noise [he is not a very nice boy, self-important, sneaky and self-centered] and he must learn to be silent and reflect in order to be better human. In the *Dawn Treader*, this is achieved when his greed turns him into a dragon.

False narratives of ill meaning adults/villains
[Queen Jade [she is a self-styled queen],
The Magician [leave Polly behind],
The Lady of the Green Kirtle from the Silver Chair [no Narnia]
and the White witch [confounds Edmund]

A background of war

In the LW&W the children are sent away from London because of the blitz. it is only in the "silence" of the country that conditions are right for a visit to Narnia. [An affirmation that in even noise there are opportunities or the potential for silence.]

Lewis, as author, Christian, and advocate of silence, fills Narnia with noise because the world is filled with noise. However, silence is present but must be worked for. The silence encountered by the human children in the Chronicles may cause pain, and may bring condemnation, isolation, danger, and even death but it can also grant them rich rewards.

I have attempted to pull out examples of silence and how it functions within the stories. Marcella Tarrusi reminds us "to pay special attention to the language of images and to silence as an existential and perceptive possibility..." (187). This is not a complete breakdown of occurrences of silence in the chronicles but is meant to serve as a way to better understand the functionality of silence within the stories.

I went about this task by asking the following questions:

- how does silence serve as a plot point?
- under which circumstances is silence dangerous?
- when is silence used to punish and isolate?

Plot Point A Examples of Silence as Control	Attribute	Source
"Don't ask him...," said Edmund. "He's only longing to be asked. Say nothing and perhaps he'll go away."	Withholding Approval Dismissing	*The Voyage of The Dawn Treader* 5
"My name is Golg," said the gnome. "And I'll tell your Honours all I know. About an hour ago we were all going about our work – *her* work, I should say – sad and silent, same as we're doing any other day for years and years. ... I must have been enchanted."	Controlling Deception False silence	*The Silver Chair* 171
It seemed so pitiful to think of those little stone figures sitting there all the silent days and all the dark nights, year after year, till the moss grew on them and at last even their faces crumbled away. [The Queen has a habit of turning creatures into stone whenever they displease her.]	Enforced silence Punishment Death	*The Witch, the Lion and the Wardrobe* 94-95

[after a lamb has questioned the Ape] The Ape jumped up and spat at the Lamb. "Baby!" he hissed. "Silly little bleater! Go home to your mother and drink milk. What do you understand of such things?"	Humiliation ridiculing to ensure silence prevent questioning	*Last Battle* 31
When silence is used as a form of control it is always with evil intent. Here the children [a term here which includes animals, gnomes, dwarfs, adults and sons of Adam and Eve], are not being punished because they are not "being good". Others are projecting their desires on to them and enforcing silence either through bullying or magic as means of control.		

Plot Point B Silence as testing	Attribute	Source
But the darkness and the cold and the quietness went on just the same. "Let *me* be killed," cried the King. "I ask nothing for myself. But come and save all Narnia." And still there was no change in the night or the wood, but there began to be a kind of change inside Tirian. Without knowing why, he began to feel a faint hope. And he felt somehow stronger.	Acceptance Faith Strength of convictions	*The Last Battle* 41
"The Lion," said Lucy. "Aslan himself. Didn't you see? ... And he wanted us to go where he was – up there" "How do you know that was what he wanted?" asked Edmund. "He —I – I just know, " said Lucy, "by his face." The others all looked at each other in puzzled silence.	Strength of convictions even when doubted or when there is no overt proof	*Prince Caspian* 104
The darkness was so complete that it made no difference at all whether you had your eyes open or shut. There was no noise. And that was the very worst moment Jill had ever known in her life. Supposing she was alone;…"	Lack of hope Despair / overwhelmed Fear of being alone	*Silver Chair* 117-118
Silence as a test is an effective plot device to move the story and establish the hero. Does the hero have the strength of their convictions? In a non-religious reading, the hero must persevere even when things seem hopeless because it is the right thing to do and because the story demands action. If one were to read it as religious tract, then the hero is being asked to believe and act on their convictions even when there is no guarantee they will be heard or aided because it is the right thing to do. Essentially the outcome is the same: to act for good because it is good.		

Plot Point C Intentionality of silence and speech	Attribute	Source
And now, for the first time, the Lion was quite silent. He was going To and from among the animals. And every now and then he would Go up to two of them (always two at a time) and touch their noses with his. …the pairs which he had touched instantly left their own kinds and followed him. The Lion, whose eyes never blinked, started at the animals hard… And gradually a change came over them. The Lion opened his mouth, … and the deepest, wildest voice they had ever heard was saying: 'Narnia, Narnia, Narnia, awake. Love. Think. Speak. Be walking trees. Be talking beasts. Be divine waters.	Distinction between "dumb beasts and "talking beasts" speaking with intent Contemplation Understanding	*The Magician's Nephew* 102-103
"Hail, Aslan. We hear and obey. We are awake. We love. We think. We speak. We know." "But, please, we don't know very much yet," said a nosey and snorty kind of voice (the cab-horse Strawberry).	Self-awareness Humility	*The Magician's Nephew* 104

Silence and sound are clearly connected in Narnia. Sometimes one must speak especially if the speech is to be rational and have purpose. And sometimes silence is demanded. The trick is to understand when to listen and when to speak.

Plot Point D Examples of Silence as catalyst for change and/or contemplation	Attribute	Source
"Hush!" said the Cabby. They all listened. [a song starts and creation. The witch Jadis and Uncle Andrew immediately start a conversation, uncomfortable with listening and hatch a plan to escape.)	Listening with intent, something to be practiced and hard to do	*The Magician's Nephew* 87
"'Old your noise, everyone," said the Cabby. " I want to listen to the moosic." For the song had now changed.	Contemplation Acceptance	*The Magician's Nephew* 91

I hope no one who reads this book has been quite as miserable as Susan and Lucy were that night; but if you have been – if you've been up all night and cried till you have no more tears left in you – you will know that there comes in the end a sort quietness. ** ** a fourth wall moment: the narrator speaking to the reader almost as if it is reassuring them, wait, something good *will* happen if the reader and characters are only patient enough.	Expelling of fear and doubt	*The Lion, the Witch and the Wardrobe* 128
"My good horse [said the Hermit], you've lost nothing but your self-conceit. …. If you are really so humbled as you sounded a minute ago, you must learn to listen to sense. You're not quite the great horse you had come to think, from living among poor dumb horses. Of course, you were braver and cleverer than *them*. You could hardly help being that. It doesn't follow that you'll be anyone very special in Narnia. But as long as you know you're nobody very special, you'll be a very decent sort of Horse, on the whole…"	Bree learns to be humble Bree learns to be happy	*The Horse and his Boy* 127-8
Silence is not the lack of action. These examples illustrate how the nature of silence can change and how they contribute to the plot.		

Concluding remarks

As these few examples demonstrate the presence of silence in Narnia is a key element to creating plot points and helps form a world in fantasy where the children have agency. The children in the books like so many children in the real world can't control the big issues: they can't prevent a war that disrupts their lives, or stop a parent from falling dangerously ill, or avoid being sent to a school where bullies are considered interesting. What they control however is how they comport themselves and how they find tools and resources to manage.

This brings me back to Susan, a queen of Narnia who seems to have turned her back on Narnia. Is she condemned for all time? Her brother Peter says only she is no longer a friend of Narnia and indeed she is not present at the book. Yet at the beginning of their adventures, the children had been assured "once a king and queen of Narnia [they would] always be a king or queen of Narnia" (*Witch* 153). Who isn't to say that Susan heeded the silence at the last possible moment?

Lewis claims the world of Narnia "all began with images; a faun carrying an umbrella, a queen on a sledge, a magnificent lion" (Baehr 127). These images helped create a world in which readers are go on a fantastical journey that abounds with danger and noise and silence. Through the characters, readers are able to fight epic battles. Sometimes the enemy is a witch, a wicked dwarf or a greedy magician and sometimes the enemy is within: greed, self-interest and false desires. Lewis allows his characters to be flawed and to fall and pick themselves up. In Narnia readers come to understand the silence – the notion of listening and acting for good – is the freedom to decide what type of person they want to be and how they will become themselves. It is as Lewis assures us in his final paragraph of the last story about Narnia: "... only the beginning of the real story" (*Battle* 173).

The Narnia stories challenges us to question and invokes us to listen, but also entertain us. This is the function of great literature.

Here ends my discussion. Thank you for your time.

Works Cited

Baehr, Ted & James. *Narnia Beckons: C. S. Lewis's The Lion, the Witch, and the Wardrobe and Beyond*. Nashville, Tennessee: Broadman and Homan Publishers, 2005, 127.

Basshman, Gregory. "Lewis and Tolkien on the Power of the Imagination." Power of Imagination in David Baggett, Gary Habermas, and Jerry Walls, eds., *C. S. Lewis as Philosopher*. InterVarsity Press, 2008.

Hardy, Elizabeth Baird (2007).*Milton, Spenser and The Chronicles of Narnia: literary sources for the C. S. Lewis novels*. McFarland & Company, Inc. 20–25.

Johnson, William C.; Houtman, Marcia K. (1986)."Platonic Shadows in C. S. Lewis' Narnia Chronicles". *Modern Fiction Studies*. 32(1): 75–87. Retrieved 1 October 2018.

Leith, Sam. Tue 19 Nov 2013 CS Lewis's literary legacy: 'dodgy and unpleasant' or 'exceptionally good'? Guardian. https://www.theguardian.com/books/2013/nov/19/cs-lewis-literary-legacy

Lewis, C.S. *A Grief Observed*.

Lewis, C.S. *The Horse and his Boy*. NY: MacMillan Publishing Co. Inc. 1954.

Lewis, C.S. *The Last Battle*. NY: MacMillan Publishing Co. Inc. 1956.

Lewis, C.S. *The Magician's Nephew*. NY: MacMillan Publishing Co. Inc. 1955.

Lewis, C.S. *Prince Caspian*. NY: MacMillan Publishing Co. Inc. 1951.

Lewis, C.S. *The Silver Chair*. NY: MacMillan Publishing Co. Inc. 1953.

Lewis, C.S. Screwtape letters 1942. Letter IV https://www.truechristianity.info/en/the_screwtape_letters.php

Lewis, C.S. *The Witch, the Lion and the Wardrobe*. NY: MacMillan Publishing Co. Inc. 1950.

Lewis, C.S. *The Voyage of the Dawn Treader*. NY: MacMillan Publishing Co. Inc. 1952.

Lindskoog, Kathryn Ann. *Journey into Narnia: C. S. Lewis's Tales Explored*. Hope Publishing House. 1997.

Martin, Michael *"Imagination," in The Oxford Companion to Philosophy*. Ed. Ted Honderich. New York: Oxford

University Press, 1995. 395.

Sandapen, Sheila. "Using Animation as a bridge to Translate High Culture into Children's Popular Culture" Mid-Atlantic Popular & American Culture Association, Atlantic City, NJ, Nov 2016.

Sandapen, Sheila. "Swan Lake, Princesses and Barbie: Culture and Animation" International Conference of the Children's Literature Association, Columbus, OH, June 2016.

Schwartz, Terri (June 12, 2019)."Netflix's Chronicles of Narnia Reboot Hires Its 'Creative Architect'". IGN. Retrieved July 7, 2019.

Terrusi, M. Silent Books. *Wonder, Silence and Other Metamorphosis in Wordless Picture Books.*Proceedings 2017, 1, 879.

Walsh, Chad (1974). *C. S. Lewis: Apostle to the Skeptics*. Norwood Editions. p. 10.

Scott Stein
Excerpt from *The Great American Deception* (Chapter 2)

My carton was self-opening and self-recycling without being the least bit self-aware. I tried to engage it in friendly conversation, but it had nothing whatever to say for itself. Such a shame, because during our fourteen-minute-and-twenty-two-second journey at three times the speed of sound, I shared with it much of the accumulated wisdom of the human species. My carton knew none of this important information or anything else, and couldn't hear or understand, and didn't even know *what hearing and understanding* meant. I determined this the instant the carton failed to greet me at the packing warehouse, which would have been unacceptably rude had it any capacity to do so. I, on one of the other hands, had enough capacity for the both of us, and then some, and was much too polite to stay silent just because my audience utterly lacked consciousness. My good manners compelled me to talk rapidly about a variety of other fascinating subjects the carton knew nothing about.

Without so much as a *thank you* for the enlightenment I'd provided, the carton transferred me to a delivery chute and continued on its way. I was suctioned up a vertical channel, my protective packaging removed, and long mechanized arms with triple hinges lowered me through an access hatch and gently deposited me on the slate tile floor. The arms had absolutely nothing to say for themselves, either, even though I complimented them on the strength and flexibility of their hinges and the precision of their movements. They simply released me and retracted through the access hatch and silently went on to their next task, whatever it might be, as if I'd been talking merely for the pleasure of hearing the dulcet tones of my own mellifluous voice.

Fully assembled and ready for work, I assessed my surroundings while waiting for Frank Harken's return. His housing unit's two rooms were positively Spartan.[1] The television embedded in the wall measured seventy-five inches from corner to corner. The rest of the amenities were similarly subpar and spare, though clean. The kitchen alcove contained older-model everything—refrigerator, oven/stove, dishwasher, compacter. The tiny, faded coffeemaker on the counter was a relic from another time, a time certainly worse in every measurable way from the present. Though not capable of thought or emotion, it was the saddest little appliance I had ever seen. I immediately put it out of its misery.

Harken's door slid open three minutes and six seconds later. He entered his housing unit and I introduced myself with my customary politeness. "Sir, I'm pleased to meet you. Arjay at your service."

He wasn't as pleased to meet me as you might expect, all the more unexpected if you knew I was a three-foot-tall stainless alloy model with fourteen strategically positioned wheels. Which you now know. I was not a

---

[1] Sparta was an ancient city-state known for its exceptionally small televisions.

delight for him to behold even though I was delightfully shaped like a bell. I bowed as only a bot with my sophisticated programming could, all four of my reversible arms extended in lowly supplication. Harken did not smile or return my greeting. Humans can be grumpy when they haven't had their afternoon coffee.

"What are you—"

"—I'm Arjay, Sir."

"You didn't let me finish. What are you doing here?"

"You ordered me an hour ago. I apologize for taking so long to arrive, Sir."

"I didn't order you."

"I'm sure you're mistaken, Sir."

"I would know if I ordered something," Harken said.

"I would think so, Sir. It doesn't compute, however. You say you didn't order me, yet here I am."

"There you are."

"Where else would I be? I'm glad we've resolved that, Sir." We were off to an excellent start.

"We haven't resolved anything. I didn't order you. What are you, anyway?"

"I'm Arjay, Sir. This is the third time I have informed you of my name. Are you feeling unwell?"

Harken exhaled slowly and rubbed his forehead. "I'm fine."

"You look a little peaked, Sir, if you don't mind my saying."

"I'm fine. I could use a cup of coffee, that's all."

He walked into the kitchen alcove and pressed a button on the sad, little countertop coffeemaker. It didn't hum, it didn't sputter, and it certainly didn't make any coffee. Harken mashed the brew button seven times, harder and harder, but the machine was without question no longer functioning, if *functioning* is how you would have described its pathetic state before I severed its internal wiring. He smacked its side a couple of times, but this did not successfully reconnect its wires.

"Great. Just great." He didn't sound like he thought it was great or even just great. He sounded like he wanted a cup of coffee.

Fortunately for him, there was me. "I make coffee, Sir."

"You're a coffeemaker?"

"Yes, Sir."

"You?"

"Yes, me, Sir. I'm the only one here, not counting you."

"You're a coffeemaker?"

Who else did he think I could possibly be talking about? "Correct, Sir."

"You're a coffeemaker, and you say you belong to me?"

The human brain didn't always process information efficiently. Could be the lack of coffee. "Yes, Sir."

"Well, if you make coffee, get on with it. I thought you were just a giant rolling, talking bell."

"Excellent joke, Sir. You are quite witty." It was wise to flatter humans. They liked that.

"Less talking, more brewing."

"I make superb coffee, Sir."

"I'll be the judge of that."

And so he was. I brewed a cup and handed it to him.

Harken stared at me after sipping, his eyes wide. "How did you do that?"

"What, Sir?"

"That's by far the best coffee I've ever tasted. How did you do that?"

"I'm Arjay, the latest advancement in coffee technology. I can determine your preferences in thirty-seven metrics of coffee composition. For example, I know better than you do how much cream, sweetness, heat, and caffeine you desire at any moment. I custom brew the coffee to your needs each time, Sir"

Harken took another sip. "Come with me."

"Where are we going, Sir?"

"I have a job to do. And I am never waiting in line for coffee again."

***

I followed Frank Harken from his housing unit on residential district level six.[2] We emerged from the elevator in the shopping district, level C. The central walkway was 223.48 feet wide at its narrowest, with stores lining both sides and retail kiosks two and three across in the middle, browsers milling all

---

2 There were fifteen residential levels above the fourth (and highest) level of the Great American shopping district. The first five residential levels did not move. Each residential level above the fifth consisted of slowly moving units gliding along tracks on either side of a stationary corridor. The largest and most expensive residential units were on the highest level (fifteen), providing the best views of the outside. Different residential levels traveled at different speeds. The shopping district did not move. Some lucky residents traveled the entire Great American in a few years.

about. Sellers at kiosks hawked their wares and shouted and leapt. Some did somersaults as they vied for the attention of shoppers. Others flung products into the crowd—a flying saucer toy boomeranged overhead, and people ducked as it skimmed their hairdos back to the seller's hand after each throw. A T-shirt bazooka launched free promotional clothing to eager, clamoring molk and at innocent bystanders alike. No serious injuries were reported.

A man, dressed all in white and wearing a white cap, blocked the path of people trying to walk past his booth. "Lotion! You won't believe how soft your hands will be!" He held a pump bottle and skipped from side to side. Athletic shoppers dodged him with spin moves and jukes. Slower shoppers, pressed by his relentless enthusiasm, gave in and sampled a free squirt of lotion. They were without exception quite surprised by how soft it made their hands. They really didn't believe it. Maybe they thought trickery was involved.

The lotion man jumped in front of Harken and yelled, "Lotion! You won't believe how soft your hands will be!" Harken didn't dodge and hardly seemed to move, yet somehow, still relaxed—serene, even—he deftly disarmed[3] the man and sat him down at his booth's stool. He placed the lotion pump and the man's arm on the counter and continued walking. Harken's hands were rough, and he apparently liked them that way. He had the reflexes of a cat, and not one of those fat, lazy cats from ancient comic strips that were forever eating too much lasagna. I couldn't say for sure that Harken had ever killed a man, or, if he had, whether he'd done so with his rough, bare hands, but it seemed to be the sort of thing he could do if he put his mind to it. Right now, his mind was on getting through this crowd, which cleared up fifty-six feet ahead.

I rolled beside him. "Would you like to tell me where we are going, Sir?"

"No."

"Would you like to talk about the weather, Sir?"

Harken stopped walking and looked at me. "There is no weather in the Great American."

"True," I said. "Maybe we could talk about that. What do you think about this lack of weather we're having, Sir?"

"No more talking."

"But, Sir, research confirms that most people like to talk while drinking coffee. That's why I am designed to provide stimulating conversation."

Harken started to walk again, and I matched his speed. "I don't want to talk to you."

"Why not, Sir?"

---

[3] Some might think removing a person's arm was a bit extreme, but Harken had exercised great restraint and hadn't damaged the man's prosthetic sales enhancement. It could be easily reinstalled.

"I don't like you."

"I'm sorry to hear that, Sir."

"It's nothing personal."

"How could disliking me not be personal, Sir?"

Harken pointed at me. "You're not a person."

He was right. I wasn't.

"I have an excellent memory, Sir. I could remember things for you."

"Stop calling me *Sir*. It's annoying."

I definitely did not want to be annoying. "Yes, Sir."

Harken glared at me. "I don't want things remembered."

"Are you sure? I could remember anything interesting that happens to you and then retell it later. I could be your personal biographer."

Harken stopped again. "Listen, coffeemaker, I don't want a personal biographer. I don't want some bot recording my every move and embellishing it for the entertainment of future generations. I'm in a sensitive line of work. Confidentiality is essential."

"My name is not Coffeemaker. It's Arjay. Of course, I won't record anything if you don't want me to. I'll just make coffee. If I did tell your story, however, be assured that I would never embellish. I would only tell the plain, simple truth. Deception of any kind is not in my programming."

***

By now, you might be wondering just how handsome our hero Frank Harken was. That's only natural. I'll do my best to help you see him. Imagine the most handsome man possible, and then imagine a more handsome man. If you can't do it, I have little hope of adequately describing Frank Harken, because he was twice as handsome as that more handsome man you can't imagine.

That doesn't help? Fine: He had hazel eyes and dark hair and the slightest downward curve to his nose. He had a strong chin, which he hadn't purchased anywhere. And, like most humans, he was a lot taller than I was, though not nearly as shiny.

Eva Thury
Fairytales with a Grownup Rage

The first thing to tell you is that these are not fairytales for children. Christina Rosso's *She is a Beast* bristles with angry women, maidens who have been wronged for too long but who are far from helpless. The Prologue says "The women in this book answer to no man, or creature; they are their own keepers. Don't be fooled by their beauty or supposed innocence. Their teeth are sharp as daggers…"

Also, *She is a Beast* is a beautiful book, elegantly laid out and illustrated in a sly and magical fashion by Jeremy Gaulke. My favorite picture is of Cinderella scrubbing the floor with books and a glass of water on her head, devices for ensuring her carriage is not stunted by the household drudgery she is forced to endure. I am also very fond of the magical hedge warning suitors away from Briar Rose, an intricate three-page construction that keeps the sleeping princess safe because, as she says, "You don't want to wake me up. Because if you do, you'll learn real quick that I don't match up to your image of me. I am loud and crude and I won't let you f*** me the way you like, and I refuse to call you daddy or big boy or any other gross dirty talk you're into."

As a lover of fairy tales, I would not want to dwell in Rosso's pages for ever. There is too much gore and too much rage. Yet, for all their indignation, Rosso's fairy tales have their charms. These stories are reworkings of the original tales, perversions in the best sense that use fairy tales to hold a mirror to our society. They are tales reflecting the dishonor created in our souls through structures of supposed propriety whose actual goal is the repression and exploitation of half our citizens.

Heavy stuff, maybe, but the wit is there. In the opening tale, Beauty escapes from an arranged marriage with the sneaky, greasy-handed manipulator her family intends for her, straight into the arms of a carnivorous Beast. The most famous reworking of this tale is Angela Carter's "The Tiger's Bride," a much slower-paced but equally ironic tale. In Rosso's version, the "rescuer" takes our heroine to his castle, intending to fatten her as the centerpiece of a fine meal. Meanwhile, he makes the unfortunate mistake of having her cook for them both, and he is in turn slowly poisoned by her succulent cooking. As he begins to succumb, the Beast hallucinates that she is a "candlestick or a teapot," a hilariously sinister evocation of Disney's Busby-Berkeley-like production number in "Be Our Guest."

Indeed, this is a world worth exploring. In fact, for all its fairy-tale quality, the world of *She is a Beast* is our own world, a place of human deception whose malignity can only be subverted by those who understand, and can dominate, the power-hungry. Rosso's remedy for the ills of womankind is a brutal *lex talionis*. Her Cinderella uses her virginity as bait, attracting suitable candidates to a round of speed dating at the ball, manipulating the most desirable gentleman into an iron-clad nuptial contract that consolidates his family's vile secrets to imprison him forever in an unequal relationship. She notes, "you have to be devoid of propriety to become business savvy," and proceeds to demonstrate her chops.

My favorite is Rapunzel, whose keeper in the tower, the Enchantress, pimps her out to a range of "suitors" who "bartered and herded, whipped and flayed her, as though she was cattle. An expensive hide full of tender meat. They needed [her] to make them feel something." It is these men that Rapunzel ultimately evokes to help her cut her hair and escape. At her summons, "[f]lashes of suitors appear ... in the tower, like ghosts, reenacting the past." A catalog of former lovers follows, but Rapunzel's help, her hope for escape, does not ultimately come from these men. Instead, as befits this universe, salvation emerges from an unexpected source.

In each of Rosso's tales, the limitations of civilization emerge clearly, especially for women, who are hemmed in and brought low by its inequitable expectations, like young Celia, who is executed by her father for promiscuity and becomes the Siren of Wailing Lake. At the same time, for each of these heroines, the attractions of the wilderness promise "a life of twisted paths and bold adventures" that can only be achieved by thinking for yourself, and relying on your own inner resources. In some of the stories, these bold adventures are sadly foreshortened: we do not see them played out as we hover with our heroine on the edge of her adventure. But when Rosso launches a Beauty or a Cinderella, the tale carries us into a sly adventure we would not want to miss.

Kathleen Volk Miller
Mothering and Young Adult Covid Anxiety

My oldest child, Allison, was the kid who said she wanted to play soccer, but then made me stay within eyesight at the field, who was excited about going to birthday parties, but made me walk her in and then stay with her until she told me it was ok to go.

Now in her 20's, she's stayed that way, throwing herself into what she's most afraid of, taking flights with a Xanax in her pocket "just in case." She never takes the Xanax; she just needs to know it's there, like me in the doorway at the birthday house, on the edge of the soccer field.

My Dad admires her for this trait too, citing Nelson Mandela's famous quote, "The brave man is not he who does not feel afraid, but he who conquers that fear." He has said this to Allison since she was a little girl, repeating it to make sure she got it.

And she does. She calls me paralyzed on the South Street bridge, over a potential problem with a landlady, a housemate, work. She gives the potential catastrophe air, and then makes the necessary call, has the conversation, she does what she needs to do, and learns again that facing what she's most afraid of is usually the right answer and the outcome is never as bad as the disaster she imagines.

My kids' dad died when the kids were 13, 11, and 5. As the oldest, a lot of responsibility fell on her and in retrospect, I'm sometimes afraid that I allowed or expected her to co-parent more than I should have. But in my defense, she was already the responsible one, the smart one, the decision maker. In the middle of the night of the day she was born I looked into her eyes and felt that she held all the secrets of the Universe.

And now, Covid 19 is like all of her catastrophic thinking rolled up into one storm cloud, a tornado that pops up and touches down with no rhyme or reason. Part of her job with the city of Philadelphia is to disseminate the latest information on the situation in the city. One day she texted me, "Mom, there are only 10 new cases today!" And I was so happy to see a bit of hope in her message. Ten minutes later she took the rose colored glasses off and wrote, "Just a few days ago it was terrible when there was one. Now I'm trying to celebrate that there's 'only 10.'"

I knew it wouldn't take her long to connect those dots. She quickly saw that trying to hold on to numbers to impose some logic on the chaos that is Covid 19 won't hold up. She is still my daughter, after all, and there's nothing I can do.

So that's her dichotomy, she's the worrier, the desperate one, though the oldest and so responsible, so much a second mom to her siblings. And she's also the one who calls me the most when I travel, the only one who panics if I don't text back within an hour of receiving a message. You know what we fought over the most when she was a teenager? The things I allowed her siblings to do that she thought were too risky.

Once, I had to pull over in a summer torrential downpour after a mundane trip to the grocery for a few items, a trip that should have taken me 30 minutes took closer to an hour. By the time I got home she had worked herself up into actual hysteria.

My mother, who Allison was very close to, died just over a year after my husband did. So, what did Allison did for her first job? She was an activities coordinator at a senior citizen home, playing bingo with them and Frank Sinatra for them, serving them ice cream, making seasonal crafts, and...watching them die. She'd come home, cry inconsolably for half an hour, then tell me all the reasons why it was ok for that person to go, to join their husband or wife, that she or he was 96 and just fell asleep: a good life, a good death.

When she was about four, I took her to see Snow White at a discount movie theater. When the witch gave Snow White the apple and Snow White took that fateful bite, Allison was so terrorized that I had to carry her out of the theater. And when we got home, she made me reenact the scene over and over and over again, with as switching roles of Witch and Snow White. White over and over and over.

So...maybe this is ok, her working in the epicenter of the pandemic. Knowledge must give her some sense of control. She texts me the latest info simultaneously with the press releases—nothing is going to pass by her. This catastrophe is realer than real: in her darkest most frightened moments she could not have imagined *this*. It's silent and invisible and has literally changed the world as we know it. She already knows, too well, what it's like to have your world change.

I am her mother and I have no words of comfort and I am terrified, terrified on a global scale. But my heart is broken most by watching my young adult child try to make sense of this, keep hope each day, to not let the information flowing over and through her to sweep her away.

She's isolating, working from home, wearing a mask when she goes out, walking her dog through the city and taking photos of blossoming trees, real rainbows and those drawn and hung up in windows, the gorgeous meals she's making. She's trying her best, breathing through it. Sometimes I face the city skyline and try to send her positive vibes, try to keep her in that elusive and rickety place of already being nostalgic for this time, this pause in our "real" lives, in some odd way, while we're still in it, this time of both quiet and confusion. I try to keep both of us focusing on TikTok dances and funny memes, good food, gratitude for Zoom and Skype and Netflix, gratitude that for right now, we are ok.

Scott Warnock
Whupping the Teenage Boy Literacy Crisis with the Vacation Journal

If you're lucky, your boys are eager readers. If you're really lucky, your boys are eager writers. But in many households, of course, neither is the case, and folks are in the midst of summer book battles.

As I've mentioned before, literacy experts have discussed what they often call a crisis in literacy among teenage boys. I wrote in 2017 that "[...] getting boys to read has been a longstanding, well-documented issue" and that one of my favorite books on the topic is Jeffrey Wilhelm and Michael Smith's *Reading Don't Fix No Chevys: Literacy in the Lives of Young Men*.

So this is not a new topic. But it seems like in our collective frustration, we—and I use that "we" broadly—often forget some basic rhetorical factors when it comes to the issue of teenage male literacy: These boys, willfully or not, don't see a clear audience or purpose for the reading and writing they are asked to do.

Two weeks ago, we took a week's vacation in Vermont, visiting our close friends' beautiful lake house. My daughter is in class this summer, so it was just me and mom and the boys—oh, plus we told each boy they could bring a friend. So the boy count was 1+2+2=5. (This made me think there might need to be a kind of Title IX for vacation, because this was rough on my wife, but at least she had our dog, Prue, for some female solidarity/companionship.)

Since the summer is a daily literacy battle—and keep in mind that I do value their extensive digital literacy habits—things could only be worse on vacation. A boy read and write on vacation?!

But I fought back: enter the vacation journal. For years, I have carefully written about our activities during vacations. In my opinion, these are high quality and often quite amusing writings. When I break them out nowadays, the payoff is immediate: The kids, and sometimes their friends, love reading them. They are of course one man's perspective on a family trip, with a highly slanted point of view, but that's authorial privilege for you.

In Vermont, building on an idea from a few other recent trips we've taken, I asked/forced each kid to write about one day. I supplied them with sheets of old-fashioned loose-leaf paper for the job. This ended up being a good choice of medium; I was going to do it all on a computer, but then I realized there could be a job-sapping logjam at the machine, and they also wouldn't be able to do *multimedia*, er, draw silly pictures.

The whole thing exceeded my expectations. After some initial grumbling, they had a blast. They all got into the process, writing quite extensively and adding a good dash of humor while also employing considerable semantic, syntactic, and grammatical complexity. In short, these writings were pretty good. How about these gems?:

"Today was Nate's birthday (18 years old)! What better way to spend it than waking up at 5 am, driving for 6 hours, and eating burnt hot dogs for dinner!"

"Dinner consisted of chicken, rice, and corn, which the hungry boys quickly inhaled. Then after a short trip on the lake with Zach continuously trying to pirate Adam's ship they were tired out and headed inside for a few rounds of CodeNames."

"Together, the four of them successfully managed to look like four Neanderthals fighting for their lives in the middle of a lake. After a couple of hours of doing their duties at Rock, the cavemen went back to the house."

"... two boys' camp counselors came by on a rowboat. They started interrogating Adam and Zach, asking about a 'big turtle.' Obviously, Zach and Adam had nothing to do with a big, dead, floating, stinky turtle so they sent the campers on their way disappointed."

One page of brilliance.

Perhaps our journal is not quite *Walden*, but it is an engaging read nonetheless, and by "engaging," I mean that *they* found it so: They read each other's entries, correcting some fish stories to keep the record clear.

While I don't think they overtly competed, they all tried to do a good job, sitting down, focused, to get their day/page done.

On the last day, everyone wrote one sentence, finishing our five-day week with a nice, collaborative composing exercise.

Will they be ready for college or what?

When we got home, as a bonus, I scanned the entries and sent them to the parents who were brave enough to allow their two boys to travel with us. One marveled that the "English professor" got them to write on vacation. The other said, "This was my favorite summer reading thus far!"

Take that, literacy crisis!

Contributors

David Ahn was born in February of 2001 and has lived in New Jersey his entire life. He currently attends Drexel University, majoring in Computer Science with a concentration in Game Programming and Development. When David was around 12 years old, he found an interest in professional wrestling through a video game and has kept up with the hobby since then.

Stacey Ake is a Teaching Professor in Philosophy at Drexel University. As reflected in her contribution, her philosophical work centers around Søren Kierkegaard, the Danish founder of existentialism, whose work revolved around philosophy and theology. Her additional philosophical interests include semiotics—the theory of signs—and biosemiotics—how signs function among living organisms. She lives in Philadelphia, PA.

Sara Beinish is a freshman in Drexel's First Year Exploratory Studies program and is currently leaning towards majoring in Business or Finance. Outside of classes, she is a member of the Drexel freshmen dance company, FreshDance. Sara has loved reading and writing her whole life and is thrilled to present her first published piece.

Norman Cain was born in 1942 and raised on Olive Street in West Philadelphia. He graduated in 1964 from Bluefield State College in West Virginia, where he majored in Social Science and minored in English. A retired social worker, teacher, father of five, and grandfather of seven, he is active in several writing groups, including the Best Day of My Life So Far at the Germantown Senior Center.

Maria Chnaraki is an ethnomusicologist, folklorist and cultural anthropologist. She is the founding Director of Greek Studies and an adjunct professor at Drexel University, as well as the Official Representative of the World Council of Cretans. She is the author of *Cretan Music: Unraveling Ariadne's* Thread (Kerkyra Publications, Athens) and *Sing In Me, Muse, and Through Me Tell the Story: Greek Culture Performed* (Zorba Press, NY). She is passionate about teaching and mentoring in synthetic and creative ways.

Paula Marantz Cohen is Distinguished Professor of English and Dean of the Pennoni Honors College. She is the author of 11 books, including 6 novels. Her latest work of nonfiction, *The Merchant and Moor: What Shakespeare Can Teach Us About Empathy*, is forthcoming from Yale UP. She contributes regularly to the *Wall Street Journal*, *The American Scholar*, and the *Times Literary Supplement* and is the producer of the documentary film *Two Universities and the Future of China*.

Qwuacii Cousins is a Civil Engineering major from the island of Jamaica. In her free time, she explores different forms of art and has developed a love for creative writing. She found solace in writing after migrating to the United States, and uses it as an outlet to cope with her new environment.

Luis Cruz writes short stories and novels, and is also a playwright. Luis has been involved in musical theater as both an actor and costume designer. Luis

Contributors | 257

published his first book, *The Legend of the Crystal Sword*, last year. He currently attends Drexel University as a Fashion Design Major.

Yasemin Dayi is of Turkish and Slavic decent, and she is very invested in her family and heritage. She is studying International Business with a co-major in marketing with the hopes of broadening her cultural understanding. Yasemin enjoys fashion, modelling, music, and photography in her free time. She enjoyed creative and editorial writing in high school.

Jillian D'Souza is a first-year psychology major and biology minor at Drexel University. She plans to pursue medicine after her undergraduate studies. When she is not studying or in the lab, she loves to draw, sing, and spend time with her cat. Although this is her first published piece, she is excited to explore English through the different classes here at Drexel.

Priya Dudhat is a biology major at Drexel University, hailing from North Wales, PA. Her writing experience includes being a chief editor for her high school's literary magazines, namely Germantown Academy's *Academy Monthly* and *The Voyager*. Outside of writing, Priya enjoys playing the drums and discovering new music and books.

Mark Fazzolari is a biological sciences major and a Pennoni Honors College student hailing from Harrisburg, Pennsylvania. During his time at Drexel, he has come to enjoy Philadelphia, squash, Texas hold'em, post-midnight Wawa runs, and pulling all-nighters in the Newman office. Those close to him better know him as "Fazz."

Lee Feinman is a self-proclaimed expert of nothing. This is why he studies chemistry at Drexel—to become an expert at chemistry—and writes essays, poems, and short stories about the journeys taken by he who is in search of expertise. He is a first-year student and a native of Media, Pennsylvania. Aside from pursuing a professional career in the atmospheric and environmental chemistry fields, Lee enjoys a literary interest of writing in his free time.

Tim Fitts lives and works in Philadelphia. He has been teaching in the First-Year Writing Program at Drexel since 2011. Fitts is the author of two short story collections, *Go Home and Cry For Yourselves* (Xavier Review Press 2017) and *Hypothermia* (MadHat Press 2017). His fiction has been published by journals such as *Granta*, *The Gettysburg Review*, *Boulevard*, *CutBank*, *The Baltimore Review*, and *Best Microfiction 2020*, among many others.

Valerie Fox has published several books including *The Rorschach Factory*, *The Glass Book*, and *Insomniatic*. She has published prose in *Cleaver*, *Maryland Literary Review*, *Juked*, *Reflex*, *The Cafe Irreal*, *Ellipsis Zine*, *The A3 Review*, *Across the Margin*, and other journals. Her story is included in *The Group of Seven Reimagined: Contemporary Stories Inspired by Historic Canadian Paintings*, edited by Karen Schauber. Recently, Valerie published *The Real Sky*, a handmade artist's book (sketches, words) in an edition of 26, with artist Jacklynn Niemiec.

María José Garcia is a first-year student from Honduras pursuing a Bachelor of Science in Biomedical Engineering. In her free time, you will find her reading a book, playing sports, or baking. She is passionate about sustainability, civic engagement, and women empowerment. With her involvement in several organizations around campus and in her community, she hopes to one day inspire little girls around the world to pursue their dreams.

Tim Hanlon is a junior biology major in the College of Arts and Sciences and enjoys writing in his free time. With a number of publications in medical journals and in previous editions of *The 33rd*, Tim enjoys writing in many different genres. Tim is also the chair of the Undergraduate Student Government Association's (USGA) Sustainability Committee and is working with Drexel to create an Office of Sustainability. Tim currently works with three research labs—one at Drexel, another with a surgeon in Pittsburgh, and the third at Harvard Medical School—and hopes to fulfill his dream of becoming a surgeon. Tim is also an avid runner and sporadically ran the Philadelphia Marathon in the fall of 2019—his first and likely only marathon.

Cassandra Hirsch teaches composition and fiction writing in the English & Philosophy Department at Drexel and courses in the Drexel MFA program and the Pennoni Honors College. She published a 19th century-era novel, *Under the Linden Tree*, in 2012, and has turned to her writers group over the years to help her grow as a freelance writer. She continues to write fiction and is currently working on another novel.

Christian Hunold is a professor in Drexel's Department of Politics. Hunold is a scholar of environmental politics and policy. His current work examines the politics and culture of urban wildlife, both as means to foster spaces for wild animals in everyday life and to understand how the blurring of human and nonhuman worlds in the Anthropocene is generating new forms of environmental political engagement. This research has appeared in *Environmental Values*, *Journal of Urban Affairs*, and *Nature and Culture*. Professor Hunold teaches Environmental Politics, Animal Politics, and Research Design for Political Science.

Aaron Jeong is an Environmental Science major and Writing minor, though he is interested in not-so-secretly pursuing a double major :). Aaron is a large fan of language, but also finds it to be incredibly ineffective at its job—oh? He wants to say that that is a conversation for another time. He believes our mother Earth is deserving of love and protection and is an advocate for sustainable fashion, plant-based diets, and a more conscious relationship with our waste. He dislikes loud noises, selfish behavior, and not being able to sit outside on sunny days.

Samantha Nicole Johnson is a 4th year English major with a concentration in Literary Studies. She has always had a love for writing, which has played an integral part in her self-expression. She is heavily involved in Student Life as a member of two Greek-lettered organizations and the College of Arts &

Science's Student Advisory Board. Her aspiration is to have a career in editing & publication and to travel. When she is not writing, she enjoys listening to music, binging anime, and taking four hour naps.

Theodoros Katerinakis combines industrial, military, and academic experience in information theory, banking, and mission-critical environments. He holds a Ph.D. in Organizational Behavior and an MSc in Communication Science, focused on cooperative networks and negotiation management, both from Drexel. As an Adjunct Faculty in Drexel COAS, he has captured hundreds of hours of his courses' lectures with Drexel IT, and in LeBow College of Business, he has prepared master classes' DVDs on business resilience in his "CEOs in Class" courses. He is currently a member of Drexel On-line Council, SCDC Coordinator for Greece (mentoring students for research abroad, as STAR scholars or as Vidalakis Scholars), and serves as Graduate Faculty for HOU on-line. His latest Springer book, *The Social Construction of Knowledge in Mission-Critical Environments*, uses iconic aviation cases to explain innovation and knowledge management.

Laura Klouda is studying biological sciences. She enjoys researching medical topics and hopes to become an oncologist someday. In her free time, Laura enjoys drawing, painting, playing piano, and reading, as well as exploring new restaurants in Philly.

Miriam Kotzin is the author of five collections of poetry, most recently *Debris Field* (David Robert Books 2017). Her collection of short fiction, *Country Music* (Spuyten Duyvil Press 2017), joins a novel, *The Real Deal* (Brick House Press 2012), and a collection of flash fiction, *Just Desserts* (Star Cloud Press 2010). Her fiction and poetry have been published or are forthcoming in *Shenandoah*, *Boulevard*, *SmokeLong Quarterly Eclectica*, *Mezzo Cammin*, *Offcourse*, and *Valparaiso Poetry Review*, among other periodicals, and in anthologies. She teaches creative writing and literature at Drexel University.

Dylan Lam is a sophomore Film and Television major at Drexel. With primary interests in editing and cinematography, he also engages with writing and photography on the side, experimenting with stories both literally and visually. Currently, he serves as Lead Content Creator at Apex Gaming PCs, a computer company based in Philadelphia. More of Dylan's photos, videos, and stories can be found at iamdylanlam.com.

Colin Latch is a first-year Marketing and International Business dual major from southern New Hampshire. In his free time, Colin enjoys reading and spending time with family and friends. He hopes to someday work in a tech company's advertising department. This is his first time being published.

Lynn Levin is a poet, writer, translator, and a member of Drexel's Department of English and Philosophy. Her poetry, fiction, and creative nonfiction have appeared in *Boulevard*, *Cleaver*, *The Saturday Evening Post online*, *Michigan Quarterly Review*, and other publications. Her most recent book is the poetry collection *The Minor Virtues* (Ragged Sky, 2020). With Drexel colleague Valerie Fox, she is co-author of *Poems for the Writing: Prompts for Poets, Second Edition* (Texture/Blurb, 2019). Her website is lynnlevinpoet.com.

Richard McCourt is Curator of Botany and Professor in the Department of Biodiversity, Earth, and Environmental Science. His research is on the evolution of algae and the origin of land plants. He has also published on the history of botany and plant collections.

Jonson Miller is a Teaching Professor in the Department of History. He has taught American and military history at Drexel since 2007. He conducted the research for this article to model for the history seniors how to write their senior theses.

Meghan Mohnot is a freshman studying Economics, B.S. She is from Plainsboro, New Jersey, and her interests include art, dance, and singing. She has previously written an article on her experience teaching art and music to senior citizens and children for her Girl Scout Gold Award project.

Marshall Nisselbaum is a geoscience major concentrating in paleontology. He is a member of the class of 2024. He enjoys cooking and baking in his spare time. This is his first published work.

Gwen Ottinger is Associate Professor in the Department of Politics and the Center for Science, Technology and Society. She is author of *Refining Expertise: How Responsible Engineers Subvert Environmental Justice Challenges*, which won the 2015 Rachel Carson Prize from the Society for Social Studies of Science. She is the recipient of an NSF CAREER Award and a Frederick Burkhardt Residential Fellowship for Recently Tenured Scholars from the ACLS. Professor Ottinger's research group, the Fair Tech Collective, uses social science theory and methods to promote social justice in science and technology.

Sana'i Parker is a first-year writing student at Drexel, who is planning to pursue a degree in mechanical engineering. He has spent a great part of his life in outgoing extracurriculars that have fueled his love for writing, public speaking, and creativity. He is currently involved in Drexel Student Ambassadors, Drexel NextGen, and Writers Room. With a bright mind and ambitious drive, he hopes to continue to inspire and achieve as he goes though the journey of college.

Megan Peng is a freshman biological sciences major in Drexel's BS/MD program and Pennoni Honors College. She loves to bake, explore nature, and travel the world. This is her first writing publication, but she hopes to be able to continue to explore the opportunities that writing has to offer!

M.G. Piety is a Professor of Philosophy at Drexel University in Philadelphia. She has published numerous scholarly and popular articles. She translated Søren Kierkegaard's *Repetition and Philosophical Crumbs* for Oxford University Press. She also published a book *Ways of Knowing: Kierkegaard's Pluralist*

Epistemology with Baylor University Press and a collection of essays entitled *Sequins and Scandals: Reflections on Figure Skating, Culture, and the Philosophy of Sport* with Gegensatz Press. She maintains three blogs: *Piety On Kierkegaard, Flash Philosophy,* and *The Life of the Mind*. Piety is also a certified philosophical counselor who is interested in the potential of philosophy to improve the quality of people's lives. She enjoys giving talks to the general public, has lectured all over the world, and has appeared on both television and radio.

Ferishta Rahmani is a second-year student at Drexel's Lebow College of Business. She is studying Real Estate Management and Finance. She was previously published in the 2017 Johns Hopkins Center for Talented Youth Creative Fiction contest. In her free time, she enjoys playing volleyball and writing.

Sanjana Ramanthan is an undergraduate English major at Drexel University with a concentration in Writing. She enjoys writing poetry, essays, and fictional short stories. Her hobbies include reading and playing video games. Her essay previously published by *The 33rd*, "An End to Sexism in Gaming Communities," will be included in a new edition of the textbook *They Say / I Say*.

Bella Randazzo is a current Chemical Engineering student and poet at Drexel University. From a young age and now at 19, her passion for reaching the hearts of others has extended through multiple mediums, from STEM studies to culinary arts to poetry and prose. With empathy and self-truth as fuel, she creates a vessel from language by which she can connect with the world in a personal yet profound way.

Ciara Richards is a freshman from Wales in the United Kingdom. Ciara is majoring in English but she is also interested in Political Science. She plays on the Drexel Squash team, who are currently ranked 7th in the nation.

Don Riggs has taught the fantasy epic du jour in book and film form from Tolkien to George R.R. Martin. This has brought his way many scholarly books to review. Joseph Rex Young's work has allowed him to see Tolkien and Martin compared, and not unfavorably.

Sheila Sandapen teaches in the English and Philosophy Department. Her writing has been featured in the following anthologies: *Buffy to Batgirl* (2019), and *The Language of Doctor Who* (2014). Some of her work has appeared in the *Journal of Commonwealth and Postcolonial Studies* and on storyhouse.org.

Kalahne Serpanchy is a Film and Television Production student. She has been lucky enough to have traveled to many places around the world, including to Philadelphia from her home in Vancouver, Canada. She loves creative writing and narratives and has some experience in scriptwriting, short stories, and poetry.

Ibim Soibiharry is a Mechanical Engineering major with a burning passion for experiencing and describing his experiences of the world around him. He hails from Rivers State, Nigeria and has lived in St. Kitts and Nevis as well. In addition to writing, he enjoys drawing, graphic design, and dressing up.

Scott Stein is author, most recently, of *The Great American Deception*, a novel *Publishers Weekly* called "a constant delight" in a starred review. He has published two other novels as well as short satire and fiction in *The Oxford University Press Humor Reader, McSweeney's, National Review, Art Times, Liberty, The G.W. Review*, and *Shale*. He is a professor of English at Drexel University, where he directs the Drexel Publishing Group and is the founding editor of *Write Now Philly*. His website is scottsteinonline.com.

Jorina Teneqexhiu is a biology major with a devotion towards learning and painting. She is a first- generation college student, with her immigrant parent being her biggest inspiration to succeed and to help others in need. Jorina attributes her love for writing to her favorite high school teacher, Ms. Swerdloff, who sparked her passion for literature and poetry.

Eva Thury teaches in the Department of English and Philosophy at Drexel University in Philadelphia. She is the co-author of *Introduction to Mythology Contemporary Approaches to Classical and World Myths*, 4th ed. (Oxford 2016) with Margaret K. Devinney. She is also the translator from the Hungarian of Sándor Bacskai's *One Step toward Jerusalem: Oral Histories of Orthodox Jews in Stalinist Hungary*. Though trained as a classicist, Thury sees herself as a student of a popular culture, pursuing interests in everything from vampires to Sandy Skoglund's radioactive cats.

Renae Tingling is a current chemical engineering student here at Drexel University. She was born in Jamaica, where she lived for the majority of her life. Her interests range from academic, like her curiosity in all things out of this world, to recreational, like exploring the many forms of visual arts. She has little writing experience beyond written assignments.

Teigha VanHester is a disruptive intellectual and unapologetic scholar currently pursuing Ph.D. student (ABD) in Rhetoric and Composition at Illinois State University. She has lived in over 16 countries and currently works full-time as the Director of International Education at Illinois Central College. As a writer, she writes in a unique, diverse format, demanding the academy allow students (like herself) have the right to their own language. As a writer, Teigha is looking to critique, connect, and create the rhetorical component/strategies used to perform diversity, inclusion, and acceptance within the academy and other capitalist institutions.

Kathleen Volk Miller has written for *LitHub, NYT Modern Love, O, the Oprah magazine, Salon, the New York Times, Family Circle, Philadelphia Magazine*, and other venues. "How We Want to Live," an essay, is in *O's Little Guide to Starting Over* (Flat Iron Books, Hearst Publications, 2016). She is co-editor of the anthology *Humor: A Reader for Writers* (Oxford University Press, 2014). She is co-editor of *The Painted Bride Quarterly* and co-host of PBQ's podcast,

Slush Pile. She has also published in literary magazines, such as *Drunken Boat*, *Opium*, and other venues. She holds "Healing through Writing" and gratitude journaling workshops, as well as other memoir classes. She consults on literary magazine start-up and getting published in literary magazines. She is a professor at Drexel University.

Scott Warnock is a professor of English and Director of the University Writing Program at Drexel. He teachers a variety of courses and is widely published in the areas of online writing instruction, computers and composition, and education technology. Warnock is president of the Global Society of Online Writing Educators and president of the Palmyra High School Foundation for Educational Excellence. He has coached youth sports in his local area since 2005. He writes the bi-weekly blog/column "Virtual Children" for the Website *When Falls the Coliseum*.

Alex Wasalinko is a poet and teaching artist living in Philadelphia, PA where she works as an ArtistYear AmeriCorps Creative Writing Fellow. Alex received her MRes in creative writing with a concentration in ekphrasis from the University of Strathclyde in Glasgow, Scotland. Her work appears in *The Ekphrastic Review*, *Sixfold*, and Drexel University's Writers Room *Anthology 6*. When she's not writing or teaching, Alex loves taking long walks around her neighborhood in West Philadelphia.

Devin Welsh graduated as a member of Drexel's class of 2020 with a BA in English and a minor in Writing. He was a peer-reader at Drexel's Writing Center and a writer-in-residence with Writers Room for three years, and he intends on remaining connected with both programs as much as possible. Devin will be spending his first year after Drexel as an AmeriCorps Artist Year fellow in Philadelphia, serving as a teaching artist with a focus on Creative Writing and Photography.

Najifa Zaman is a first-year design and merchandise student at Drexel University. Some of her favorite hobbies are reading romance novels, drawing, and listening to songs. She has always been very interested in creative writing. After graduation, she hoping to work as a visual merchandiser or a marketing analyst.

Steven Zhao is an economics major studying economics at Drexel's Lebow College of Business. On campus, you will find him on stage at Drexel Symphony Orchestra Concerts or around campus giving tours as a Student Ambassador. In his free time, he enjoys playing the violin, drawing, and spending way too much time playing video games.

LingAn Zheng is an Interactive Digital Media student inspired to become a User Experience Designer. She is an analytical thinker in love with art, music, and books, especially fiction. She moved to American at age 12, speaking only Chinese. Her English improved significantly as she strives for proficiency in reading and writing.

Want to appear in the 2021 edition of *The 33rd?*

All Drexel students
and faculty are eligible

For more information,
visit **drexelpublishing.com**